M000267513

Algorithms of the Intelligent Web

SECOND EDITION

DOUGLAS G. MCILWRAITH
HARALAMBOS MARMANIS
DMITRY BABENKO

MANNING
SHELTER ISLAND

For online information and ordering of this and other Manning books, please visit
www.manning.com. The publisher offers discounts on this book when ordered in quantity.
For more information, please contact

> Special Sales Department
> Manning Publications Co.
> 20 Baldwin Road
> PO Box 761
> Shelter Island, NY 11964
> Email: orders@manning.com

Manning Publications Co.
20 Baldwin Road
PO Box 761
Shelter Island, NY 11964

Development editor:	Jennifer Stout
Technical development editors:	John Guthrie, Michael Williams
Technical proofreader:	David Fombella Pombal
Review editor:	Ozren Harlovic
Project editor:	Tiffany Taylor
Copy editor:	Linda Recktenwald
Proofreader:	Tiffany Taylor
Typesetter:	Dottie Marsico
Cover designer:	Marija Tudor

ISBN 9781617292583
Printed in the United States of America
1 2 3 4 5 6 7 8 9 10 – EBM – 21 20 19 18 17 16

This book is dedicated to Elly, mon petit pois.

—*D.M.*

contents

foreword

The World Wide Web is the underlying infrastructure of an internet-based information society. It is the primary tool that billions of people use to interact on the internet. Industrial progress is made by developing information services on the internet. Today, with the maturity of cloud computing and wireless communications, the web is becoming not only a platform for publishing and accessing information, but also a platform where information services can be developed, deployed, and delivered to billions of users anytime and anywhere. Big data provides rich content for building versatile services and also constitutes the means for enriching the services with intelligence and thus improving the user experience of services on the web. With such intelligent services, the web is changing our lives: it guides us to find the right restaurant, helps us to make the ideal holiday arrangements, enables us to purchase almost anything, and builds communities for a variety of purposes. Such intelligence is achieved through analyzing the data generated from interactions between users and the contents of the web. Building web intelligence is therefore central to today's development of data science.

It is my great pleasure to present to you this excellent book, *Algorithms of the Intelligent Web, Second Edition*, revised by a young but very experienced data scientist: Dr. Douglas McIlwraith. This book aims to reveal the soul of intelligent web applications: the underlying algorithms that realize the intelligence. This is an ambitious goal. What amazes me is that Doug has managed to present this broad subject comprehensively in plain English in less than 250 pages.

This book covers the most popular methods for a wide spectrum of applications. It provides a concise description of algorithms with their mathematical foundations and sample code in Python. I thoroughly enjoyed reading the book, and I hope you will share my enjoyment when you read it. More important, I hope that after you finish reading, you find yourself equipped with the skill and knowledge to make the web more intelligent.

YIKE GUO
PROFESSOR AND DIRECTOR
DATA SCIENCE INSTITUTE,
IMPERIAL COLLEGE LONDON

preface

We consider ourselves lucky to be working in one of the most exciting fields of technology that our time has to offer. In a few short years, we've moved from a nascent internet to a fully developed World Wide Web, whereby each and every one of us have the power of communication in our pockets and the ability to answer almost any question in seconds.

The development of intelligent algorithms to make sense and utility of this information has played no small part in the development of this new paradigm. A certain beauty of symmetry strikes us: that we rely more and more on intelligent algorithms to help us lead our lives both on and off the internet, and this in turn has provided us with deeper insight and data on which to train and test our algorithms. Just a few years ago, neural networks had fallen out of favor in research circles; but now, with the advent of large, accessible datasets, we've been able to show their utility again.

We *just about* live in a world where we can talk to our phone and have it predict our needs, book our appointments, and reach our contacts. A bit further into the future, we can see self-driving cars and virtual reality. All of these applications are firmly rooted in the application of computer science to real-world problems. Intelligent algorithms are part of this and are here to stay.

Unfortunately, entering the world of machine learning and data science can be daunting. It's a math- and statistics-heavy field where often your intuition will get you into trouble! We wanted to revise this book in order to recognize our progress since the first edition and to provide a guiding hand for those new to the field. Within the pages of this book, you'll find easy-to-understand examples and real-world solutions with code snippets. Where possible, we've tried to emphasize the core principles of a technique over a mathematics-heavy approach. This is a tricky line to tread, and we hope that we've done it well.

As you'll see, the book is arranged into eight core chapters, each covering an important area of the intelligent web from an algorithmic standpoint. The book ends with an appendix that looks at the intelligent web from a data-processing vantage. We've included it so that, as a practitioner in the space, you can appreciate how crucial (and difficult) it is to move high-velocity data around a system effectively.

acknowledgments

Thanks to everyone at Manning who made this book possible: publisher Marjan Bace and everyone on the editorial and production teams, including Janet Vail, Kevin Sullivan, Tiffany Taylor, Dottie Marsico, Linda Recktenwald, and many others who worked behind the scenes.

Thanks also to all the reviewers of this manuscript in its various stages: Nii A-Okine, Tobias Bürger, Marius Butuc, Carlton Gibson, John Guthrie, Pieter Gyselinck, Peter-John Hampton, Dike Kalu, Seth Liddy, Radha Ranjan Madhav, Kostas Passadis, Peter Rabinovitch, Srdjan Santic, Dennis Sellinger, Dr. Joseph Wang, and Michael Williams. We know how much time and effort it takes to read and re-read such a text, so thanks to you all. You provided invaluable feedback that is now reflected in the text.

A special thanks must go to David Fombella Pombal for providing an invaluable technical review, to Dr. Michael Davy for reviewing chapter 3, and to Matthew Sword for reviewing chapter 7. Thank you all.

In this book, we draw on many systems, libraries, and packages that weren't written by us. The community of developers, data scientists, and machine-learning experts working in this field do us all credit. Thank you, each and every one of you.

Looking back to the initial discussions about revising *Algorithms of the Intelligent Web*, I remember thinking, "Hey, the first edition was a great book. How much work could it be?!" Well, as it turns out, a lot. Things move so quickly in this space, and there was so much interesting work that I wanted to share with you, that I had to think very carefully about what to leave in, what to remove, what to revise and what to add. Consequently, this book took up a lot more time than I expected. But I'm very lucky to be surrounded by so many great people who provided support, motivation, and patience when I needed it.

First and foremost, I want to thank my fiancée, Elly. Darling, your love, patience, and support are much-appreciated constants in my life, and I'm certain that without them, this book would never have been written. I love you.

Second, I'd like to thank my parents and family, who have always fostered my curiosity and supported me when I've foundered. I hope you enjoy this book and realize how grateful I am for your nurture and care.

Third, I'd like to mention my friends and colleagues, who are too numerous to name. I've been lucky enough to work and play alongside some extraordinary people, and this has made every day a pleasure. Thank you all.

I'd also like to thank both of my editors, Jeff Bleiel and Jennifer Stout. You've been instrumental in getting the book to this stage. Jennifer, your positivity and energy kept me going at the end, so thank you.

DOUGLAS MCILWRAITH

I'd like to thank my parents, Eva and Alexander. They've instilled in me the appropriate level of curiosity and passion for learning that keeps me writing and researching late into the night. The debt is too large to pay in one lifetime.

I wholeheartedly thank my cherished wife, Aurora, and our three sons: Nikos, Lukas, and Albert—the greatest pride and joy of my life. I'll always be grateful for their love, patience, and understanding. The incessant curiosity of my children has been a continuous inspiration for my studies on learning. A huge acknowledgment is due to my parents-in-law, Cuchi and Jose; my sisters, Maria and Katerina; and my best friends, Michael and Antonio for their continuous encouragement and unconditional support.

I'd be remiss if I didn't acknowledge the manifold support of Drs. Amilcar Avendaño and Maria Balerdi, who taught me a lot about cardiology and funded my early work on learning. My thanks also are due to Professor Leon Cooper, and many other amazing people at Brown University, whose zeal for studying the way that our brain works trickled down to folks like me and instigated my work on intelligent applications.

To my past and present colleagues, Ajay Bhadari, Kavita Kantkar, Alexander Petrov, Kishore Kirdat, and many others, who encouraged and supported all the intelligence-related initiatives at work: there are only a few lines that I can write here, but my gratitude is much larger than that.

HARALAMBOS MARMANIS

First and foremost, I want to thank my beloved wife Elena.

I'd also like to thank all of my past and present colleagues, who influenced my professional life and served as an inspiration: Konstandin Bobovich, Paul A. Dennis, Keith Lawless, and Kevin Bedell.

DMITRY BABENKO

about this book

Algorithms of the Intelligent Web was written to provide you with a roadmap to the design and creation of intelligent algorithms. It draws on many areas of computer science, including machine learning and artificial intelligence, but has been written with the practitioner in mind. It's a cookbook of sorts and provides the relative newcomer in this field with several real-world, worked examples that can be modified for your own purpose.

Who should read this book

This book is firmly aimed at those who are new to writing intelligent algorithms but who have a firm grasp of programming and basic math and statistics. Wherever possible, we've tried to write the book so the mathematical rigor can be glossed over, leaving you with an overall impression of the applicability of an approach. Of course, if you're more mathematically inclined, we encourage you to follow the detail. Ideally, readers of this book should have had at least some exposure to a programming language and have attended a first-year undergraduate mathematics course.

Roadmap

This book is organized into eight chapters and one appendix:

- Chapter 1 provides an overview of intelligent algorithms and outlines some key characteristics. It also provides you with guiding principles for the rest of the book.
- Chapter 2 discusses the concept of structure within your data. In particular, it introduces the concept of the feature space. In this chapter, we introduce expectation maximization and eigenvectors.

- Chapter 3 introduces recommender systems. We introduce collaborative filtering techniques and discuss the Netflix Prize.
- Chapter 4 outlines classification techniques and introduces logistic regression. We use logistic regression to perform fraud detection.
- Chapter 5 presents a case study on click prediction for online advertising. We outline how online advertising works behind the scenes and provide you with a worked example of click prediction using a publicly available web-click dataset.
- Chapter 6 is about deep learning and neural networks. We provide a whistle-stop tour of neural networks from their humble beginnings and discuss recent advances in learning with deep networks.
- Chapter 7 outlines how to make the right choice. We discuss statistical significance for A/B testing and several approaches for online learning using multi-armed bandits.
- Chapter 8 presents a forward-looking summary of the intelligent web.
- The appendix discusses how we might process high-velocity event streams and build intelligent algorithms that use them. We discuss several design patterns for web-log processing and outline some key pitfalls to avoid.

For the most part, the chapters can be read independently. But note that chapter 5 is a case study and relies on knowledge of logistic regression that's introduced in chapter 4.

Downloads

All the code and data required to run the examples in this book are available to download from the publisher's website (www.manning.com/books/algorithms-of-the-intelligent-web-second-edition) and from GitHub (https://github.com/dougmcilwraith/aiw-second-edition). The only notable exception is the Criteo Display Challenge Dataset, which must be downloaded directly from Criteo due to its size. Instructions are provided in chapter 5.

All code has been tested in Ubuntu 14.04.2 using Python 2.7.10. Various dependencies exist; these can be found in the requirements file provided with the downloads. In this file we also include instructions to ensure that your environment is compatible with the code samples in this book.

Code conventions

This book provides copious examples. Source code in listings and code terms in text are in a fixed-width font like this to separate them from ordinary text. In some places, we've added line breaks and reworked indentation to accommodate the available page space in the book. When even this was not enough, listings include line-continuation markers (➡). Additionally, comments in the source code have often been removed from the listings when the code is described in the text. Code annotations accompany some of the source code listings, highlighting important concepts.

Math conventions

In the text, you'll find many equations that support the code and concepts introduced. We follow a standard convention for the notation throughout. Matrices are represented by upright, capital, bold characters, such as **M**. Upright, lowercase, bold characters represent vectors: **v**. Scalar values are expressed using lowercase italic, as in the case of λ.

About the authors

DR. DOUGLAS MCILWRAITH earned his first degree at Cambridge in computer science before completing a PhD at Imperial College in London. He is a machine learning expert currently working as a data scientist for a London-based advertising network. He has made research contributions to the fields of distributed systems, ubiquitous computing, pervasive sensing, and robotics and security—and he gets excited when technology has a positive impact on people's lives.

DR. HARALAMBOS MARMANIS is a pioneer in the adoption of machine learning techniques for industrial solutions. He has 25 years of experience in developing professional software.

DMITRY BABENKO has designed and built a wide variety of applications and infrastructure frameworks for banking, insurance, supply-chain management, and business intelligence companies. He received a MS degree in computer science from Belarussian State University of Informatics and Radioelectronics.

Author Online

Purchase of *Algorithms of the Intelligent Web* includes free access to a private web forum run by Manning Publications where you can make comments about the book, ask technical questions, and receive help from the authors and from other users. To access the forum and subscribe to it, point your web browser to www.manning.com/books/algorithms-of-the-intelligent-web-second-edition. This page provides information on how to get on the forum once you're registered, what kind of help is available, and the rules of conduct on the forum.

Manning's commitment to our readers is to provide a venue where a meaningful dialog between individual readers and between readers and the author can take place. It is not a commitment to any specific amount of participation on the part of the authors, whose contribution to Author Online remains voluntary (and unpaid). We suggest you try asking the authors some challenging questions, lest their interest stray! The Author Online forum and the archives of previous discussions will be accessible from the publisher's website as long as the book is in print.

About the cover illustration

The illustration on the cover of *Algorithms of the Intelligent Web, Second Edition*, is taken from a French book of dress customs, *Encyclopedie des Voyages by J. G. St. Saveur,* published in 1706. Travel for pleasures was a relatively new phenomenon at the time, and illustrated guides such as this one were popular, introducing both the tourist and the armchair traveler to the inhabitants of other far-off regions of the world, as well as to the more familiar regional costumes of France and Europe.

The diversity of the drawings in the *Encyclopedie des Voyages* speaks vividly of the uniqueness and individuality of the world's countries and peoples just 200 years ago. This was a time when the dress codes of two regions separated by a few dozen miles identified people uniquely as belonging to one or the other, and when members of a social class or a trade or a tribe could be easily distinguished by what they were wearing. This was also a time when people were fascinated by foreign lands and faraway places, even though they couldn't travel to these exotic destinations themselves.

Dress codes have changed since then, and the diversity by region, so rich at the time, has faded away. It's now often hard to tell the inhabitants of one continent from another. Perhaps, trying to view it optimistically, we've traded a world of cultural and visual diversity for a more varied personal life, or a more varied and interesting intellectual and technical life.

We at Manning celebrate the inventiveness, the initiative, and the fun of the computer business with book covers based on native and tribal costumes from two centuries ago, brought back to life by pictures like those from this travel guide.

Building applications for the intelligent web

This chapter covers

- Recognizing intelligence on the web
- Types of intelligent algorithms
- Evaluating intelligent algorithms

The intelligent web means different things to different people. To some it represents the evolution of the web into a more responsive and useful entity that can learn from and react to its users. To others it represents the inclusion of the web into many more aspects of our lives. To me, far from being the first iteration of Skynet, in which computers take over in a dystopian future, the intelligent web is about designing and implementing more naturally responsive applications that make our online experiences better in some quantifiable way. There's a good chance that every reader has encountered machine intelligence on many separate occasions, and this chapter will highlight some examples so that you'll be better equipped to recognize these in the future. This will, in turn, help you understand what's really happening under the hood when you interact with intelligent applications again.

Now that you know this book isn't about writing entities that will try to take over the world, we should perhaps discuss some other things that you won't find within these pages! First, this is very much a back-end book. In these pages, you won't learn about beautiful interactive visualizations or platforms. For this, we refer you to excellent publications by Scott Murray,[1] David McCandless,[2] and Edward Tufte.[3] Suffice to say that we don't have space here to do this topic justice along with what we're about to cover. Also, this book won't teach you statistics; but to gain the most from the book we'll assume you have a 101 level of knowledge or higher, in that you should have at least taken a course in statistics at some point in the past.

This is also not a book about data science. A plethora of titles are available that will help the data science practitioner, and we do hope that this book will be useful to data scientists, but these chapters contain little detail about how to be a data scientist. For these topics we refer you to the texts by Joel Grus[4] and Foster Provost and Tom Fawcett.[5]

Nor is this a detailed book about algorithm design. We'll often skim over details as to the design of algorithms and provide more intuition than a deep dive into specifics. This will allow us to cover much more ground, perhaps at the cost of some rigor. Think of each chapter as a trail of breadcrumbs leading you through the important aspects of that approach and nudging you toward resources where you can learn more.

Although many of the examples within the pages of this book are written using scikit-learn (http://scikit-learn.org), this isn't a book about scikit-learn! That is merely the tool by which we can demonstrate the approaches presented in this book. We'll never provide an example without at least an intuitive introduction as to why the algorithm works. In some cases we'll go deeper, but in many cases you should continue your research outside this book.

So what, then, is this book about? We'll cover the tools that provide an end-to-end view of intelligent algorithms as we see them today. We'll talk about the information that's collected about you, the average web user, and how that information can be channeled into useful streams so that it can be used to make predictions about your behavior—changing those predictions as your behavior changes. This means we'll often deviate from the standard "algorithm 101" book, in favor of giving you a flavor (!) of all the important aspects of intelligent algorithms.

We'll even discuss (in the appendix) a publish/subscribe technology that allows large quantities of data to be organized during ingestion. Although this has no place in a book that's strictly about data science or algorithms, we believe that it has a fundamental place in a book about the intelligent web. This doesn't mean we ignore data science or algorithms—quite the contrary! We'll cover most of the important algorithms used by the majority of the leading players in the intelligent-algorithm space.

[1]   Scott Murray, *Interactive Data Visualization for the Web* (O'Reilly, 2013).
[2]   David McCandless, *Information Is Beautiful* (HarperCollins, 2010).
[3]   Edward Tufte, *The Visual Display of Quantitative Information* (Graphics Press USA, 2001).
[4]   Joel Grus, *Data Science From Scratch: First Principles with Python* (O'Reilly, 2015).
[5]   Foster Provost and Tom Fawcett, *Data Science for Business* (O'Reilly Media, 2013).

Where possible, we reference known examples of these in the wild, so that you can test your knowledge against the behavior of such systems—and no doubt impress your friends!

But we're getting ahead of ourselves. In this chapter, we'll provide several examples of the application of intelligent algorithms that you should find immediately recognizable. We'll talk more about what intelligent algorithms can't do, before providing you with a taxonomy of the field that can be used to hang your newly learned concepts on. Finally, we'll present you with a number of methods to evaluate intelligent algorithms and impart to you some useful things to know.

We already hear you asking, "What is an intelligent algorithm?" For the purposes of this book, we'll refer to any algorithm that uses data to modify its behavior as *intelligent*. Remember that when you interact with an algorithm, you're merely interacting with a set of distinct rules. Intelligent algorithms differ in that they can change their behavior as they run, often resulting in a user experience that many would say is intelligent. Figure 1.1 summarizes this behavior. Here you see an intelligent algorithm responding to events within the environment and making decisions. By ingesting data from the context in which it operates (which may include the event itself), the algorithm is evolving. It evolves in the sense that the decision is no longer deterministic given the event. The intelligent algorithm may make different decisions at different points, depending on the data it has ingested.

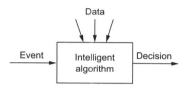

Figure 1.1　Overview of an intelligent algorithm. Such algorithms display intelligence because the decisions they make change depending on the data they've received.

1.1　*An intelligent algorithm in action: Google Now*

To demonstrate this concept, we'll try to deconstruct the operation of Google Now. Note that the specific details of this project are proprietary to Google, so we'll be relying on our own experience to illustrate how this system might work internally.

For those of you with Android devices, this product may be immediately recognizable, but for the iOS users among us, Google Now is Google's answer to Siri and has the product tagline "The right information at just the right time." This is essentially an application that can use various sources of information and alert you about nearby restaurants, events, traffic jams, and the like that it believes will be of interest to you. To demonstrate the concept of an intelligent algorithm, let's take an even more concrete example from Google Now. When it detects a traffic jam on your normal route to work, it will show you some information before you set off from home. Neat! But how might this be achieved?

First, let's try to understand exactly what might be happening here. The application knows about your location through its GPS and registered wireless stations, so at any given time the application will know where you are, down to a reasonable level of granularity. In the context of figure 1.1, this is one aspect of the data that's being used to change the behavior of the algorithm. From here it's a short step to determine home and work locations. This is performed through the use of *prior knowledge*: that is, knowledge that has somehow been distilled into the algorithm before it started learning from the data. In this case, the prior knowledge could take the form of the following rules:

- The location most usually occupied overnight is home.
- The location most usually occupied during the day is work.
- People, in general, travel to their workplace and then home again almost every day.

Although this is an imperfect example, it does illustrate our point well—that a concept of work, home, and commuting exists within our society, and that together with the data and a *model*, inference can be performed: that is, we can determine the likely home and work locations along with likely commuting routes. We qualify our information with the word *likely* because many models will allow us to encapsulate the notion of probability or likelihood of a decision.

When a new phone is purchased or a new account is registered with Google, it takes Google Now some time to reach these conclusions. Similarly, if users move to a different home or change jobs, it takes time for Google Now to relearn these locations. The speed at which the model can respond to change is referred to as the *learning rate*.

In order to display relevant information regarding travel route plans (to make a *decision* based on an *event*), we still don't have enough information. The final piece of the puzzle is predicting when a user is about to leave one location and travel to the other. Similar to our previous application, we could model leaving times and update this over time to reflect changing patterns of behavior. For a given time in the future, it's now possible to provide a likelihood that a user is in a given location and is about to leave that location in favor of another. If this likelihood triggers a threshold value, Google Now can perform a traffic search and return it to the user as a notification.

This specific part of Google Now is quite complex and probably has its own team devoted to it, but you can easily see that the framework through which it operates is an intelligent algorithm: it uses *data* about your movements to understand your routine and tailor personalized responses for you (*decisions*) based on your current location (*event*). Figure 1.2 provides a graphical overview of this process.

One interesting thing to note is that the product Google Now is probably using an entire suite of intelligent algorithms in the background. Algorithms perform text searches of your Google Calendar, trying to make sense of your schedule, while interest models churn away to try to decide which web searches are relevant and whether new content should be flagged for your interest.

As a developer in the intelligent-algorithm space, you'll be called on to use your skills in this area to develop new solutions from complex requirements, carefully identifying each subsection of work that can be tackled with an existing class of intelligent

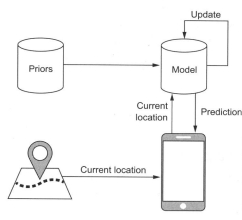

Figure 1.2   Graphical overview of one aspect of the Google Now project. In order for Google Now to make predictions about your future locations, it uses a model about past locations, along with your current position. Priors are a way to distill initially known information into the system.

algorithm. Each solution that you create should be grounded in and built on work in the field—much of which you'll find in this book. We've introduced several key terms here in italics, and we'll refer to these in the coming chapters as we tackle individual algorithms in more depth.

1.2   *The intelligent-algorithm lifecycle*

In the previous section, we introduced you to the concept of an intelligent algorithm comprising a black box, taking data and making predictions from events. We also more concretely drew on an example at Google, looking at its Google Now project. You might wonder then how intelligent-algorithm designers come up with their solutions. There is a general lifecycle, adopted from Ben Fry's *Computational Information Design,*[6] that you can refer to when designing your own solutions, as shown in figure 1.3.

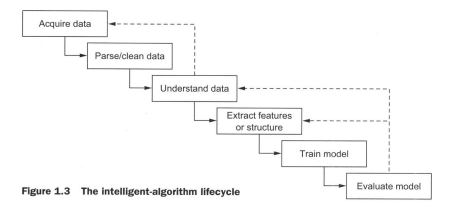

Figure 1.3   The intelligent-algorithm lifecycle

---

[6]   Ben Fry, PhD thesis, *Computational Information Design* (MIT, 2004).

When designing intelligent algorithms, you first must acquire data (the focus of the appendix) and then parse and clean it, because it's often not in the format you require. You must then understand that data, which you can achieve through data exploration and visualization. Subsequently, you can represent that data in more appropriate formats (the focus of chapter 2). At this point, you're ready to train a model and evaluate the predictive power of your solution. Chapters 3 through 7 cover various models that you might use. At the output of any stage, you can return to an earlier stage; the most common return paths are illustrated with dotted lines in figure 1.3.

1.3   *Further examples of intelligent algorithms*

Let's review some more applications that have been using algorithmic intelligence over the last decade. A turning point in the history of the web was the advent of search engines, but a lot of what the web had to offer remained untapped until 1998 when link analysis emerged in the context of search. Since this time Google has grown, in less than 20 years, from a startup to a dominant player in the technology sector, initially due to the success of its link-based search and later due to a number of new and innovative applications in the field of mobile and cloud services.

Nevertheless, the realm of intelligent web applications extends well beyond search engines. Amazon was one of the first online stores that offered recommendations to its users based on their shopping patterns. You may be familiar with that feature. Let's say that you purchase a book on JavaServer Faces and a book on Python. As soon as you add your items to the shopping cart, Amazon will recommend additional items that are somehow related to the ones you've just selected; it might recommend books that involve AJAX or Ruby on Rails. In addition, during your next visit to the Amazon website, the same or other related items may be recommended. Another intelligent web application is Netflix, which is the world's largest online movie streaming service, offering more than 53 million subscribers access to an ever-changing library of full-length movies and television episodes that are available to stream instantly.

Part of its online success is due to its ability to provide users with an easy way to choose movies from an expansive selection of movie titles. At the core of that ability is a recommendation system called Cinematch. Its job is to predict whether someone will enjoy a movie based on how much they liked or disliked other movies. This is another great example of an intelligent web application. The predictive power of Cinematch is of such great value to Netflix that, in October 2006, it led to the announcement of a million-dollar prize for improving its capabilities. By September 2009, a cash prize of $1 million was awarded to team BellKor's Pragmatic Chaos. In chapter 3, we offer coverage of the algorithms that are required to build a recommendation system such as Cinematch and provide an overview of the winning entry.

Using the opinions of the collective in order to provide intelligent predictions isn't limited to book or movie recommendations. The company PredictWallStreet collects the predictions of its users for a particular stock or index in order to spot trends in the opinions of the traders and predict the value of the underlying asset. We don't suggest that you should withdraw your savings and start trading based on this company's predictions, but it's yet another example of creatively applying the techniques in this book to a real-world scenario.

1.4 *Things that intelligent applications are not*

With so many apparently intelligent algorithms observable on the web, it's easy to think that, given sufficient engineering resources, we can build or automate any process that comes to mind. To be impressed by their prevalence, however, is to be fooled into thinking so.

> *Any sufficiently advanced technology is indistinguishable from magic.*
>
> —Arthur C. Clarke

As you've seen with Google Now, it's tempting to look at the larger application and infer some greater intelligence, but the reality is that a finite number of learning algorithms have been brought together to provide a useful but limited solution. Don't be drawn in by apparent complexity, but ask yourself, "Which aspects of my problem can be learned and modeled?" Only then will you be able to construct solutions that appear to exhibit intelligence. In the following subsections, we'll cover some of the most popular misconceptions regarding intelligent algorithms.

1.4.1 *Intelligent algorithms are not all-purpose thinking machines*

As mentioned at the start of this chapter, this book isn't about building sentient beings but rather about building algorithms that can somehow adapt their specific behavior given the data received. In my experience, the business projects that are most likely to fail are those whose objectives are as grand as solving the entire problem of artificial intelligence! Start small and build, reevaluating your solution continuously until you're satisfied that it addresses your original problem.

1.4.2 *Intelligent algorithms are not a drop-in replacement for humans*

Intelligent algorithms are very good at learning a specific concept given relevant data, but they're poor at learning new concepts outside their initial programming. Consequently, intelligent algorithms or solutions must be carefully constructed and combined to provide a satisfactory experience.

Conversely, humans are excellent all-purpose computation machines! They can easily understand new concepts and apply knowledge learned in one domain to another. They come with a variety of actuators (!) and are programmable in many different languages (!!). It's a mistake to think that we can easily write code-driven solutions to replace seemingly simple human processes.

Many human-driven processes in a business or organization may at first glance appear simple, but this is usually because the full specification of the process is unknown. Further investigation usually uncovers a considerable level of communication through different channels, often with competing objectives. Intelligent algorithms aren't well suited to such domains without process simplification and formalization.

Let's draw a simple but effective parallel with the automation of the motor-vehicle assembly line. In contrast to the early days of assembly-line automation pioneered by Henry Ford, it's now possible to completely automate steps of the construction process through the use of robotics. This was not, as Henry Ford might have imagined, achieved by building general-purpose robotic humanoids to replace workers! It was made possible through the abstraction of the assembly line and a rigorous formalization of the process. This in turn led to well-defined subtasks that *could* be solved by robotic aides. Although it is, in theory, possible to create automated learning processes for existing manually achieved optimization tasks, doing so would require similar process redesign and formalization.

1.4.3 *Intelligent algorithms are not discovered by accident*

The best intelligent algorithms are often the result of simple abstractions and mechanisms. Thus they appear to be complex, because they learn and change with use, but the underlying mechanisms are conceptually simple. Conversely, poor intelligent algorithms are often the result of many, many layers of esoteric rules, added in isolation to tackle individual use cases. To put it another way, always start with the simplest model that you can think of. Then gradually try to improve your results by combining additional elements of intelligence in your solution. KISS (Keep it simple, stupid!) is your friend and a software engineering invariant.

1.5 *Classes of intelligent algorithm*

If you recall, we used the phrase *intelligent algorithm* to describe any algorithm that can use data to modify its behavior. We use this very broad term in this book to encompass all aspects of intelligence and learning. If you were to look to the literature, you'd more likely see several other terms, all of which share a degree of overlap with each other: *machine learning* (ML), *predictive analytics* (PA), and *artificial intelligence* (AI). Figure 1.4 shows the relationship among these fields.

Although all three deal with algorithms that use data to modify their behavior, in each instance their focus is slightly different. In the following sections, we'll discuss each of these in turn before providing you with a few useful nuggets of knowledge to tie them together.

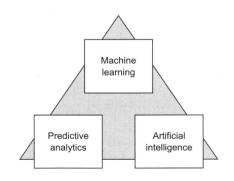

Figure 1.4 Taxonomy of intelligent algorithms

1.5.1 Artificial intelligence

Artificial intelligence, widely known by its acronym AI, began as a computational field around 1950. Initially, the goals of AI were ambitious and aimed at developing machines that could think like humans.[7] Over time, the goals became more practical and concrete as the full extent of the work required to emulate intelligence was uncovered. To date, there are many definitions of AI. For example, Stuart Russell and Peter Norvig describe AI as "the study of agents that receive percepts from the environment and perform actions,"[8] whereas John McCarthy states, "It is the science and engineering of making intelligent machines, especially intelligent computer programs."[9] Importantly, he also states that "intelligence is the computational part of the ability to achieve goals in the world."

In most discussions, AI is about the study of agents (software and machines) that have a series of options to choose from at a given point and must achieve a particular goal. Studies have focused on particular problem domains (Go,[10] chess,[11] and the game show Jeopardy![12]), and in such constrained environments, results are often excellent. For example, IBM's Deep Blue beat Garry Kasparov at chess in 1997, and in 2011 IBM's Watson received the first-place prize of $1 million on the U.S. television show Jeopardy! Unfortunately, few algorithms have come close to faring well under Alan Turing's *imitation game*[13] (otherwise known as the Turing test), which is considered by most the gold standard for intelligence. Under this game (without any visual or audio cues—that is, typewritten answers only), an interrogator must be fooled by a machine attempting to act as a human. This situation is considerably harder, because the machine must possess a wide range of knowledge on many topics; the interrogator isn't restricted in the questions they may ask.

1.5.2 Machine learning

Machine learning (ML) refers to the capability of a software system to generalize based on past experience. Importantly, ML is about using these generalizations to provide answers to questions relating to previously collected data as well as data that hasn't been encountered before. Some approaches to learning create explainable models—a layperson can follow the reasoning behind the generalization. Examples of explainable models are decision trees and, more generally, any rule-based learning

---

7 Herbert Simon, *The Shape of Automation for Men and Management* (Harper & Row, 1965).

8 Stuart Russell and Peter Norvig, *Artificial Intelligence: A Modern Approach* (Prentice Hall, 1994).

9 John McCarthy, "What Is Artificial Intelligence?" (Stanford University, 2007), http://www-formal.stanford.edu/jmc/whatisai.

10 Bruno Bouzy and Tristan Cazenave, "Computer Go: An AI Oriented Survey," *Artificial Intelligence* (Elsevier) 132, no. 1 (2001): 39–103.

11 Murray Campbell, A. J. Hoane, and Feng-hsiung Hsu, "Deep Blue," *Artificial Intelligence* (Elsevier) 134, no. 1 (2002): 57–83.

12 D. Ferrucci et al., "Building Watson: An Overview of the DeepQA Project," *AI Magazine* 31, no. 3 (2010).

13 Alan Turing, "Computing Machinery and Intelligence," *Mind* 59, no. 236 (1950): 433–60.

method. Other algorithms, though, aren't as transparent to humans—neural networks and support vector machines (SVM) fall in this category.

You might say that the scope of machine learning is very different than that of AI. Whereas AI looks at the world through the lens of *agents* striving to achieve *goals* (akin to how a human agent may operate at a high level in their environment), ML focuses on learning and generalization (more akin to how a human operates internally). For example, ML deals with such problems as classification (how to recognize data labels given the data), clustering (how to group similar data together), and regression (how to predict one outcome given another).

In general, machine-learning practitioners use *training data* to create a *model*. This model generalizes the underlying data relationships in some manner (which depends on the model used) in order to make predictions about previously unseen data. Figure 1.5 demonstrates this relationship. In this example, our data consists of three *features*, named A, B, and C. Features are elements of the data; so, for example, if our classes were male and female and our task was to separate the two, we might use features such as height, weight, and shoe size.

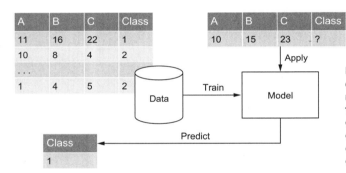

Figure 1.5 The machine-learning data flow. Data is used to train a model, which can then be applied to previously unseen data. In this case, the diagram illustrates classification, but the diagrams for clustering and regression are conceptually similar.

In our training data, the relationship between the *features* and *class* is known, and it's the job of the model to encapsulate this relationship. Once trained, the model can be applied to new data where the class is unknown.

1.5.3 *Predictive analytics*

Predictive analytics (PA) isn't as widely addressed in the academic literature as AI and ML. But with the developing maturity in big data processing architectures and an increasing appetite to operationalize data and provide value through it, it has become an increasingly important topic. For the purposes of this book, we use the following definition, extended from the OED definition of *analytics*. Note that the italicized text extends the existing definition:

> Predictive analytics: The systematic computational analysis of data or statistics *to create predictive models.*

You may ask, "How is this different from ML, which is also about prediction?" This is a good question! In general, ML techniques focus on understanding and generalizing the underlying structure and relationships of a dataset, whereas predictive analytics is often about scoring, ranking, and making predictions about future data items and trends, frequently in a business or operational setting. Although this may appear to be a somewhat fuzzy comparison, there's a large degree of overlap among the intelligent-algorithm classes we've introduced, and these categories aren't concrete and definite.

Confusingly, analysts don't usually create PA solutions. Predictive analytics is about creating models that, given some information, can respond quickly and efficiently with useful output that predicts some future behavior. Software engineers and data scientists often create such systems. Just to add to the confusion, PA models may use ML and AI approaches!

PREDICTIVE ANALYTICS EXAMPLES

To provide you some intuition, we'll demonstrate several examples of PA solutions in the wild. For our first example, we look toward the online-advertising world. An astute web user may notice that advertisements often follow them around as they browse the web. If you've just been looking at shoes on Nike's shopping page, then as you browse other pages, you'll often find ads for those very shoes alongside the text of your favorite site! This is known as *retargeting*. Every time a page hosting advertisements is loaded, hundreds of decisions are made by multiple different parties, all wanting to show you a different ad. This is facilitated through an ad exchange whereby each party submits the price it's willing to pay to show an ad to you, with the highest bidder winning that right. Because all of this must happen in several milliseconds, an intelligent algorithm trying to predict or score the value of this user in advance reaches this price. This PA solution makes decisions based on past user behavior and provides an advantage over randomly selecting users for advertising display. We'll revisit this example in chapter 5, where you'll see how many online advertisers have solved this problem.

For our second example, we turn to the world of consumer credit. Whenever we try to obtain credit for a store card, credit card, mobile phone, or mortgage, retailers are exposing themselves to an element of risk (and also an element of reward!). In order to balance this, retailers want to know that they're mostly providing credit to credit-worthy individuals, while rejecting those who are more likely to default on their payments. In practice, this decision is referred to specialist credit agencies that will, for a fee, provide the retailer with an estimate, or credit score, on an individual. This is generated by a PA solution based on historical data for the population and is a number that has a high degree of correlation with the risk of the individual. The higher the score, the more creditworthy the individual and the less likely the chance of default. Note that this provides you with only a statistical advantage, because people with high credit scores can still default (although if the model works, at a lower frequency than those with a lower credit score).

1.6 Evaluating the performance of intelligent algorithms

Thus far, we've talked about the high-level classes of intelligent algorithms and provided several motivating examples. But how does the intelligent-algorithm practitioner evaluate their algorithm? This is of great importance for several reasons. First, without an objective evaluation, it's not possible to track performance, and so it's impossible to know if modifications have improved operation. Second, if you can't measure performance, then justification becomes difficult. From a business perspective, managers and technologists will always try to measure value against cost, and being able to solidly evaluate your solution will help keep it in production!

Let's now return to each class of intelligent algorithm and discuss strategies for performance measurement. Although we'll touch on how to evaluate intelligence, this section is largely about evaluating predictions (that is, for machine learning and predictive analytics). Evaluating (and defining) intelligence is a big subject and could fill a book like this on its own! Rather than delve into this topic, we refer you to Linda Gottfredson,[14] James Flynn,[15] and Alan Turing.[16]

1.6.1 Evaluating intelligence

In the preceding text, we mentioned Turing's imitation game, but there may be a call to evaluate systems that are less grand in their approach to intelligence: for example, intelligent systems that play chess or compete on Jeopardy! Such systems would hardly be able to imitate a human, but they excel in one specific task. Sandeep Rajani's approach to the evaluation of artificial intelligence[17] separates performance into four categories:

- *Optimal*—Not possible to perform better
- *Strong super-human*—Performs better than all humans
- *Super-human*—Performs better than most humans
- *Sub-human*—Performs worse than most humans

For example, the current state of the art in AI can create systems that are optimal at Tic-Tac-Toe, super-human (and perhaps strong super-human) at chess, and sub-human at natural language translation.

1.6.2 Evaluating predictions

Although interesting, the majority of solutions in this book won't seek to create artificial intelligence, and so we should provide more relevant evaluation metrics. Recall that in both ML and PA, the objective is to make a prediction based on the data and

---

[14] Linda S. Gottfredson, "Mainstream Science on Intelligence: An Editorial with 52 Signatories, History, and Bibliography," *Wall Street Journal*, December 13, 1994.

[15] James R. Flynn, *What Is Intelligence? Beyond the Flynn Effect* (Cambridge University Press, 2009).

[16] Alan Turing, "Computing Machinery and Intelligence."

[17] Sandeep Rajani, "Artificial Intelligence - Man or Machine," *International Journal of Information Technology and Knowledge Management* 4, no. 1 (2011): 173–76.

the relationship between the features and the target (or class). Consequently, we have a concrete framework for evaluation and may look to statistics for a formal treatment of performance.

Table 1.1 presents a demonstration (toy) dataset that will be used to illustrate how the performance of a predictor can be calculated. Features of the data are labeled with letters of the alphabet, and the ground truth and predicted (Boolean) classes are presented alongside. Imagine that predictions have been generated from a test set that the original model hasn't been exposed to. This test set has had the ground truth withheld, and so the model must base its output on the value of the features alone.

Table 1.1 A sample dataset to illustrate intelligent-algorithm evaluation

A	B	...	Ground truth	Prediction
10	4	...	True	False
20	7	...	True	True
5	6	...	False	False
1	2	...	False	True

It's immediately clear that there are a few simple metrics we may wish to apply to judge the performance of this classifier. First, we might look at the true positive rate (TPR), which is the total number of positives that are correctly identified divided by the total number of positives in the dataset. This is sometimes known as the *sensitivity* or *recall*. Note, however, that this is only half the picture! If we built a classifier that always returned true, regardless of the features of the data, we would still have excellent recall. Consequently, this metric must be considered in the context of another metric, known as the *specificity* or true negative rate (TNR): that is, the total number of negative classes that were correctly identified as such as a percentage of the total number of negative data items. A perfect classifier will provide a TPR and TNR of 100%.

Unfortunately, most classifiers are far from perfect, and so we must reason about their performance with respect to their error. The false positive rate (FPR) is determined as 1 minus the TNR, whereas the false negative rate (FNR) is 1 minus the TPR. These are known as *type I* and *type II* errors, respectively. Table 1.2 summarizes these relationships.

Table 1.2 Performance metrics used in the evaluation of intelligent algorithms

Metric	Calculation
True positive rate (TPR)	Predicted true positives / ground truth true positives
True negative rate (TNR)	Predicted true negatives / ground truth true negatives
False positive rate (FPR)	1 − true negative rate
False negative rate (FNR)	1 − true positive rate

To drive home the concept, let's apply the metrics from table 1.2 to our dataset in table 1.1. By carefully working through the definitions, you'll see that the TPR and TNR are equal to 1/2, and by implication so are the FPR and FNR.

Let's imagine that our algorithms have an internal mechanism that's used to adjust their behavior. We can imagine this as some sort of threshold, or knob, that adjusts the sensitivity of the algorithm. As we twist the knob to zero, the algorithm might be extremely desensitized and classify everything as false (TNR=1, TPR=0). Conversely, if we crank the knob all the way up to 11, the algorithm may classify everything as true (TNR=0, TPR=1). Clearly, neither of these options is desirable. Ideally, we'd like a classifier that returns true if and only if an item is true and false if and only if the item is false (TNR=1, TPR=1). This idealized classifier is unlikely for anything other than a toy problem, but we can look at how our classifier behaves as we twist this knob and use this to evaluate our algorithm; see figure 1.6.

Figure 1.6 gives what is known as the receiver operating characteristic (ROC) curve of two imaginary classifiers. This curve traces the TPR and FPR as we twist our conceptual knob, thereby changing the parameters of the classifier. As mentioned previously, the ideal is a classifier with TPR=1 and TNR=1 (FPR=0); thus models that trace a line closer to the top-left corner of the graph are conceptually better, because they do a better job at separating negative and positive classes correctly. In this graph, classifier 2 clearly does a better job and should be chosen over classifier 1. Another way to encode this performance is by looking at the area under the ROC curve, sometimes known as the AUC (area under the curve). The larger the AUC, the better the performance of the model.

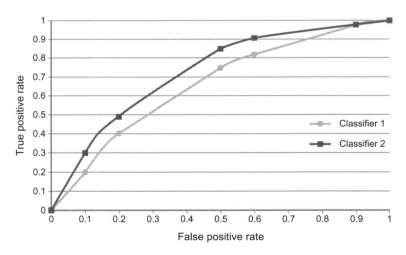

Figure 1.6   ROC curves for two theoretical classifiers. As we modify the algorithm parameter, we see a change in behavior against a given dataset. The closer the trace gets to touching the top-left corner of the diagram, the closer that classifier is to being ideal, because the TPR=1 and the TNR=1 (because TNR=1 – FPR).

So far, so sensible! Be aware, however, that for predictive analytics solutions, things may not always be so easy. Take, for example, the issue of credit scoring. When you provide a score, you may not always be able to follow up on the behavior of that user in the future. Also, in these cases you're usually not attempting to provide the answer but rather some indicator that's correlated with a target variable (such as creditworthiness). Although the ROC curve can be used in these cases, there can be a few more hoops to jump through to get there.

1.7   Important notes about intelligent algorithms

Thus far we've covered a lot of introductory material. By now, you should have a fairly good, albeit high-level, understanding of intelligent algorithms and how you're going to use them. You're probably sufficiently motivated and anxious to dive into the details. We won't disappoint you. Every following chapter is loaded with new and valuable code. But before we embark on our journey into the exciting and (for the more cynical among us) financially rewarding world of intelligent applications, we'll present some useful things to know, many of which have been adapted from Pedro Domingos's excellent and easy-to-read paper on the subject.[18] These should help guide you as you progress through this book and, later on, the field of intelligent algorithms.

1.7.1   Your data is not reliable

Your data may be unreliable for many reasons. That's why you should always examine whether the data you'll work with can be trusted before you start considering specific intelligent-algorithmic solutions to your problem. Even intelligent people who use very bad data will typically arrive at erroneous conclusions. The following is an indicative but incomplete list of the things that can go wrong with your data:

- The data that you have available during development may not be representative of the data that corresponds to a production environment. For example, you may want to categorize the users of a social network as "tall," "average," or "short" based on their height. If the shortest person in your development data is 6 feet tall (about 184 cm), you're running the risk of calling someone short because they're "just" 6 feet tall.
- Your data may contain missing values. In fact, unless your data is artificial, it's almost certain to contain missing values. Handling missing values is a tricky business. Typically, you either leave the missing values or fill them in with some default or calculated values. Both conditions can lead to unstable implementations.
- Your data may change. The database schema may change, or the semantics of the data in the database may change.

---

[18] Pedro Domingos, "A Few Useful Things to Know About Machine Learning," *Communications of the ACM* 55, no. 10 (2012): 78–87.

- Your data may not be normalized. Let's say that you're looking at the weight of a set of individuals. In order to draw any meaningful conclusions based on the value of the weight, the unit of measurement should be the same for all individuals—pounds or kilograms for every person, not a mix of measurements in pounds and kilograms.
- Your data may be inappropriate for the algorithmic approach you have in mind. Data comes in various shapes and forms, known as *data types*. Some datasets are numeric, and some aren't. Some datasets can be ordered, and some can't. Some numeric datasets are discrete (such as the number of people in a room), and some are continuous (for example, the temperature or the atmospheric pressure).

1.7.2   *Inference does not happen instantaneously*

Computing a solution takes time, and the responsiveness of your application may be crucial for the financial success of your business. You shouldn't assume that all algorithms on all datasets will run within the response-time limits of your application. You should test the performance of your algorithm within the range of your operating characteristics.

1.7.3   *Size matters!*

When we talk about intelligent applications, size does matter! The size of your data comes into the picture in two ways. The first is related to the responsiveness of the application, as mentioned earlier. The second is related to your ability to obtain meaningful results on a large dataset. You may be able to provide excellent movie or music recommendations for a set of users when the number of users is around 100, but the same algorithm may result in poor recommendations when the number of users involved is around 100,000.

Second, subject to the curse of dimensionality (covered in chapter 2), getting more data to throw at a simple algorithm often yields results that are far superior to making your classifier more and more complicated. If you look at large corporations such as Google, which use massive amounts of data, an equal measure of achievement should be attributed to how they deal with large volumes of training data as well as the complexity and sophistication of their classification solutions.

1.7.4   *Different algorithms have different scaling characteristics*

Don't assume that an intelligent-application solution can scale just by adding more machines. Don't assume that your solution is scalable. Some algorithms are scalable, and others aren't. Let's say that you're trying to find groups of news stories with similar headlines among billions of titles. Not all clustering algorithms can run in parallel. You should consider scalability during the design phase of your application. In some cases, you may be able to split the data and apply your intelligent algorithm on smaller datasets in parallel. The algorithms you select in your design may have parallel (concurrent) versions, but you should investigate this from the outset, because typically you'll build a lot of infrastructure and business logic around your algorithms.

1.7.5   *Everything is not a nail!*

You may have heard the phrase, "When all you have is a hammer, everything looks like a nail." Well, we're here to tell you that all of your intelligent-algorithm problems can't be solved with the same algorithm!

Intelligent-application software is like every other piece of software—it has a certain area of applicability and certain limitations. Make sure you test your favorite solution thoroughly in new areas of application. In addition, it's recommended that you examine every problem with a fresh perspective; a different algorithm may solve a different problem more efficiently or more expediently.

1.7.6   *Data isn't everything*

Ultimately, ML algorithms aren't magic, and they require an inductive step that allows you to reach outside the training data and into unseen data. For example, if you already know much regarding the dependencies of the data, a good representation may be graphical models—which can easily express this prior knowledge.[19] Careful consideration of what's already known about the domain, along with the data, helps you build the most appropriate classifiers.

1.7.7   *Training time can be variable*

In certain applications, it's possible to have a large variance in solution times for a relatively small variation of the parameters involved. Typically, people expect that when they change the parameters of a problem, the problem can be solved consistently with respect to response time. If you have a method that returns the distance between any two geographic locations on Earth, you expect that the solution time will be independent of any two specific geographic locations. But this isn't true for all problems. A seemingly innocuous change in the data can lead to significantly different solution times; sometimes the difference can be hours instead of seconds!

1.7.8   *Generalization is the goal*

One of the most common pitfalls with practitioners of ML is to get caught up in the process and to forget the final goal—to generalize the process or phenomenon under investigation. At the testing phase, it's crucial to employ methods that allow you to investigate the generality of your solution (hold out test data, cross validate, and so on), but there's no substitute for having an appropriate dataset to start with! If you're trying to generalize a process with millions of attributes but only a few hundred test examples, chasing a percentage accuracy is tantamount to folly.

---

[19] Judea Pearl, *Probabilistic Reasoning in Intelligent Systems* (Morgan Kaufmann Publishers, 1988).

1.7.9 *Human intuition is problematic*

As the feature space grows, there's a combinatorial explosion in the number of values the input may take. This makes it extremely unlikely that for any moderate-sized feature set you'll see even a decent fraction of the total possible inputs. More worrisome, your intuition breaks down as the number of features increases. For example, in high dimensions, counter to intuition, most of the mass of a multivariate Gaussian distribution isn't near the mean but in a "shell" around it.[20] Building simple classifiers in a low number of dimensions is easy, but increasing the number of dimensions makes it hard to understand what's happening.

1.7.10 *Think about engineering new features*

You've probably heard the phrase "garbage in, garbage out." This is especially important when it comes to building solutions using ML approaches. Understanding the problem domain is key here, and deriving a set of features that exposes the underlying phenomena under investigation can mean all the difference to classification accuracy and generalization. It's not good enough to throw all of your data at a classifier and hope for the best!

1.7.11 *Learn many different models*

Model ensembles are becoming increasingly common, due to their ability to reduce the variance of a classification with only a small cost to the bias. In the Netflix Prize, the overall winner and runner-up recommenders were both stacked (in which the output of each classifier is passed to a higher-level classifier) ensembles of more than 100 learners. Many believe that future classifiers will become more accurate through such techniques, but it does provide an additional layer of indirection for the non-expert to understand the mechanics of such a system.

1.7.12 *Correlation is not the same as causation*

This often-labored point is worth reiterating—and can be illustrated by a tongue-in-cheek thought experiment stating, "Global warming, earthquakes, hurricanes, and other natural disasters are a direct effect of the shrinking numbers of pirates since the 1800s."[21] Just because two variables are correlated, this doesn't imply causation between the two. Often there is a third (or fourth or fifth!) variable that isn't observable and is at play. Correlation should be taken as a sign of potential causation, warranting further investigation.

---

[20] Domingos, "A Few Useful Things to Know About Machine Learning."

[21] Bobby Henderson, "An Open Letter to Kansas School Board," *Verganza* (July 1, 2005), www.venganza .org/about/open-letter.

1.8   Summary

- We provided the 50,000–foot view of intelligent algorithms, providing many specific examples based on real-world problems.
- An intelligent algorithm is any that can modify its behavior based on incoming data.
- We provided some intelligent-algorithm design anti-patterns that will hopefully serve as a warning flag for practitioners in the space.
- You've seen that intelligent algorithms can be broadly divided into three categories: artificial intelligence, machine learning, and predictive analytics. We'll spend the most time on the latter two in this book, so if you glanced over these sections, it would be worth rereading them to ensure good foundational knowledge.
- We introduced some key metrics such as the receiver operating characteristic. The area under the ROC curve is often used to assess the relative performance of models. Be warned that there are many ways to evaluate performance, and here we only introduced the basics.
- We provided you with some useful facts that have been learned collectively by the intelligent-algorithm community. These can provide an invaluable compass by which to navigate the field.

Extracting structure
from data: clustering and
transforming your data

In the previous chapter, you got your feet wet with the concept of intelligent algorithms. From this chapter onward, we're going to concentrate on the specifics of machine-learning and predictive-analytics algorithms. If you've ever wondered what types of algorithms are out there and how they work, then these chapters are for you!

This chapter is specifically about the structure of data. That is, given a dataset, are there certain patterns and rules that describe it? For example, if we have a data set of the population and their job titles, ages, and salaries, are there any general rules or patterns that could be used to simplify the data? For instance, do higher

Figure 2.1   Visualizing structure in data. x- and y-axis values are arbitrary and unimportant. This data shows three different classes of data, all colored differently. You see that the x and y values appear to cluster around certain areas of the x, y plot dependent on their class. You also see that higher values of x correlate to higher values of y regardless of the class. Each of these properties relates to the structure of the data, and we'll cover each in turn in the remainder of this chapter.

ages correlate with higher salaries? Is a larger percentage of the wealth present in a smaller percentage of the population? If found, these generalizations can be extracted directly either to provide evidence of a pattern or to represent the dataset in a smaller, more compact data file. These two use cases are the purpose of this chapter, and figure 2.1 provides a visual representation.

> **NOTE TO PRINT BOOK READERS: COLOR GRAPHICS**   Many graphics in this book are best viewed in color. The eBook versions display the color graphics, so they should be referred to as you read. To get your free eBook in PDF, ePub, and Kindle formats, go to www.manning.com/books/algorithms-of-the-intelligent -web-second-edition to register your print book.

We'll embark on this subject by laying down some fundamental terms and defining the meaning of structure as it relates to data. We'll also discuss the concepts of bias and noise, which can color your collected data in unexpected ways. You'll also find a discussion about the curse of dimensionality and the feature space. Simply put, this helps us reason about the relationship between the number of data features, the number of data points, and the phenomenon that we're trying to capture in an intelligent algorithm.

We'll move on to talk about a specific method of capturing structure, known as *clustering*, which seeks to group data points together based on their similarity—equivalent to coloring the data as in figure 2.1. Clustering has a wide range of applications, because we often want to know which things are similar to each other. For example, a business might want to find customers who are similar to each other in the hope that the purchase characteristics of one will be similar to those of the others. This might be useful if you're trying to identify your best clients and to grow your user base by locating more people who are like them. Whatever your reason for clustering, there are many ways to perform it, and we'll zero in on a specific type of clustering method known as *k-means*. K-means seeks to partition its input data into k distinct regions or clusters. Although conceptually simple, the k-means algorithm is widely used in practice, and we'll provide you with all the required code to get your very own implementation off the ground using scikit-learn. As part of our discussion of k-means, you'll see how the clusters are learned through the use of an iterative training algorithm called *expectation maximization* (EM). This key concept will be revisited again in this chapter when we discuss our second clustering method using the *Gaussian mixture model* (GMM).

Using a GMM to cluster can be seen as an extension of the k-means algorithm. It's possible to achieve exactly the same results with GMM and k-means if you provide certain limitations to your GMM. We'll discuss this in much more detail in the coming sections, but for now, you can think of GMM as a slightly more expressive model that assumes and captures some additional information about the distribution of data points. This model is also trained using the EM algorithm, and we'll investigate and discuss how and why these two versions of EM differ slightly.

In the final section, we'll review an important method for investigating the structure of data and for reducing the total number of features in your dataset without sacrificing the information contained in your data. This topic is equivalent to understanding how your variables vary together in a data set. In figure 2.1, it's equivalent to understanding that x increases with y regardless of the class of data. The method we'll cover is known as *principal component analysis* (PCA). Used on its own, this algorithm uncovers the principal directions of variance in your data—helping you understand which of your features are important and which are not. It can also be used to map your data into a smaller feature space—that is, one with fewer data features—without losing much of the information it captures. Consequently, it can be used as a preprocessing step to your clustering algorithms (or any other intelligent algorithm). This can often impact the training time of your algorithm positively without compromising the algorithm's efficacy. So without further delay, let's investigate the world of data and structure!

2.1   *Data, structure, bias, and noise*

For the purposes of this book, *data* is any information that can be collected and stored. But not all data is created equal. For intelligent algorithms on the web, data is collected in order to make predictions about a user's online behavior. With this in mind, let's add a little color to the terms *structure, bias,* and *noise.*

In general, when we talk about structure, we're referring to some implicit grouping, ordering, pattern, or correlation in the data. For example, if we were to collate the heights of all individuals in the UK, we might find two distinct groups relating to the average heights of male and female individuals. Bias might be introduced to the data if the person or people collecting the data consistently underreported their measurements, whereas noise might be introduced if those same people were careless and imprecise with their measurements.

To investigate these concepts further, we're going to explore some real data known as the *Iris dataset.* This commonly used dataset originated in 1936 and presents 150 data samples from 3 species of flower. For each data item, four measurements (features) are available. Let's begin by interrogating the data; see the following listing.

Listing 2.1 Interrogating the Iris dataset in scikit-learn (interactive shell)

```
>>> import numpy as np
>>> from sklearn import datasets                    ⟵——— Imports scikit-learn datasets
>>>
>>> iris = datasets.load_iris()
>>> np.array(zip(iris.data,iris.target))[0:10]      ⟵
array([[array([ 5.1,   3.5,   1.4,   0.2]), 0],      ⟵      Creates an array of both the
        [array([ 4.9,   3. ,   1.4,   0.2]), 0],            data and the target, and
        [array([ 4.7,   3.2,   1.3,   0.2]), 0],            displays the first 10 lines
        [array([ 4.6,   3.1,   1.5,   0.2]), 0],
        [array([ 5. ,   3.6,   1.4,   0.2]), 0],     Contents of the first 10 rows
        [array([ 5.4,   3.9,   1.7,   0.4]), 0],     of the array displayed
        [array([ 4.6,   3.4,   1.4,   0.3]), 0],
        [array([ 5. ,   3.4,   1.5,   0.2]), 0],
        [array([ 4.4,   2.9,   1.4,   0.2]), 0],
        [array([ 4.9,   3.1,   1.5,   0.1]), 0]], dtype=object)
```

Loads in the Iris dataset

Listing 2.1 presents an interactive Python session using scikit-learn to interrogate the Iris dataset. After firing up a Python shell, we imported NumPy and the datasets package, before loading in the Iris dataset. We used the `zip` method to create a 2-D array in which `iris.data` appeared alongside `iris.target`, and we selected the first 10 entries in the array.

But what are `iris.data` and `iris.target`? And what did we create? Well, the `iris` object is an instance of `sklearn.datasets.base.Bunch`. This is a dictionary-like object with several attributes (for more details, see the scikit-learn documentation). `Iris.data` is a 2-D array of feature values, and `iris.target` is a 1-D array of classes. For each row in listing 2.1, we printed out an array of the attributes (or *features*) of the flower, along with the class of the flower. But what do these feature values and classes relate to? Each feature relates to the length and width of the petal and sepal, whereas the class relates to the type of flower that was sampled. The next listing provides a summary of this information. Note that the features are presented in the same order as in listing 2.1.

Listing 2.2 Interrogating the Iris dataset in scikit-learn (interactive shell, continued)

```
>>> print(iris.DESCR)
Iris Plants Database

Notes
-----
Data Set Characteristics:
    :Number of Instances: 150 (50 in each of three classes)
    :Number of Attributes: 4 numeric, predictive attributes and the class
    :Attribute Information:
        - sepal length in cm
        - sepal width in cm
        - petal length in cm
        - petal width in cm
        - class:
```

```
                        - Iris-Setosa
                        - Iris-Versicolour
                        - Iris-Virginica
     :Summary Statistics:
     ============== ==== ==== ======= ===== ====================
                    Min  Max  Mean    SD    Class Correlation
     ============== ==== ==== ======= ===== ====================
     sepal length:  4.3  7.9  5.84    0.83   0.7826
     sepal width:   2.0  4.4  3.05    0.43  -0.4194
     petal length:  1.0  6.9  3.76    1.76   0.9490  (high!)
     petal width:   0.1  2.5  1.20    0.76   0.9565  (high!)
     ============== ==== ==== ======= ===== ====================
     :Missing Attribute Values: None
     :Class Distribution: 33.3% for each of 3 classes.
     :Creator: R.A. Fisher
     :Donor: Michael Marshall (MARSHALL%PLU@io.arc.nasa.gov)
     :Date: July, 1988
```

Using the DESCR attribute, you can obtain and print to the console some information that has been recorded about the Iris dataset. You can observe that, for each row of iris.data, the features consist of the sepal length (cm), the sepal width (cm), the petal length (cm), and the petal width (cm), in that order. The classes of flower, given by iris.target, are Iris-Setosa, Iris-Versicolour, and Iris-Virginica. Referring back to listing 2.1, you see that these are encoded by integers. It's easy to understand which class names relate to which integer class labels by using the target_names attribute, which stores the values in the same order in which they're encoded. The following code shows that 0 relates to Setosa, 1 to Versicolour, and 2 to Virginica:

```
>>> iris.target_names
array(['setosa', 'versicolour', 'virginica'],
      dtype='|S10')
```

Although we're working with a simple dataset, the concepts that you can learn here are universal among machine-learning algorithms. You'll see later in this chapter how you can draw on machine learning to extract the structure of the data and how different techniques can be adopted to achieve this.

To illustrate the concept of structure, let's try some thought experiments with the Iris dataset. It may be that all Virginicas are much bigger than the other flowers, such that the lengths and widths of the sepals and petals have significantly higher values. It may also be that one of the flowers is characterized by having long, thin petals, whereas the rest have short, rounded petals. At this stage, you don't know what the underlying structure or organization of the data is, but you may wish to employ automatic techniques to uncover this information. You may go further than this. What you might want is for your automated algorithm to uncover this structure and determine these subgroups or clusters and then assign each data point to one of the clusters. This is known as *clustering*.

As mentioned earlier, not all data is equal! Assuming that these measurements characterize the flowers well, and that they somehow capture the uniqueness of the individual species, there are a few other issues to watch out for. For example, what if the data was collected early in the flower-growing season? What if the flowers were immature and hadn't grown to their full size? This would mean the flowers are systematically different from the overall population—this is known as *bias*. Clusters generated from this data may be fine within the dataset being used, but due to their differences from the rest of the population, the clusters may not generalize well.

Conversely, what if the data-collection task was delegated to many different people? These people would likely perform measurement in different ways and with different levels of care. This would introduce a higher level of randomness to the data, known as *noise*. Depending on the structure of the data, this might be enough to obfuscate any underlying structure or pattern. For maximum generality and performance, both bias and noise should be minimized when collecting data.

2.2 *The curse of dimensionality*

Although the dataset contains only four features at the moment, you may wonder why we can't collect hundreds or thousands of measurements from each of the flowers and let the algorithm do all the work. Despite the practical challenges in obtaining so many measurements, there are two fundamental problems when collecting data with high dimensionality that are particularly important when finding structure. The first problem is that the large number of dimensions increases the amount of space available for spreading data points. That is, if you keep the number of data points fixed and increase the number of attributes you want to use to describe them, the density of the points in your space decreases exponentially! So, you can wander around in your data space for a long time without being able to identify a formation that's preferable to another one.

The second fundamental problem has a frightening name. It's called the *curse of dimensionality*. In simple terms, it means if you have *any* set of points in high dimensions and you use *any* metric to measure the distance between these points, they'll all come out to be roughly the same distance apart! To illustrate this important effect of dimensionality, let's consider the simple case illustrated in figure 2.2.

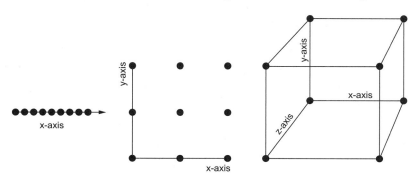

Figure 2.2   The curse of dimensionality: every point tends to have the same distance from any other point.

If you look at figure 2.2 from left to right, you'll see that the dimensionality increases by 1 for each drawing. We start with eight points in one dimension (x-axis) distributed in a uniform fashion: say, between 0 and 1. It follows that the minimum distance we need to traverse from any given point until we meet another point is $\min(D) = 0.125$, whereas the maximum distance is $\max(D) = 1$. Thus, the ratio of $\min(D)$ over $\max(D)$ is equal to 0.125. In two dimensions, the eight data points are again distributed uniformly, but now we have $\min(D) = 0.5$ and $\max(D) = 1.414$ (along the main diagonal); thus, the ratio of $\min(D)$ over $\max(D)$ is equal to 0.354. In three dimensions, we have $\min(D) = 1$ and $\max(D) = 1.732$; thus, the ratio of $\min(D)$ over $\max(D)$ is equal to 0.577. As as the dimensionality continues to increase, the ratio of the minimum distance over the maximum distance approaches the value of 1. This means no matter which direction you look and what distance you measure, it all looks the same!

What that this means practically for you is that the more attributes of the data you collect, the bigger the space of possible points is; it also means the similarity of these points becomes harder to determine. In this chapter, we're looking at the structure of data, and in order to determine patterns and structure in the data, you might think it's useful to collect lots of attributes about the phenomenon under investigation. Indeed it is, but be careful—the number of data points required to generalize patterns grows more quickly than the number of attributes you're using to describe the phenomenon. In practical terms, there's a trade-off to be made: you must collect highly descriptive attributes but not so many that you can't collect enough data to generalize or determine patterns in this space.

2.3   *K-means*

K-means seeks to partition data into k distinct clusters, characterizing these by their means. Such an outcome is often obtained using Lloyd's algorithm,[1] which is an iterative approach to finding a solution. It is often known as the *k-means algorithm* due to its widespread adoption. Usually, when people say they're applying k-means, they understand that they're using Lloyd's algorithm to solve for k-means. Let's look at a simple example of this algorithm operating on only a single dimension. Consider the number line presented in figure 2.3.

Here we present a dataset containing 13 points. You can clearly see that there's some structure to the data. The leftmost points might be considered to be clustered in the range 0–6, whereas the points to the right might be clustered in the range 9–16. We don't necessarily know that this is a good clustering, but if we were to use our judgment, we might hazard a guess that they're significantly different enough to be considered different groups of points.

This is essentially what all clustering algorithms seek to do: to create groups of data points that we may consider to be clusters of points or structure in the data. We'll dig further into this example before using k-means on some real data, but it's worth

---

[1]   Stuart P. Lloyd, "Least Squares Quantization in PCM," *IEEE Transactions on Information Theory* 28 (1982): 129-137.

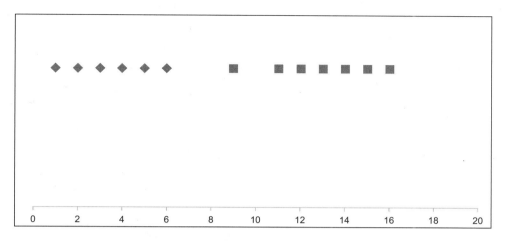

Figure 2.3 A number line containing two possible clusters in a single dimension. An entry indicates the existence of that number in the dataset. Data points represented by the same shape indicate one possible intuitive clustering of the data.

mentioning that this simple one-dimensional example demonstrates the concept without loss of generalization. In reality, nontrivial patterns and structure would be found from higher-dimensional data, subject, of course, to the curse of dimensionality.

Lloyd's algorithm works by iteratively trying to determine the means of the clusters in the dataset. The algorithm takes as a parameter k, the number of clusters that are to be learned; it may also take k estimates of the means of these clusters. These are the initial means of the clusters, but don't worry if these aren't correct yet—the algorithm will iteratively update them in order to provide the best solution it can. Let's revisit the data given in figure 2.3 and see if we can work through an example using this data.

Let's first imagine that we don't know the clusters or the means of these clusters (a sound assumption for a clustering algorithm), but all that we have is the 13 data points. Let's assume that we're also good guessers and we think there are two clusters to the data, so we'll start with k=2. The algorithm then proceeds as follows. First, we must calculate some non-identical estimates for the k means. Let's select these randomly as 1 and 8 for k_1 and k_2, respectively. We denote these by a triangle and a circle in figure 2.4, respectively. These values are our best guesses, and we'll update these as we go.

Now, for each data point in the dataset, we'll assign that point to the nearest cluster. If we work this through, all the points below 4.5 will be assigned to cluster k_1, and all the points above 4.5 will be assigned to cluster k_2. Figure 2.5 shows this with the data points belonging to k_1 shaded green (diamonds, in the print version of this book) and those belonging to k_2 shaded red (squares).

Not a bad start, you might think, but we can do better. If we revisit the data, we see that it looks more like points below 7 belong to the leftmost cluster, k_1, and points above 7 belong to the rightmost cluster, k_2. In order to make a cluster centroid better

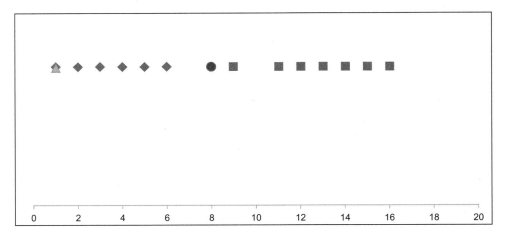

Figure 2.4 Initial assignment of the means of the k clusters. The mean of cluster k_1 is denoted by a triangle, and a circle denotes the mean of cluster k_2.

represent this, new means are calculated based on the average values in that cluster: that is, the new mean for cluster k_1 is given by the mean of the green data points, and the new mean for cluster k_2 is given by the mean of the red data points. Thus, the new means for k_1 and k_2 are 2.5 and 11.2, respectively. You can see the updated means in figure 2.6. Essentially, both cluster means have been dragged up by the data points assigned to them.

We now proceed with the second iteration. As before, for each data point, we assign it to the cluster with the closest centroid. All of our points below approximately 6.8 are now assigned to cluster k_1, and all of our points above this number are

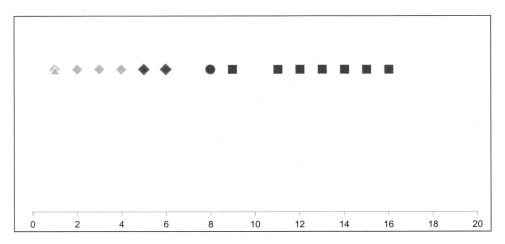

Figure 2.5 Initial assignment of data points to clusters. Those data points assigned to cluster k_1 are shaded green (diamonds), and those assigned to cluster k_2 are shaded red (squares).

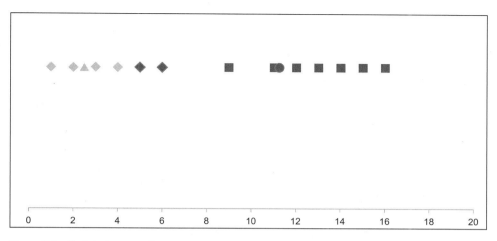

Figure 2.6 Updated means given the new cluster assignment. Cluster centroids have been updated to better represent the data points that have been assigned to them.

assigned to cluster k_2. If we continue as before and calculate the new means of the clusters, this gives centroids of 3.5 and 12.8. At this point, no number of additional iterations will change the assignment of the data points to their clusters, and thus the cluster means won't change. Another way of saying this is that the algorithm has *converged*.[2] Figure 2.7 shows the final assignment.

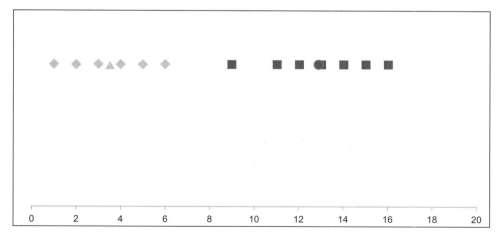

Figure 2.7 Final assignment of the data points to the clusters. Final cluster centroids are given by the triangle and circle, respectively. Data points below 6.8 have been assigned to cluster k_1, and data points above this have been assigned to cluster k_2. Additional iterations of the k-means algorithm won't change this clustering.

---

[2] The same nomenclature is used when learning the parameters for any algorithm. When a cost function is minimized, practitioners say that the training algorithm has converged. In this book, we'll mostly rely on scikit-learn libraries to reach convergence for us during training.

Note that this final assignment is exactly the means we would have chosen if we had manually performed clustering (that is, we visually determined the clusters and calculated their means); thus the algorithm has automatically determined an intelligent clustering of the data with minimal intervention from the developer!

Be aware that although the algorithm provably converges if you use the Euclidean distance function,[3] there's no guarantee that convergence reaches a global minimum; that is, the final clustering reached may not be the best. The algorithm can be sensitive to initial starting conditions and identify different (local minima) cluster means. Consequently, in application you might consider multiple starting points, rerunning the training several times. One approach then to getting closer to the global minima is to use the average of each resultant centroid group as the starting centroids for a final run. This may put you in a better starting position to reach the best clustering. No such guarantees are given, though.

Listing 2.3 provides the pseudo-code that summarizes these execution steps. In the first case, we must initialize the centroids, one for each k that we're defining at the start of the algorithm. We then enter a loop, which is broken by convergence of the algorithm. In the previous example, we knew intuitively that the algorithm had converged because the cluster centroids and data-point assignment wouldn't change, but in reality, this may not be the case. It's more common to look at the change in the means. If this change drops below a certain tolerance value, you can safely assume that only a small number of points are being reassigned and thus the algorithm has converged.

> **Listing 2.3   K-means pseudo-code: expectation maximization**

```
Initialize centroids                                    Expectation step
while(centroids not converged):
    For each data item, assign label to that of closest centroid.
    Calculate the centroid using data items assigned to it    Maximization
                                                              step
```

The expectation step assigns a centroid to every data item based on the Euclidean distance to that centroid (the closest is chosen). The maximization step then recalculates the centroids based on the data items that have been assigned to it; that is, each dimension in the feature space is averaged to obtain the new centroid.

This, in essence, creates a loop in which data is captured by a cluster, which is made to look more like the data it clusters, which then captures more data in the cluster, and so on. Convergence occurs when clusters stop capturing data and become steady. This is a specific implementation of Lloyd's algorithm, and more generally of a class of algorithms known as *expectation maximization*. From here on, we'll refer to this as the k-means algorithm for convenience. We'll revisit the concept of expectation maximization in the following sections of this chapter.

---

[3]   Leon Bottou and Yoshua Bengio, "Convergence Properties of the K-Means Algorithms," *Advances in Neural Information Processing Systems* 7 (1994).

2.3.1 *K-means in action*

Let's now run the k-means algorithm over a higher-dimensional dataset: the Iris dataset introduced earlier. The following listing shows a simple code snippet to load in the Iris dataset and execute the k-means implementation provided with scikit-learn. It prints to screen the derived clusters of the data and then terminates.

Listing 2.4   The k-means algorithm in action

```
from sklearn.cluster import KMeans
from sklearn import datasets

iris = datasets.load_iris()
X = iris.data
km = KMeans(n_clusters=3)
km.fit(X)

print(km.labels_)
```

Contains only the data, not the labels

Passes in the value of k, which in this case is equal to 3

Given the Iris dataset, the basic example shown here uses k-means to see if, in the absence of any ground truth data relating to the type of the flower, we can detect any intrinsic pattern in the data. In other words, can the algorithm find any structure such that it separates the Iris dataset into three distinct clusters? Try running this now. You'll see that, yes, the algorithm does indeed separate the data into three clusters! This is great, but you'd learn more if you could look at these clusters in comparison to the data. The next listing provides the code to visualize this.

Listing 2.5   Visualizing the output of k-means

```
from sklearn.cluster import KMeans
from sklearn import datasets
from itertools import cycle, combinations
import matplotlib.pyplot as pl

iris = datasets.load_iris()
km = KMeans(n_clusters=3)
km.fit(iris.data)

predictions = km.predict(iris.data)

colors = cycle('rgb')
labels = ["Cluster 1","Cluster 2","Cluster 3"]
targets = range(len(labels))

feature_index=range(len(iris.feature_names))
feature_names=iris.feature_names
combs=combinations(feature_index,2)

f,axarr=pl.subplots(3,2)
axarr_flat=axarr.flat

for comb, axflat in zip(combs,axarr_flat):
        for target, color, label in zip(targets,colors,labels):
                feature_index_x=comb[0]
                feature_index_y=comb[1]
```

```
axflat.scatter(iris.data[predictions==target,feature_index_x],
iris.data[predictions==target,feature_index_y],c=color,label=label)
            axflat.set_xlabel(feature_names[feature_index_x])
            axflat.set_ylabel(feature_names[feature_index_y])
f.tight_layout()
pl.show()
```

This listing provides the code to plot all 2-D combinations of the Iris feature set, as seen in figure 2.8. Color and shape of the data points denote the cluster to which the point belongs—as discovered by k-means.

In this figure, all combinations of the Iris features are plotted against each other in order to assess the quality of clustering. Note that each point is assigned to the cluster with the centroid closest to it in four-dimensional space. The two-dimensional plots are color-coded such that the color-coding is consistent across the plots.

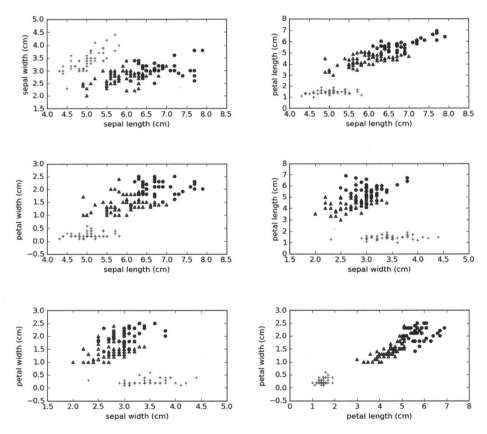

Figure 2.8 K-means clustering of the Iris dataset. This is achieved through the execution of listing 2.5. Note that k-means represents the centroids of the clusters in *n*-dimensional space, where *n* is the number of features (four, in the case of the Iris dataset). For visualization purposes, we plot all combinations of features against each other.

A quick glance over the data seems to suggest that plotting petal length against petal width provides the best way to visualize the data (bottom-right). It also appears that these two variables are highly correlated and that looking at this feature alone can probably separate the three clusters. If this is indeed true, then it begs the question, if a single feature could be used to separate the flowers, why do we need four? Excellent question!

The short answer is that we probably don't, but this wasn't known at the time of collection. With the benefit of hindsight, we might have changed the data that was collected; we did not, however, have that benefit.

In section 2.6, we'll revisit this problem and propose a solution in the form of principal component analysis. This method can generate new axes for your data in which the directions are those with maximal variance in the data. Don't worry about that for now; you can just think of it as distilling all of your features into one or two that have been designed to best illustrate your data.

But before we do this, we're going to continue with a bit more modeling. We'd like to show you another partitional algorithm based on a conceptual modeling approach. In contrast to k-means, this method uses an underlying distribution to model its data—and because the parameters of this distribution must be learned, this type of model is known as a *parametric model*. We'll discuss later how this differs from k-means (a non-parametric model) and under what conditions the two algorithms could be considered equivalent. The algorithm we're going to look at uses the Gaussian distribution as its heart and is known as the *Gaussian mixture model*.

2.4   *The Gaussian mixture model*

In the previous section, we introduced k-means clustering, which is one of the most widely used approaches for clustering. This non-parametric method for extracting structure has some excellent properties that make it ideal for many situations. In this section, we'll look at a parametric method that uses the Gaussian distribution, known as the Gaussian mixture model (GMM). Both approaches use the expectation maximization (EM) algorithm to learn, so we'll revisit this in more detail in the following sections.

Under certain circumstances, the k-means and GMM approaches can be explained in terms of each other. In k-means, the cluster whose centroid is the closest is assigned directly to a data point, but this assumes that the clusters are scaled similarly and that feature covariance is not dissimilar (that is, you don't have some really long clusters along with really short clusters in the feature space). This is why it often makes sense to normalize your data before using k-means. Gaussian mixtures, however, don't suffer from such a constraint. This is because they seek to model feature covariance for each cluster. If this all seems a little confusing, don't worry! We'll go through these concepts in much more detail in the following sections.

2.4.1 *What is the Gaussian distribution?*

You may have heard of the Gaussian distribution, sometimes known as the normal distribution, but what exactly is it? We'll give you the mathematical definition shortly, but qualitatively it can be thought of as a distribution that occurs naturally and very frequently.

Using a simple example, if you were to take a random large sample of the population, measure their height, and plot the number of adults in certain height ranges, you'd end up with a histogram that looks something like figure 2.9. This illustrative and wholly fictional data set shows that, from 334 people surveyed, the most common height range lies 2.5 cm on either side of 180 cm.

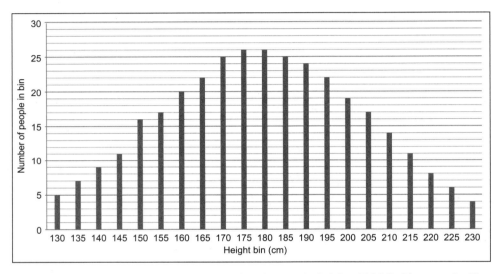

Figure 2.9 Histogram of a normal distribution, in this case the height of 334 fictitious people. The modal (most frequently occurring) bin is centered at 180 cm.

This clearly looks like a Gaussian distribution; but in order to test this assumption, let's use the formulaic definition of a Gaussian to see if we can fit this data through trial and error. The probability density of the normal distribution is given by the following equation:

$$f(x|\mu,\sigma^2) = \frac{1}{\sqrt{2\sigma^2\pi}}\, e^{-\frac{(x-\mu)^2}{2\sigma^2}}$$

This has two parameters, which we need to learn in order to fit this equation to the data: the mean given by the parameter μ and the standard deviation given by the parameter σ. The mean is a measure of the center of the distribution, and if we had to make an informed guess, we might say it was around 180 cm. The standard deviation is a measure of the distribution of the data around the mean. Armed with the knowledge that, for a normal distribution, 95% of the data is always within two standard deviations from the mean, we might guess that somewhere between 25 and 30 is a good value for this parameter, because most of the collected data does seem to lie between 120 cm and 240 cm.

Recall that the previous equation is a probability density function (PDF). That is, if you plug in a value for *x*, given a known set of parameters, the function will return a probability density. One more thing, though, before you rush off and implement this! The probability distribution is normalized, such that the area underneath the curve is equal to 1; this is necessary to ensure that returned values are in the range of allowed values for a probability. What this means here is that if we wish to determine the probability of a particular range of values, we must calculate the area under the curve between these two values to determine the likelihood of occurrence. Rather than calculate this area explicitly, we can easily achieve the same results by subtracting the results of the cumulative density function (CDF) for the values of *x* that define the range. This works because the CDF for a given value of *x* returns the probability of a sample having a value less than or equal to *x*.

Let's now return to the original example and see if we can informally evaluate the selected parameters against the collected data. Suppose that we're going to define the data bins in terms of a probability. Each bin corresponds to the probability that, given we select one of the 334 users randomly, the user is in that bin. We can achieve this by dividing the counts on the y-axis by the number of people surveyed (334) to give a probability. This data can be seen in the red plot (the bar on the left in each pair) in figure 2.10. If we now use the cumulative density function to calculate the probabilities of falling in the same bins, with parameters μ=180,σ=28, we can visually inspect how accurate the model is.

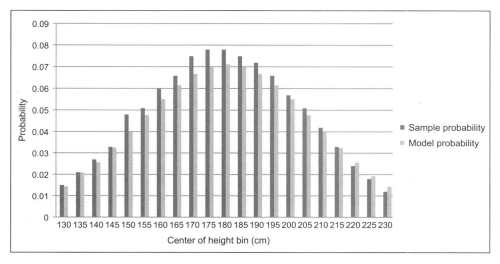

Figure 2.10 Fictional data on the height of 334 people. The sample probability of a given user occurring in a given height range is shown in red (the bar on the left in each pair). The probability from a Gaussian model, with parameters μ=180,σ =28, is shown in green (the bar on the right).

A brief look at figure 2.10 shows that our initial guess of 180 for the mean and 28 for the standard deviation isn't bad. The standard deviation looks reasonable, although it could potentially be decreased slightly. Of course, we could continue to change the parameters here to obtain a better fit, but it might be much better if this was done algorithmically! This process is known as *model training*. We can use the expectation-maximization algorithm to do just this, and you'll see this in the following section.

There's an important distinction to make here about the difference between sample and population distribution. First, we assume that data from the 334 users is representative of the entire population. We're also making an assumption that the underlying distribution that generates the data is Gaussian and that the sample data is drawn from this. As such, it's our best chance at estimating the underlying distribution, but it's just that: an estimate! We're hoping that in the limit (that is, if we collected more and more samples), height tends to a Gaussian, but there will always be an element of uncertainty. The purpose of model training is to minimize this uncertainty under the assumptions of the model.

2.4.2 *Expectation maximization and the Gaussian distribution*

The previous section presented an intuitive approach to fitting a Gaussian model to a given dataset. In this section, we'll formalize this approach so that model fitting can occur algorithmically. We'll do this by expressing some of the concepts that we used intuitively in a more rigorous manner. When determining whether a model was a good fit, we were looking at the sample probability and seeing whether this was approximated by the model probability. We then changed the model, so that the new model better matched the sample probability. We kept iterating through this process a number of times until the probabilities were very close, after which we stopped and considered the model trained.

We'll do exactly the same thing algorithmically, except we now need something other than a visual evaluation to assess fit. The approach we'll use is to determine the likelihood that the model generates the data; that is, we'll calculate the expectation of the data given the model. We'll then seek to maximize the expectation by updating the model parameters μ, σ. This cycle can then be iterated through until the parameters are changing by only a very small amount at each cycle. Note the similarity to the way in which we trained the k-means algorithm. Whereas in that example we updated only the centroids at the maximization, under a Gaussian model we'll update two parameters: the mean and the variance of the distribution.

2.4.3 *The Gaussian mixture model*

Now that you understand what a Gaussian distribution is, let's move on to discuss the Gaussian mixture model. This is a simple extension to a Gaussian model that uses multiple Gaussian distributions to model the distribution of data. Let's take a concrete example of this to illustrate. Imagine that instead of measuring the height of users randomly, we now wish to account for both male and female heights in our model.

If we assume that a user can be either male or female, then our Gaussian distribution from earlier is the result of sampling from two separate and overlapping Gaussian distributions. Rather than modeling the space using a single Gaussian, we can now use two (or more!) such distributions:

$$p(x) = \sum_{i=1}^{K} \phi_i \frac{1}{\sqrt{2\sigma_i^2 \pi}} e^{-\frac{(x-\mu_i)^2}{2\sigma_i^2}}$$

This equation is extremely similar to the one earlier in the chapter, save for a few details. First, note that instead of a single Gaussian, the probability is made up from the sum of K separate Gaussian distributions, each with its own set of parameters μ,σ. Also note the inclusion of a weighting parameter, φ_i, for each separate distribution. Weights must be positive, and the sum of all weights must equal 1. This ensures that this equation is a true probability density function; in other words, if we integrate this function over its input space, it will be equal to 1.[4]

Returning to the previous example, women may be distributed normally with a lower average height than men, resulting in an underlying generating function drawn from two distributions! See figure 2.11.

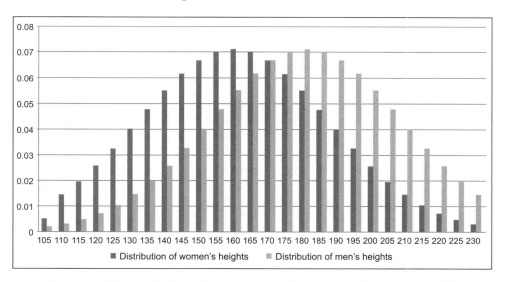

Figure 2.11 Probability distributions of height for men and women. Note that these probabilities are conditioned on the fact that gender is known: so, for example, given that we know a particular person is a woman, her probability of having a height in a particular bucket can be read off the y-axis.

[4] Unlike the previous equation, where the parameters are explicitly represented on the left-hand side of the equation, in this case, the parameters are omitted and implied.

The probabilities given on the y-axis in figure 2.11 are conditioned on the fact that we know the gender of the person. In general, for the purposes of this example, we wouldn't necessarily have that data at hand (maybe it wasn't recorded at measurement time). Thus we'd need to learn not only the parameters of each distribution but also the gender split in the sample population (φ_i). When determining the expectation, this can be calculated by multiplying the probability of being male by the probability of the height bin for a male, and adding this to a similar calculation derived with the data from the distribution over women.

Note that, although doing so is slightly more complicated, we can still use the same technique for model training as specified previously. When working out the expectation (probability that the data is generated by the mixture), we can use the equation presented at the beginning of section 2.4.3. We just need a strategy for updating the parameters to maximize this. Let's use a scikit-learn implementation on the dataset and see how the parameter updates have been calculated.

2.4.4 An example of learning using a Gaussian mixture model

In the rather simple example shown previously, we worked with only single-dimension Gaussians: that is, only a single feature. But Gaussians aren't limited to one dimension! It's fairly easy to extend their mean into a vector and their variance into a covariance matrix, allowing n-dimensional Gaussians to cater to an arbitrary number of features. In order to demonstrate this in practice, let's move on from the height example and return to the Iris dataset, which, if you recall, has a total of four features; see the next listing. In the following sections, we'll investigate the implementation of a Gaussian mixture model using scikit-learn and visualize the clusters obtained through its use.

> **Listing 2.6   Clustering the Iris dataset using a Gaussian mixture model**

```
from sklearn.mixture import GMM
from sklearn import datasets
from itertools import cycle, combinations
import matplotlib as mpl
import matplotlib.pyplot as pl
import numpy as np

# make_ellipses method taken from: http://scikit-
# learn.org/stable/auto_examples/mixture/plot_gmm_classifier.html#example-
# mixture-plot-gmm-classifier-py
# Author: Ron Weiss <ronweiss@gmail.com>, Gael Varoquaux
# License: BSD 3 clause

def make_ellipses(gmm, ax, x, y):
    for n, color in enumerate('rgb'):
    row_idx = np.array([x,y])
    col_idx = np.array([x,y])
        v, w = np.linalg.eigh(gmm._get_covars()[n][row_idx[:,None],col_idx])
        u = w[0] / np.linalg.norm(w[0])
        angle = np.arctan2(u[1], u[0])
        angle = 180 * angle / np.pi  # convert to degrees
```

```
            v *= 9
            ell = mpl.patches.Ellipse(gmm.means_[n, [x,y]], v[0], v[1],
                                  180 + angle, color=color)
            ell.set_clip_box(ax.bbox)
            ell.set_alpha(0.5)
            ax.add_artist(ell)

iris = datasets.load_iris()

gmm = GMM(n_components=3,covariance_type='full', n_iter=20)
gmm.fit(iris.data)

predictions = gmm.predict(iris.data)

colors = cycle('rgb')
labels = ["Cluster 1","Cluster 2","Cluster 3"]
targets = range(len(labels))

feature_index=range(len(iris.feature_names))
feature_names=iris.feature_names
combs=combinations(feature_index,2)

f,axarr=pl.subplots(3,2)
axarr_flat=axarr.flat

for comb, axflat in zip(combs,axarr_flat):
    for target, color, label in zip(targets,colors,labels):
        feature_index_x=comb[0]
        feature_index_y=comb[1]
        axflat.scatter(iris.data[predictions==target,feature_index_x],

    iris.data[predictions==target,feature_index_y],c=color,label=label)
        axflat.set_xlabel(feature_names[feature_index_x])
        axflat.set_ylabel(feature_names[feature_index_y])
        make_ellipses(gmm,axflat,feature_index_x,feature_index_y)
pl.tight_layout()
pl.show()
```

The vast majority of the code in listing 2.6 is identical to that of listing 2.5, where we visualized the output from the k-means algorithm. The notable differences are these:

- Using `sklearn.mixture.GMM` instead of `sklearn.cluster.KMeans`
- Defining and using the `make_ellipses` method

You'll notice that, in the former, method initialization is almost exactly the same, aside from some additional parameters. Let's take a look at these. In order to initialize GMM, we pass the following parameters:

- `n_components`—The number of Gaussians in our mixture. The previous example had two.
- `covariance_type`—Restricts the covariance matrix properties and therefore the shape of the Gaussians. Refer to the following documentation for a graphical interpretation of the differences: http://scikit-learn.org/stable/modules/mixture.html.
- `n_iter`—Number of EM iterations to perform.

So in actual fact, the two code snippets are remarkably similar. The only additional decisions that need to be made relate to the relationships of the variances (covariances) that will affect the shape of the resulting clusters.

The remainder of the code presented consists of the `make_ellipses` method. This is a helper method that allows us to present the output of the GMM in a graphical manner. This is taken from the scikit-learn documentation, so you may recognize the code from there. Take a look at the output of listing 2.6 in figure 2.12 before delving into the explanation.

The figure shows the output of our Gaussian mixture model with four dimensions. Three 4-D clusters have been projected onto each set of two dimensions with a representation of the resultant cluster in 2-D through the `make_ellipses` method.

The `make_ellipses` method[5] is conceptually simple. It takes as its arguments the `gmm` object (the trained model), a plot axis (relating to one of the six tiles in figure 2.12), and two indices, x and y, which relate to the parameters against which the four-

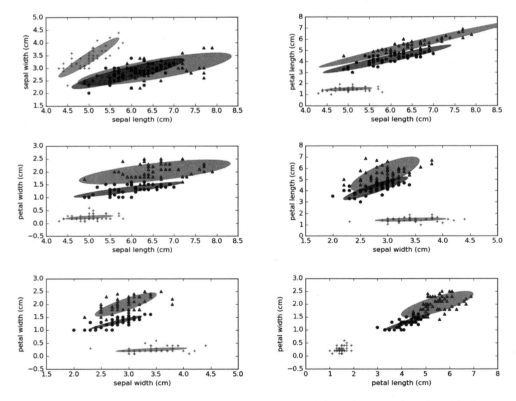

Figure 2.12   Output from listing 2.6. Each panel shows the 4-D Gaussian clustering of the Iris dataset mapped onto two of the axes. The colored clusterings are representations of the underlying four-dimensional Gaussian in two dimensions only.

---

[5] Ron Weiss and Gael Varoquaux, "GMM classification," *scikit-learn*, http://mng.bz/uKPu.

dimensional plot will be reduced. It returns nothing, but it operates over the axis object, drawing the ellipses in the plot.

> **A word about make_ellipses**
>
> The method `make_ellipses` is derived from `plot_gmm_classifier`, written by Ron Weiss and Gael Varoquaz for scikit-learn. By extracting the covariance matrix in the two dimensions you're plotting, you can find the first and second directions of maximal variance, along with their respective magnitudes. You then use these to orient and draw ellipses relating to the shape of the learned Gaussian. These directions and magnitudes are known as *eigenvectors* and *eigenvalues*, respectively, and will be covered in more detail in section 2.6.

2.5　*The relationship between k-means and GMM*

K-means can be expressed as a special case of the Gaussian mixture model. In general, the Gaussian mixture is more expressive because membership of a data item to a cluster is dependent on the shape of that cluster, not just its proximity.

The shape of an *n*-dimensional Gaussian is dependent on the covariance across the dimensions in each cluster. It's possible to obtain the same results with GMM and k-means if additional constraints are placed on the learned covariance matrices.

In particular, if covariance matrices for each cluster are tied together (that is, they all must be the same), and covariances across the diagonal are restricted to being equal, with all other entries set to zero, then you'll obtain spherical clusters of the same size and shape for each cluster. Under such circumstances, each point will always belong to the cluster with the closest mean. Try it and see!

As with k-means, training a Gaussian mixture model with EM can be sensitive to initial starting conditions. If you compare and contrast GMM to k-means, you'll find a few more initial starting conditions in the former than in the latter. In particular, not only must the initial centroids be specified, but the initial covariance matrices and mixture weights must be specified also. Among other strategies,[6] one approach is to run k-means and use the resultant centroids to determine the initial starting conditions for the Gaussian mixture model.

As you can see, there's not a great deal of magic happening here! Both algorithms work similarly, with the main difference being the complexity of the model. In general, all clustering algorithms follow a similar pattern: given a series of data, you can train a model such that the model is in some way a generalization of the data (and hopefully the underlying process generating the data). This training is typically achieved in an iterative fashion, as you saw in the previous examples, with termination occurring when you can't improve the parameters to make the model fit the data any better.

---

[6]　Johannes Blomer and Kathrin Bujna, "Simple Methods for Initializing the EM Algorithm for Gaussian Mixture Models," 2013, http://arxiv.org/pdf/1312.5946.pdf.

2.6 *Transforming the data axis*

So far in this chapter, we've concentrated on clustering data as it's presented in its original feature space. But what if you were to change this feature space into a more appropriate one—perhaps one with fewer features that's more descriptive of the underlying structure?

This is possible using a method known as *principal component analysis* (PCA). This transforms your data axis in such a way that you use the directions of maximal variance in your data as a new data basis (instead of y=0, x=0 that form the standard x-axis and y-axis, respectively). These directions are given by the eigenvectors of your data, and the amount of variance in these directions is given by an associated eigenvalue. In the following sections, we'll discuss these terms in more detail before providing an example of PCA applied to the Iris dataset. You'll see how to reduce the number of features from four to two without losing the ability to cluster the Iris data effectively in the new feature space.

2.6.1 *Eigenvectors and eigenvalues*

Eigenvectors and eigenvalues[7] are characteristics of a square matrix (a matrix having the same number of rows and columns); that is, they're descriptors of a matrix. What they describe, however, is quite special and quite subtle! In this section, we'll provide some of the intuition behind these terms, before demonstrating the power of these constructs with a dataset. Mathematically, eigenvectors and eigenvalues are defined in the following manner

$$\mathbf{Cv} = \lambda \mathbf{v}$$

where $\mathbf{C}$ is a square matrix (it has the same number of rows and columns), $\mathbf{v}$ is an eigenvector, and λ is the corresponding eigenvalue relating to that eigenvector. This may seem a little confusing at first, but with a bit of illustration you should be able to see why this is so powerful.

Let's imagine that the matrix $\mathbf{C}$ corresponds to some shear transformation in two-dimensional space and is thus a 2×2 matrix. Just to hit home with this, given a two-dimensional data set, $\mathbf{C}$ could be applied to every data point to create a new transformed (sheared) data set.

What you have then is an equation to solve! Can you find a number of vectors (directions) such that after the application of the shear matrix $\mathbf{C}$, they remain unchanged save for a difference in magnitude given by λ? The answer is yes, you can! But what does this mean? And why is it important?

Thinking carefully about this, you can see that we're providing a shorthand, or compact form, of the shear transformation. This set of eigenvectors describes the directions unaffected by the application of the shear. But what does the eigenvalue

---

[7]   K. F. Riley, M. P. Hobson, and S. J. Bence, *Mathematical Methods for Physics and Engineering* (Cambridge University Press, 2006).

represent? It represents how much the shear operates in a given direction: that is, the magnitude of that operation. As such, the eigenvalues are a measure of importance of that direction. Thus, you could describe most of the operation of the shear matrix by recording only the eigenvectors with the largest eigenvalues.

2.6.2 *Principal component analysis*

Principal component analysis[8] uses the eigenvector/eigenvalue decomposition in a specific way in order to obtain the *principal components* of a dataset. Given a dataset with n features, you can work out the covariance matrix, which has the form shown at right.

$$\begin{bmatrix} x_{11} & x_{12} & \cdots & x_{1n} \\ x_{21} & x_{22} & \cdots & \cdots \\ \cdots & \cdots & \cdots & \cdots \\ x_{n1} & \cdots & \cdots & x_{nn} \end{bmatrix}$$

The covariance matrix describes the pairwise variance of each feature in the dataset: that is, $x_i x_j$ is the covariance of feature i and feature j. This could be described as a measure of the shape and size of the variation of the dataset. What do you notice about the shape of the matrix? Well, for starters, because you calculate the variance of each feature against all other features, the matrix is always square. That is, the number of rows is the same as the number of columns. In this case, both are equal to n, the number of features in the dataset.

Do you notice anything else about the matrix? That's right: it's symmetrical! Because $x_i x_j = x_j x_i$, you could transpose the matrix (flip it across the diagonal), and the matrix would be the same. Keep these two properties in mind, because they'll come in handy in a few moments.

Let's go back to what the covariance matrix represents. Remember, this is the measure of the shape and size of variation in the dataset. What do you get if you calculate the eigenvectors and eigenvalues of the covariance matrix? One way to understand the covariance matrix is as a relation (via Cholesky decomposition[9]) to a transformation that takes randomly sampled Gaussian data (say, with a covariance matrix where $x_{ij}=1, i=j$ and zero elsewhere) and outputs data distributed in the same manner as the original dataset. Thus, the eigenvectors of the covariance matrix represent the vectors unchanged by this transform variation, otherwise known as the *principal components* of the dataset. But wait, there's more! Because the covariance matrix is symmetrical, the (non-equal) eigenvectors of this matrix are orthogonal! To illustrate, take a look at figure 2.13.

What's great about this decomposition is that you can now express each data point as the linear combination of eigenvectors (due to their orthogonality). For high-dimensional data, this can provide a way to compress your data, because for every data point, you need only store the distance along the eigenvectors of interest. Often, the most variance will be expressed by the first two or three eigenvectors; thus an arbitrarily high-dimensional data point can now be expressed as only a vector with only two or three dimensions.

---

[8] Jonathon Shlens, "A Tutorial on Principal Component Analysis," eprint arXiv:1404.1100, 2014.
[9] Claude Brezinski, "The Life and Work of Andre Cholesky," *Numer. Algorithms* 43 (2006):279-288.

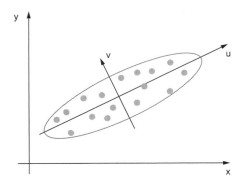

Figure 2.13 The two principal components of a two-dimensional feature set. The eigenvector u has the largest eigenvalue because it provides the largest direction of variance. The vector v has a smaller value in relation. The two vectors are orthogonal: that is, at 90 degrees from each other. In general, for higher dimensions, the dot product of any two pairs of eigenvectors will equal zero.

2.6.3 An example of principal component analysis

Now that you understand eigenvectors, eigenvalues, and PCA, you can get your hands dirty and apply these concepts to some data. As before, we'll use the Iris dataset to demonstrate this concept in scikit-learn. Consider the following listing.

Listing 2.7 Principal component analysis of the Iris dataset

```
import numpy as np
import matplotlib.pyplot as pl

from sklearn import decomposition
from sklearn import datasets
from itertools import cycle

iris = datasets.load_iris()
X = iris.data
Y = iris.target

targets = range(len(iris.target_names))
colors = cycle('rgb')

pca = decomposition.PCA(n_components=2)
pca.fit(X)

X = pca.transform(X)

for target,color in zip(targets,colors):
    pl.scatter(X[Y==target,0],
               X[Y==target,1],
               label=iris.target_names[target],c=color)
pl.legend()
pl.show()
```

❶ Initializes a PCA decomposition with two components

❷ Fits the data: solves the eigenvector decomposition

❸ Transforms the data into the basis. Because we chose to keep only two components, this has two dimensions.

❹ For each iris category, plots (in a different color) the coordinates in the new coordinate axis

This PCA transformation of the Iris data yields the output given by figure 2.14. You load in the Iris dataset as before and then initialize a PCA decomposition with two components. At this point, no decomposition has been performed (for a start, no data has been passed in); you merely prepare the Python objects for the next stage. The next stage is the fit method ❷, where the data axis is transformed.

In this single line, the covariance matrix is calculated for the dataset, which in the case of Iris will result in a 4 × 4 square matrix, and the matrix is solved for the eigenvectors. This line performs the heavy lifting, finding the directions of the dataset that account for the maximal variance in the data. The next line obtains the data transformed into the new data axis ❸. The original data is now expressed as a combination of the two eigenvectors with the largest eigenvalues (because you restrict the number of components to two in ❶), which you can now plot as per figure 2.14 ❹. It should now be fairly clear that the x-axis (y=0) and the y-axis (x=0) are the directions (in four dimensions in Iris) of the highest variance and second-highest variance, respectively. The values plotted correspond to the distance along that line of the original data. Thus, you've transformed a 4-D dataset down to a 2-D dataset, while keeping the majority of variance of the data in the new data space.

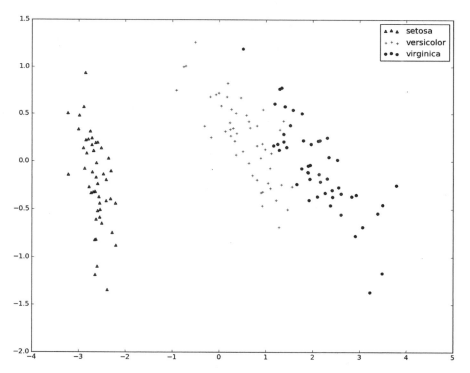

Figure 2.14 Eigenvector decomposition of the Iris dataset using the first two eigenvectors. The x-axis shows the direction in which the data has maximal variance. This is the first eigenvector, and its corresponding eigenvalue is maximal relative to all solutions given this data. The y-axis represents the second eigenvector, and its corresponding eigenvalue has the second-largest value of all solutions given this data. Points in the scatter plot are transformed from the original data into this new axis with respect to these first two eigenvectors.

Principal component analysis is a powerful tool that can help you to calculate a more efficient representation of the data while minimizing loss to that data's discriminatory power. Although we used this on a relatively simple dataset here, it can be, and often is, applied to real-world data as a first pass—as a preprocessing step to the classification and regression problems that we'll spend more time on later in the book. Note, however, that complexity grows faster as the number of features in your dataset grows, so removing redundant and irrelevant features as a step before PCA may pay dividends.

2.7   *Summary*

- Bias is a systematic offset, applied to all elements of your dataset, whereas noise is a random addition distributed around the true values being measured.
- The feature space is the space containing all feature vectors, for a given number of features. You learned about the curse of dimensionality: the more features collected about a phenomenon, the more data points are required to generalize that phenomenon. The practitioner of machine learning must walk this trade-off carefully. Too many features, and it will be impossible to collect enough data points to generalize the phenomenon under investigation; too few, and the phenomenon is not appropriately captured.
- We looked closely at data structure, covering in detail the k-means algorithm and the Gaussian mixture model. Both of these algorithms perform well in practice, and we explored the relationship between the two. In machine learning, many algorithms can be considered equivalent to others under certain conditions, as is the case here.
- Expectation Maximization (EM) is a general class of algorithms that can be used to fit data to a model through a series of iterations. First, the expectation that the model generated the data is calculated, and then the model is changed by a small amount to make it more likely that the new model is responsible for the data. This has the effect of learning (and approximating) the original distribution of the data that underlies the training samples.
- An algorithm is only as good as its data! If the features collected about a phenomenon aren't sufficiently descriptive, then no amount of machine learning will be able to achieve satisfactory results. The onus is on the practitioner to remove irrelevant and redundant features and to minimize the size of the dataset without sacrificing discriminatory power. This often leads to improved results for the same dataset. Toward this end, we examined principal component analysis, which can be used to distill many features into few without sacrificing the original variance in the dataset.

Recommending relevant content

In today's world, we're overwhelmed with choices, with a plethora of options available for nearly every aspect of our lives. We need to make decisions on a daily basis, from automobiles to home theatre systems, from finding Mr. or Ms. "Perfect" to selecting attorneys or accountants, from books and newspapers to wikis and blogs. In addition, we're constantly being bombarded by information—and occasionally misinformation! Under these conditions, the ability to recommend a choice is valuable, and even more so if that choice is aligned with the person receiving the recommendation.

In the business of influencing your choice, no one is interested in good results more than advertising companies. The raison d'être of these entities is to convince you that you really *need* product *X* or service *Y*. If you have no interest in products like *X* or services like *Y*, they'll be wasting their time, and you'll be annoyed. The broadcasting approach of traditional advertising methods (such as billboards, TV ads, and radio ads) suffers from that problem. The goal of broadcasting is to alter your preferences by incessantly repeating the same message. An alternative, more pleasant, and more effective approach would be targeted to your preferences. It would entice you to select a product based on its relevance to your personal wants and desires. That's where the online world and the intelligent advertising businesses on the internet distinguish themselves.

In this chapter, we'll tell you everything you need to know about building a recommendation engine. You'll learn about *collaborative filtering* and content-based recommendation engines. Throughout this chapter, we'll use the example of recommending movies in an online movie store, and we'll generalize it so that the proposed solutions are applicable to a variety of circumstances.

The online movie store is a simple example, but it's concrete and detailed, making it easy to understand all the basic concepts involved in the process of writing a recommendation engine. We'll look in detail at the definition of similarity between users and introduce the mechanisms by which this similarity metric can be used to perform recommendation. We'll also further delve into a more complex technique known as *singular value decomposition* (SVD) that clusters the user and movie groups together via implicit relationships within the data. By the end of this chapter, you'll be able to perform recommendation using a sizable dataset and understand the different mechanisms by which this is achieved.

Once we cover all the basic concepts in the online movie store, we'll make things a lot more interesting by presenting more-complicated cases. We'll cover recommendation engines that are crucial in the online movie industry, for online bookstores, and for internet shopping carts.

3.1 Setting the scene: an online movie store

Let's say that you have an online movie service that sells or makes money from movie downloads and streaming. Registered users log in to your application and can watch trailers of available movies. If a user likes a particular movie, she can add it to her shopping cart and purchase it later when she's ready to check out from your store. Naturally, when users complete their purchase, or when they land on the pages of your hypothetical application, you want to suggest more movies to them. There are millions of movies and TV shows available, drawn from many different genres. In addition, many people are sensitive to the kind of shows and movies that they don't like, so when you display content for a user, you want to target the genre the user likes and avoid those they don't. If that sounds difficult, fear not. Recommendation engines are here to help you deliver the right content to your users.

A recommendation engine examines the selections that a user has made in the past and identifies the degree to which he would like a certain item that he hasn't seen yet. It can be used to determine what types of shows your user prefers and the extent to which he does so, by comparing the *similarity* of his preferences with the characteristics of genres. For a more creative twist, you could help people establish a social network on that site based on the *similarity* of their movie and TV show tastes. It quickly becomes apparent that the crucial functional element of recommendation engines is the ability to define how similar to each other two (or more) users or two (or more) items are. That similarity can later be used to provide recommendations.

3.2 Distance and similarity

Let's take some data and start exploring these concepts in detail. In the following sections, we'll work with items, users, and ratings. In the context of recommendation engines, *similarity* is a measure that allows you to compare the proximity of two items in much the same way that the physical distance between two cities tells you how close they are to each other geographically. Distance and similarity differ only by the frame of reference or the coordinate space used. Consider that two cities may be geographically similar in that their distance in physical space is low, but culturally they may be very different, in that their distance as a measure of the interests and habits of the general population is very high. In general, the same distance calculation may be performed over different spaces to gain different measures of similarity.

For two cities, you'd use their longitude and latitude coordinates to calculate their geographical proximity. Think of the ratings as the coordinates in the space of items or users. Let's look at these concepts in action. We'll select three users and associate with them a list of movies (items) and their hypothetical rankings. As is typically the case, ratings will range between 1 and 5 (inclusive). The assignments for the first two users (Frank and Constantine) involve ratings that are either 4 or 5—these people really like all the movies we selected. But the third user's ratings (Catherine's) are between 1 and 3. So clearly, we expect the first two users to be similar to each other and be dissimilar to the third user. When we load the example data in the script, we have available the users, movies, and ratings shown in table 3.1.

Table 3.1   Ratings for the users show that Frank and Constantine agree more than Frank and Catherine. This data was modified, with permission, from the MovieLens database.[a]

User	Movie	Rating
0: Frank	0: Toy Story	5
	1: Jumanji	4
	2: Grumpier Old Men	5
	3: Waiting to Exhale	4
	4: Father of the Bride Part II	5
	5: Heat	4
	6: Sabrina	5

a. GroupLens Research, MovieLens dataset, http://grouplens.org/datasets/movielens/.

Table 3.1   Ratings for the users show that Frank and Constantine agree more than Frank and Catherine. This data was modified, with permission, from the MovieLens database.[a] (continued)

User	Movie	Rating
1: Constantine	0: Toy Story	5
	2: Grumpier Old Men	5
	4: Father of the Bride Part II	4
	5: Heat	5
	7: Tom and Huck	5
	8: Sudden Death	4
	9: Goldeneye	5
2: Catherine	0: Toy Story	1
	2: Grumpier Old Men	2
	3: Waiting to Exhale	2
	6: Sabrina	3
	9: Goldeneye	2
	10: American President, The	1

a. GroupLens Research, MovieLens dataset, http://grouplens.org/datasets/movielens/.

Let's begin by looking at the similarity between these users based on their ratings of different movies. The following listing provides the code. We use a cut-down and modified version of the MovieLens dataset, which contains the ratings of the 11 unique movies in table 3.1. These data files can be found in the resources associated with this book.

Listing 3.1   Calculating the similarity of users based on their ratings of movies

```
dat_file = 'ratings-11.dat'
item_file = 'movies-11.dat'

names = ['Frank','Constantine','Catherine']

userdict = read_user_data_from_ratings(dat_file)
itemdict = read_item_data(item_file)

similarity(0,1,sim_type=0)
similarity(0,1,sim_type=1)
similarity(0,2,sim_type=0)
similarity(1,2,sim_type=0)
similarity(2,1,sim_type=0)
similarity(0,0,sim_type=0)
similarity(0,0,sim_type=1)
```

Reads in the data using a helper method

Similarity of Frank and Constantine under both measures of similarity

Similarity of Frank with himself under both measures of similarity

We've provided two definitions of similarity, which are invoked by providing a different value in the third argument of the similarity method introduced in listing 3.1.

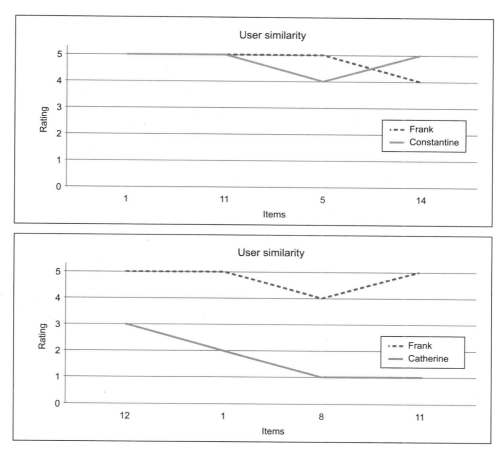

Figure 3.1 The similarity between two users can be measured by evaluating the extent of overlap (if any) between the two lines in plots like this. Thus, Frank and Constantine (top) are more similar than Frank and Catherine (bottom).

We'll describe the detailed implementation of that code shortly, but first look at figure 3.1, which shows the results that we get if we compare among the three users considering the ratings only. As you can clearly see, Frank's preferences in movies are more similar to Constantine's than they are to Catherine's.

The similarity between two users doesn't depend on the order in which we pass the arguments in the similarity method. The similarity of Frank with himself is equal to 1.0, which we take to be the maximum value of similarity between any two entities. These properties stem from the fact that many similarity measures are based on distances, like the geometric distance between two points on a plane that you learned about in high school. In general, mathematical distances have the following four important properties:

- All distances are greater than or equal to zero. In most cases, we constrain the similarities to be nonnegative like distances. In fact, we constrain the similarities within the interval [0,1].

- The distance between any two points, say A and B, is zero if and only if A is the same point as B. In the example, and based on our implementation of similarity, this property is reflected in the fact that when two users have exactly the same ratings, the similarity between them will be equal to 1.0. You'll see that this is true if you run listing 3.1, where we used the same user twice to show that the similarity is 1.0. Of course, you can create a fourth user and prove that the similarity will be equal to 1.0, provided the users have watched the same movies.

- The third property of distances is symmetry—the distance between A and B is exactly the same as the distance between B and A. This means if Catherine's movie taste is similar to Constantine's movie taste, the reverse will also be true by exactly the same amount. Quite often we want the measure of similarity to preserve the symmetric property of distances, with respect to its arguments.

- The fourth property of mathematical distances is the triangle inequality, because it relates the distances between three points. In mathematical terms, if $d(A,B)$ denotes the distance between points A and B, then the triangle inequality states that $d(A,B) <= d(A,C) + d(C,B)$ for any third point C. Looking at the output of listing 3.1, Frank is similar to Constantine by 0.391 and Constantine is similar to Catherine by 0.002, whereas Frank is similar to Catherine by 0.006, which is less than the sum of the first two similarities. Nevertheless, that property doesn't hold, in general, for all similarities.

Relaxing the fourth fundamental property of distances when you pass on to similarities is fine; there's no imperative to carry over the properties of distances to similarities. You should always be cautious to ensure that the mathematics involved is in agreement with what you consider reasonable, though. There's a century-old counterexample to the triangle inequality when it comes to similarities that's attributed to William James:[1] "A flame is similar to the moon because they are both luminous, and the moon is similar to a ball because they are both round, but in contradiction to the triangle inequality, a flame is not similar to a ball." For an interesting account of similarities in relation to cognition, we recommend *Classification and Cognition* by W. K. Estes.[2]

In figure 3.1, we show a visual representation of the similarity by plotting mutual ratings for our three example users. The closer the lines of the ratings, the more similar the users are; the farther apart the lines, the less the similarity. At the top of the figure, you can see that the lines for Frank and Constantine are close, depicting the similarity between them. At the bottom of the figure, where we show the ratings of Frank versus those of Catherine, the lines diverge and are far apart, which is in accordance with the low similarity value that we got during our calculation.

---

[1] William James, *Principles of Psychology* (Holt, 1890).
[2] W. K. Estes, *Classification and Cognition* (Oxford University Press, 1994).

The plots of the ratings in figure 3.1 clearly display the somewhat reciprocal nature of distance and similarity. The greater the distance between the two curves, the smaller the similarity between the two users; the smaller the distance between the two curves, the greater the similarity between the two users. As you'll see in the next section, the evaluation of similarity often involves the evaluation of some kind of distance, although that's not always necessary. The concept of distance is more familiar. The concept of distance and the concept of similarity are special cases of the general concept of a metric.

3.2.1 *A closer look at distance and similarity*

Now, let's examine the code that helped us find the similarity between the users and look closely at how to calculate similarity. The code in the next listing shows the details of the similarity method, which accepts three arguments: the IDs of the two users we wish to compare and the kind of similarity we want to use.

Listing 3.2 Calculating the similarity between two users

```
def similarity(user_id_a,user_id_b,sim_type=0):
    user_a_tuple_list = userdict[user_id_a].get_items()
    user_b_tuple_list = userdict[user_id_b].get_items()
    common_items=0
    sim = 0.0
    for t1 in user_a_tuple_list:
        for t2 in user_b_tuple_list:
            if (t1[0] == t2[0]):
                common_items += 1
                sim += math.pow(t1[1]-t2[1],2)
    if common_items>0:
        sim = math.sqrt(sim/common_items)
        sim = 1.0 - math.tanh(sim)
        if sim_type==1:
            max_common = min(len(user_a_tuple_list),len(user_b_tuple_list))
            sim = sim * common_items / max_common
    print "User Similarity between",
        ➥names[user_id_a],"and",names[user_id_b],"is", sim
    return sim                                    ⟵——  If no common items, returns zero
```

We include two similarity formulas in the code to show that the notion of similarity is fairly flexible and extensible. Let's examine the basic steps in the calculation of these similarity formulas. First, we take the differences between all the ratings of movies that the users have in common, square them, and add them together. The square root of that value is called the *Euclidean distance*; and as it stands, it's not sufficient to provide a measure of similarity:

$$d_{a,b} = \sqrt{\sum_i \left(rating_{a,i} - rating_{b,i}\right)^2}$$

This equation states the definition of the Euclidean distance between user *a* and user *b*, $d_{a,b}$. It's expressed as the square root of the sum of squares between the ratings of the users for the same film. $rating_{a,i}$ expresses the rating that user *a* has given to film *i*.

As we mentioned earlier, the concepts of distance and similarity are somewhat reciprocal, in the sense that the smaller the value of the Euclidean distance, the more similar the two users are. As a first naïve attempt, we could create a similarity score by adding 1 to the Euclidean score and inverting it. This would have the effect that large distances have small scores and vice versa. It would also ensure that a distance of zero returns a similarity score of 1.0.

At first sight, it appears that inverting the distance (after adding the constant value 1) might work. But this seemingly innocuous modification suffers from shortcomings. If two users have watched only one movie, one of them rated the movie 1, and the other gave a rating of 4, the sum of their differences squared is 9.0. In that case, the naïve similarity, based on the Euclidean distance, would result in a similarity value of 0.25. The same similarity value can be obtained in other cases. If the two users had watched three movies, and among these three movies their ratings differed by $\sqrt{3}$ (for each movie), their similarity would also be 0.25, according to the naïve similarity metric. Intuitively, we expect these two users to be more similar than those who watched a single movie and whose opinions differed by three units (out of five).

The naïve similarity "squeezes" the similarity values for small distances (because we add 1) while leaving large distances (values of the distance much larger than 1.0) unaffected. What if we add another value? The general form of the naïve similarity is $y = beta / (beta + x)$, where *beta* is our free parameter and *x* is the Euclidean distance. Figure 3.2 shows what the naïve similarity would look like for various values of the parameter *beta* between 1.0 and 2.0.

Keeping in mind the shortcomings of the naïve similarity, let's look at the first (default) similarity definition between two users as shown in listing 3.2, where `sim_type=0`. If the users have some movies in common, we divide the sum of their squared differences by the number of common movies, take the positive square root, and pass on that value to a special function. This function is called the *hyperbolic tangent function*. We subtract the value of the hyperbolic tangent from 1.0, so that the final value of similarity ranges between 0.0 and 1.0, with 0.0 implying dissimilarity and 1.0 implying the highest similarity. Voilà! We've arrived at our first definition of similarity of users based on their ratings.

The second similarity definition that we present in listing 3.2, in the case where `sim_type=1`, improves on the first similarity by taking into account the ratio of the common items versus the number of all possible common items. That's a heuristic that intuitively makes sense. If I've watched 30 movies and you've watched 20, we could have up to 20 common movies. Let's say that we have only 5 movies in common, and we agree fairly well on these movies, which is nice; but why don't we have more movies in common? Shouldn't that somehow be reflected in our similarity? This is exactly the aspect of the problem that we're trying to capture in the second similarity

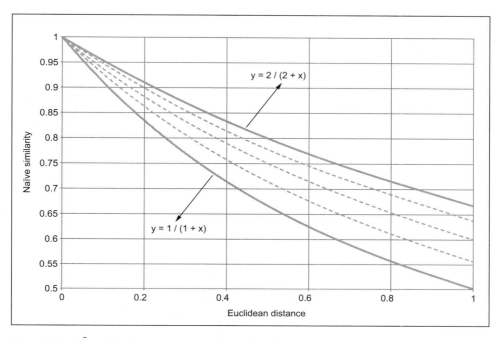

Figure 3.2 Naïve similarity curves as functions of the Euclidean distance

formula. In other words, the extent to which we watch the same movies should some-how affect the degree of our similarity as movie enthusiasts.

3.2.2 *Which is the best similarity formula?*

It may be clear by now that you can use many formulas to establish the similarity between two users—or between two items, for that matter. In addition to the two similarities introduced earlier, we could've used a metric formula known as the *Jaccard similarity* between users, which is defined by the ratio of the intersection over the union of their item sets—or, in the case of item similarity, the ratio of the intersection over the union of the user sets. In other words, the Jaccard similarity between two sets, A and B, is defined by *intersection(A,B) / union(A,B)*.

Of course, you may naturally wonder, "Which similarity formula is more appropriate?" The answer, as always, is, "It depends." In this case, it depends on your data. In one of the few large-scale comparisons of similarity metrics,[3] the simple Euclidean distance–based similarity showed the best empirical results among seven similarity metrics, despite the fact that other formulas were more elaborate and intuitively expected to perform better. Their measurements were based on 1,279,266 clicks on related community recommendations from September 22, 2004, through October 21, 2004 on the social networking website Orkut.

---

[3] Ellen Spertus, Mehran Sahami, and Orkut Buyukkokten, "Evaluating Similarity Measures: A Large-Scale Study in the Orkut Social Network," Proceedings of KDD 2005.

We don't advise that you randomly choose your similarity metric, but if you're in a hurry, consider the Euclidean or the Jaccard similarity first. It should give you decent results. You should try to understand the nature of your data and what it means for two users or two items to be similar. If you don't understand the reasons why a particular similarity metric (formula) is good or bad, you're setting yourself up for trouble. To stress this point, think of the common misconception "The shortest path between two points is a straight line that joins them." That statement is true only for what we call *flat geometries*, such as a football field. To convince yourself, compare the distance of going over a tall but narrow hill versus going around the hill's base. The straight line won't be the shortest path for a wide range of hill sizes.

In summary, one of the cornerstones of recommendations is the ability to measure the similarity between any two users and the similarity between any two items. We've provided a number of similarity measures that you can use off the shelf, and the movie store exemplified the typical structure of the data you'd deal with in order to create recommendations. We'll now move on to examine the types of recommendation engines and how they work.

3.3   *How do recommendation engines work?*

Now that you're armed with a good understanding of what similarity between two users or two items means, we can proceed with our description of recommendation engines. Generally speaking, there are two categories of recommendation engines. The first broad category is based on the analysis of the content—associated with the items or the users or both. The main characteristic of this content-based approach is the accumulation and analysis of information related to both users and items. That information may be provided either by the software system or through external sources. The system can collect information about the users *explicitly* through their response to solicited questionnaires or *implicitly* through the mining of each user's profile or news-reading habits, emails, blogs, and so on. We won't cover this category of recommendation engines in detail because it requires a large degree of manual design, and intervention is rather application specific.

The second goes under the label *collaborative filtering (CF)*. The first incarnation of CF appeared in an experimental mail system (circa 1992) developed at the Xerox Palo Alto Research Center (PARC).[4] CF relies on the breadcrumbs that a user leaves behind through interaction with a software system. Typically, these breadcrumbs are the user's ratings, such as the movie ratings that we described in the previous section. Collaborative filtering isn't limited to one-dimensional or discrete variables; its main characteristic is that it depends on past behavior rather than the content of each item in the collection of interest. CF requires neither domain knowledge nor preliminary gathering and analysis work to produce recommendations. It can be typically classified further into one of three types: item-based, user-based, and model-based.

---

[4] David Goldberg et al., "Using Collaborative Filtering to Weave an Information Tapestry," *Communications of the ACM* 35, no. 12 (December 1992), http://mng.bz/eZpM.

In item-based CF, we're most interested in the similarity of items. For example, in the case of our movie recommendation example, we'd typically build a matrix of movies whereby matrix entries express some degree of similarity. Movies can then be recommended that are most similar to those that users have already seen or liked. Conversely, with user-based CF, the similarity of users is considered important. In this scenario, users may be recommended content if they're similar to those who have seen or liked a particular item. In model-based CF, neither item-item similarity nor user-user similarity is calculated explicitly, but a model is introduced to capture the interaction between users and items.

In the following sections, we'll provide an example of user-based CF, leaving the implementation of item-based CF as an exercise for you. We'll then move on to an explicit implementation of model-based CF that uses singular value decomposition (SVD) in section 3.5.

Item-based CF vs. user-based CF

Depending on the data, there can be a distinct performance profile in the use of each of these methods of CF. If you consider the problem of movie recommendations, you'll note that there are probably more users than there are movies; thus the user-user similarity matrix is much larger and therefore more expensive to calculate. If you take two users who have rated numerous films, you aren't guaranteed much overlap in the films they've seen, because users probably watch only a small subset of available films. Conversely, the item-item matrix is cheaper to calculate, because it's smaller. If you take two films with many ratings, it may (arguably, but again, depending on the data) be more likely that there is a reasonable degree of overlap in the users who have reviewed them, because there are likely more reviews for a film from individuals than a given individual has watched films. This makes the user-user similarity matrix harder to calculate and the item-item matrix (relatively) easier.

Despite the user-user similarity matrix being harder to calculate in a fully deployed movie recommendation system, we'll be providing an implementation of user-based CF. In reality, the approach is identical, and the concept of user similarity with respect to the films users have rated is easier to reason about than the concept of item similarity with respect to the users who have rated them.

3.4 User-based collaborative filtering

An ancient Greek proverb (with similar variants in nearly every culture of the world) states, "Show me your friends, and I'll tell you who you are." Collaborative filtering based on neighborhoods of similar users is more or less an algorithmic incarnation of that proverb. In order to evaluate the rating of a particular user for a given item, you look for the ratings of similar users (neighbors or friends, if you prefer) on the same item. Then, you multiply the rating of each friend by a weight and add them—it's that simple! The following listing shows the code to provide a recommendation based on user similarity. We use the same data as we did to demonstrate different measures of similarity—the data given in table 3.1.

Listing 3.3 User-based CF recommendation

```
data = Data()
format = {'col':0, 'row':1, 'value':2, 'ids': 'int'}
data.load(dat_file, sep='::', format=format)

similarity_matrix = SimilarityMatrix()
recommend(0,10)
recommend(1,10)
recommend(2,10)
```

Provides the top 10 recommendations for user 0 (Frank)

Provides the top 10 recommendations for user I (Constantine)

Provides the top 10 recommendations for user 2 (Catherine)

Listing 3.3 provides the high-level code to perform user-based CF. We read in the data using the load method in `recsys.datamodel.data`. The `recommend` method is then used to provide recommendations of movies that the user should consider. More accurately, the method provides a prediction of the ratings that the user would give for particular movies. These are ordered, and the top 10 are returned. The `recommend` method predicts ratings for only those items that haven't already been rated by the user. With the dataset used, there are fewer than 10 movies unseen for each user; hence, this limit is never hit. You might also come across the "None" rating. This occurs only where the user hasn't rated the movie and no other users in the dataset have rated it, either. Thus, this represents not a zero rating but a lack of rating.

To provide an example, if you run the code, you'll see that Constantine is recommended *Jumanji*, *Waiting to Exhale*, and *Sabrina*, mainly because Frank has rated these films. Constantine is similar to Frank (as you saw previously), and Frank has rated them highly. It seems that our recommendation engine is working well. You'll note that the recommendations for each user are only for films that they haven't seen or rated themselves, and that recommendations appear to be made based on the tastes of similar users.

How did the `recommend` class arrive at these conclusions? How can it find the similar users (friends) for any given user? How can it recommend movies from the list of movies that a user has never watched? Let's go through the basic steps to understand what happens. Recommendation engines that are based on collaborative filtering proceed in two steps. First they calculate the similarity between either users or items. Then they use a weighted average to calculate the rating that a user would give to a yet-unseen item. Let's delve further into the `recommend` method, shown in the following listing, to see this in action.

Listing 3.4 recommend method

```
def recommend(user_id, top_n):
    #[(item,value),(item1, value1)...]
    recommendations = []
    for i in itemdict.keys():
        if (int(i) not in items_reviewed(int(user_id),userdict)):
            recommendations.append((i,predict_rating(user_id, i)))
    recommendations.sort(key=lambda t: t[1], reverse=True)
    return recommendations[:top_n]
```

This listing demonstrates that the `recommend` method is relatively simple and relies heavily on the `predict_rating` method. `recommend` takes a `user_id` and the top number of recommendations that should be returned. It iterates through every item in the item dictionary, and if the user has not yet rated the item, `predict_rating` is called and the result is appended to the recommendations list. The recommendations list is then sorted and passed back to the caller. The next listing shows the inner workings of the `predict_rating` method.

Listing 3.5 Predicting the ratings of a user

```
def predict_rating(user_id, item_id):
    estimated_rating = None;
    similarity_sum = 0;
    weighted_rating_sum = 0;

    if (int(item_id) in items_reviewed(user_id,userdict)):
        return get_score_item_reviewed(user_id,item_id,userdict)
    else:
        for u in userdict.keys():
            if (int(item_id) in items_reviewed(u,userdict)):
                item_rating = get_score_item_reviewed(u,item_id,userdict)
                user_similarity =
  ➥similarity_matrix.get_user_similarity(user_id,u)
                weighted_rating = user_similarity * item_rating
                weighted_rating_sum += weighted_rating
                similarity_sum += user_similarity

        if (similarity_sum > 0.0):
            estimated_rating = weighted_rating_sum / similarity_sum

    return estimated_rating
```

In this listing, you see that `predict_rating` takes two parameters: the ID of the user of interest and the ID of the item of interest. It returns a prediction of the rating that this user may give to this item.

Stepping through the code line by line, you see that if the user has already rated the item, we don't attempt to predict the rating; we merely return the actual rating given to the item by that user. If the user hasn't rated the item, then we proceed as per user-based CF. That is, for each user in the system, we check whether that user has reviewed the item for which we wish to make a prediction. If they have, we get the score that they input, along with a calculation of how similar this user is to the one for whom we wish to make a prediction. We then calculate a weighted rating, which is the similarity of the two users multiplied by the rating given by this new user. In order to calculate a value that considers all the users in the system, we calculate the sum of such `weighted_ratings` along with the sum of the similarities. The latter is used to normalize the values back to the range [0,5]. Provided that there are some users in the dataset who are in some way similar to the user we're attempting to make the recommendation for, and that they have rated the item we're interested in, we're guaranteed to be able to make an estimation regarding the rating with this code.

Although the code works perfectly well for our purposes, note that already there are some serious performance issues that we might want to look at. Considering listings 3.4 and 3.5 together, you can see that we're essentially looping though every item and every user in the system. We might wish to think about other data structures that could avoid this; for example, we might consider storing users in a dictionary keyed by items rated (which would result in only the users who have rated an item being iterated through, rather than all users as in listing 3.5). This is just one of many performance improvements that might be considered for a production system with user-based CF.

So far, we've presented a broad outline of our user-based CF system, but we're missing some specific details from the implementation in listing 3.5: the calculation of the similarity matrix. The next listing outlines the class responsible for this calculation.

Listing 3.6 `SimilarityMatrix` class

```
class SimilarityMatrix:

    similarity_matrix = None                                    Calculates only values of
                                                                v that are larger than
    def __init__(self):                                         the current value of u
        self.build()                                            (upper triangular form)

    def build(self):
        self.similarity_matrix = np.empty((len(userdict),len(userdict),))

        for u in range(0,len(userdict)):
            for v in range(u+1,len(userdict)):
                rcm = RatingCountMatrix(int(u),int(v))
                if(rcm.get_agreement_count()>0):
                    self.similarity_matrix[u][v] =
                    rcm.get_agreement_count()/rcm.get_total_count()
                else:
                    self.similarity_matrix[u][v] = 0
            self.similarity_matrix[u][u]=1

    def get_user_similarity(self,user_id1, user_id2):
        return
        self.similarity_matrix[min(user_id1,user_id2),max(user_id1,user_id2)]
```

Calls the build method on instantiation

The similarity between a user and themselves is 1.

Due to the upper triangular form, we have to do additional work to get the similarity. The smaller of the two users must be the row index to the matrix, whereas the larger must be the column index. Otherwise, the returned similarity would be zero (not calculated by build()).

If users agree on something, returns the similarity between the users using RatingCountMatrix

The `SimilarityMatrix` class encapsulates the storage, calculation, and access to the matrix that defines how similar each user is with respect to another. When it's first instantiated, it calls the `build` method, which calculates the similarities of the users stored in the `userdict` dictionary object. There are two important things to note about this. First, we use the upper triangular form of the matrix. As we mentioned in section 3.2, it may be sensible for our similarities to have the property of symmetry. That is, if Catherine is similar to Frank, then Frank is similar to Catherine. We do indeed take this property for our implementation of user similarity, and because of this we can use the upper triangular form of the similarity matrix. Put simply, there's no point in storing the similarity between a and b if we already have the similarity between b and a. This halves the size of the similarity matrix along with the amount of computation required to calculate it.

The second thing you may note is the use of another helper class called `Rating-CountMatrix`, the definition of which is presented in the following listing.

Listing 3.7 `RatingCountMatrix` class

```python
class RatingCountMatrix:
    user_id_a = None
    user_id_b = None
    matrix = None

    def __init__(self, user_id_a, user_id_b):
        num_rating_values = max([x[0] for x in data])
        self.user_id_a = user_id_a
        self.user_id_b = user_id_b
        self.matrix = np.empty((num_rating_values,num_rating_values,))
        self.matrix[:] = 0
        self.calculate_matrix(user_id_a,user_id_b)

    def get_shape(self):
        a = self.matrix.shape
        return a

    def get_matrix(self):
        return self.matrix

    def calculate_matrix(self,user_id_a, user_id_b):
        for item in items_reviewed(user_id_a, userdict):
            if int(item) in items_reviewed(user_id_b, userdict):
                i = get_score_item_reviewed(user_id_a,item, userdict)-1
                j = get_score_item_reviewed(user_id_b,item, userdict)-1
                self.matrix[i][j] +=1

    def get_total_count(self):
        return self.matrix.sum()

    def get_agreement_count(self):
        return np.trace(self.matrix) #sum across the diagonal
```

The `RatingCountMatrix` class is used to calculate the degree of similarity between the users, based on the items that both have rated and on their level of agreement in those ratings. As you can see, it's not enough for two users to have both rated a movie; they also must broadly agree on its quality. `RatingCountMatrix` encapsulates this through the use of a matrix that captures the covariance of their ratings. For users who always agree on the ratings for the movies they've seen, we'd expect the diagonal of the matrix to be populated with higher numbers: that is, $\mathbf{M}_{ij}$ where $i=j$. For those who never agree or who have opposing views, we'd expect those entries farthest away from the diagonal to be populated: that is, $\mathbf{M}_{ij}$ where $i=\min(rating)$, $j=\max(rating)$ or $\mathbf{M}_{ij}$ where $i=\max(rating)$ and $j=\min(rating)$.

The calculation of similarity falls out of the matrix intuitively, as you saw in listing 3.6. We can use the total number of ratings that the users have agreed on, divided by the total number of items that both users have provided a rating for. Note again that our computational performance characteristics are likely far below optimal, because we recalculate the `RatingCountMatrix` every time we wish to determine the similarity score of two users. This is acceptable for our illustrative example but would be far from appropriate for a reasonably large system.

Thus far, we've focused on a user-based CF system. You should easily be able to see how we might flip this system on its head (so that users are treated as items and items as users). Rather than provide comprehensive coverage of this here, we'll leave the exercise of completing an item-based CF system to you and move on to another form of collaborative filtering known as model-based CF.

Specifically, the model we'll use is *singular value decomposition (SVD)*. Model-based approaches are powerful and in this case help us understand a deeper relationship between users and movies. For SVD, this model consists of a third, unobservable space that we'll call a *latent space*. This captures that there is some unobservable reason why users make certain choices (affinity to certain genres of movies, for example). Rather than ignoring this as with user- and item-based CF, we attempt to capture it.

3.5 Model-based recommendation using singular value decomposition

In the previous example, we essentially clustered users in a way that allows for the most similar users to contribute to the predicted ratings for a user. Both in this case and in item-based CF, we don't presume anything about the distributions between users and item similarities. Herein lies the principal difference between user-based and item-based CF when compared with model-based CF.

In model-based CF, an additional assumption or model is added to the approach. In this case, using SVD, we assume that items and users are related through some latent space, not captured by either users or items. If this sounds somewhat exotic, don't worry. All it means is that users map to items, and items map to users through some other, third space. You can think of this as a genre space if you like, although it's technically not quite correct. If a user's preference is determined by the algorithm as equal parts drama, romance, and action, and a film is similarly (and automatically) determined as such, then they may be given a recommendation for that film provided they haven't already seen it. In reality, this latent space of genres isn't labeled as such and is determined automatically by the algorithm. This should give you a flavor of how SVD works as a recommender—but if not, never fear; we'll cover the details in this section.

3.5.1 *Singular value decomposition*

SVD is a method of factorizing a matrix. *Factorizing* just means splitting something up, such that if you multiply these elements together you get the original item that was factorized. For numbers, this is relatively simple (10 can factorize into 2×5, for example), but for matrix multiplication this can be a little harder to do in your head.

Wolfram MathWorld[5] tells us that a given matrix $\mathbf{A}$, which has m rows and n columns, with $m>n$, can be written in the form

$$\mathbf{A} = \mathbf{UDV}^T$$

where $\mathbf{U}$ is $m \times m$, $\mathbf{D}$ is $m \times n$, and $\mathbf{V}$ is $n \times n$. $\mathbf{D}$ only has entries along the diagonal, and both $\mathbf{U}$ and $\mathbf{V}$ have orthogonal columns (that is, $\mathbf{U}^T\mathbf{U}=\mathbf{I}=\mathbf{V}^T\mathbf{V}$). This last point is important because it means the directions that make up the latent space are all at orthogonal; that is, they can't be expressed as linear combinations of the others. We'll return to this in a moment.

You might think this is all very well, but what does it have to do with recommender systems? Actually, quite a lot. Let's imagine that matrix $\mathbf{A}$ is $m \times n$, where m is the number of users and n is the number of films. An entry in the matrix indicates a rating that user m has given to film n. Now, what if we could split that into $\mathbf{U}$, an $m \times r$ matrix that provides information regarding users' affinity to a new smaller space of size r? Similarly, we do the same with $\mathbf{V}^T$, such that we create an $r \times n$ matrix, which provides the affinity to movies to each dimension in size r. Finally, we try to understand how important each dimension of r is in predicting the scores users give to items. These are known as the *singular values* of the factored matrix and are placed on the diagonal of $\mathbf{D}$ in non-increasing order, with the columns and rows of the user ($\mathbf{U}$) and item ($\mathbf{V}^T$) matrix, respectively, being organized appropriately.

Note that in this example we use a latent space of size r. In general, you may choose to keep the top number of singular values—say, k—to capture the most important dimensions in the latent space while maintaining as compact a form as possible. You may notice a similarity to the concept of dimensionality reduction through eigenvalue decomposition from chapter 2. This isn't a coincidence! If you're interested, I refer you to Gerbrands[6] for more information regarding the relationship between the two concepts.

To return to the orthogonality of the latent space in $\mathbf{U}$ and $\mathbf{V}$, this conceptually makes a lot of sense. Let's take an example with matrix $\mathbf{U}$. If we pick any two columns, then the dot product of the two column vectors will equal zero. Latent features are selected such that the features are as far away as possible from each other with regard to viewership, thus being maximally descriptive. Another way to think about this is

[5] "Singular Value Decomposition," *Wolfram MathWorld*, 2015, http://mng.bz/TxyY.

[6] Jan J. Gerbrands, "On the Relationships between SVD, KLT and PCA," Conference on Pattern Recognition (1980).

that it makes sense to select features that are far away from each other in user space. If sci-fi fans never watch romantic comedies and vice versa, then such a feature would be useful in providing a recommendation. Simultaneously, we know that for any two columns in **V**, or equivalently any two rows in $\mathbf{V}^T$, they're also orthogonal. That is, latent features are selected such that the features are as far away as possible from each other with regard to film membership. To return to our imperfect, genre parallel, genres are created such that they're far away from each other in film space. For example, sci-fi films are never comedies. It's important to stress that these features aren't actually genres, as we've used in the illustration, but rather some other property that encapsulates the relationship between films and viewers.

Working through an example, if we already have **A** factorized, it's trivial to see how an individual rating can be calculated. The user's position in this r-dimensional latent space is looked up (a bit like their percentage interest in r different orthogonal genres) before multiplying each r with its relative importance globally. This leaves us with a vector of magnitude r. Finally, the coordinate in r dimensions is also looked up for the item for which we want to predict (a bit like its percentage affinity to r different orthogonal genres) before taking the dot product of the two. This leaves us with a number, which is the predicted rating for that user and that movie. Note that even though we're using the concept of genres here, this is for illustration only. Although it might be possible to overlay semantic meaning onto these dimensions after training, they have no such explicit meaning in reality.

Training a recommender system is equivalent to performing matrix factorization. Recommendations can be looked up directly from the factored matrix form, mirroring the example provided in the last paragraph. If this is a little surprising, consider that the factorization is trying to make the connections between the users, movies, and latent space that it thinks should be there. Essentially, it's trying to rationalize the factorization and minimize its error in order to model the underlying relationship. If you think about it carefully, you'll realize that recommendations spring from the error in the factorization. We'll cover this in more detail in the next section, where you'll see a recommendation system based on SVD.

3.5.2 *Recommendation using SVD: choosing movies for a given user*

In this section, we're going to use SVD to provide recommendations of movies to users. As before, we'll use the MovieLens dataset, but rather than select only a few movies and users to demonstrate the concept, we'll use all the data available to us. Recall that the MovieLens dataset contains numerous user-movie recommendations. We'll use the power of SVD to build a latent-space matrix—that is, to understand whether there is some pattern between users given the movies that they rate highly.

We'll also introduce a new package here that isn't found in scikit-learn. The python-recsys package[7] is lightweight yet powerful enough for us to easily demonstrate the use of SVD for recommendation, so we'll use this package throughout this section; see the following listing. Make sure you have it installed before running the code examples.

---

[7] ACM RecSys Wiki, www.recsyswiki.com/wiki/Python-recsys.

Listing 3.8   SVD for recommendation

```
svd = SVD()
recsys.algorithm.VERBOSE = True                              Sends back progress
                                                             to the screen
dat_file = './ml-1m/ratings.dat'                             User ratings
item_file = './ml-1m/movies.dat'                             Movie info

data = Data()
data.load(dat_file, sep='::',
          format={'col':0, 'row':1, 'value':2, 'ids': int})

items_full = read_item_data(item_file)
user_full = read_user_data_from_ratings(dat_file)

svd.set_data(data)
```

This listing provides a high-level overview of how we use the recsys package to perform SVD on the freely available Movielens ml-1m dataset, which you should download. This dataset contains 1 million user ratings, and we'll use all of them to build a recommender. We start by creating an instance of the SVD object and reading in both the user ratings for a movie and further information regarding that movie (genres, year of release, and so on). Although the model doesn't use the additional data, we could use it to reason about how sensible the recommendations returned are. In the final line, we pass only the data file to the SVD object, specifying the format of the file.

As in previous examples, we've yet to actually do any learning. Data has been passed to an object that will perform this learning, but the actual computation has been deferred. The next listing shows the code to train the model, or rather factorize the matrix that was created through the `load` method of the `Data` class.

Listing 3.9   Factorizing a matrix using SVD for recommendation

```
k = 100
svd.compute(k=k, min_values=10,
            pre_normalize=None, mean_center=True, post_normalize=True)

films = svd.recommend(10, only_unknowns=True, is_row=False)
```

We call `svd.compute` with five parameters. These parameters control the execution of matrix factorization. For completeness, we reproduce the documentation here[8] and discuss the impact of these options on factorization:

- `min_values`—Remove rows or columns that have fewer than `min_values` non-zeros.
- `pre_normalize`—Normalize the input matrix. Possible values are these:
  - `tfidf` (default)—Treat the matrix as terms-by-documents. It's important, then, how the data is loaded. Use the `format` param in `svd.load_data()` to determine the order of the fields of the input file.

---

[8]   Oscar Celma, Python Recsys v1.0 documentation, http://mng.bz/UBiX.

- – `rows`—Rescale the rows of the input matrix so that they all have unit Euclidean magnitude.
- – `cols`—Rescale the columns of the input matrix so that they all have unit Euclidean magnitude.
- – `all`—Rescale the rows and columns of the input matrix, by dividing both the rows and the columns by the square root of their Euclidean norm.
- `mean_center`—Center the input matrix (aka mean substraction).
- `post_normalize`—Normalize every row of **UD** to be a unit vector. Thus, row similarity (using cosine distance) returns [-1.0 .. 1.0].
- `savefile`—Output file to store SVD transformation (**U**, **D**, **V** ^{T} vectors).

You see here that the majority of the options control data pre- or post-processing. In the first parameter, we have the option to remove movies or users with fewer than 100 ratings. This should reduce the matrix size significantly and concentrate on only those movies or users with enough data to provide recommendations for. The second and third parameters provide normalization and centering of the data. Normalization is important because it provides guarantees regarding the variance of the data. Centering modifies the point of reference for this variance. Both parameters can help with the stability of the algorithm performing SVD, which in this case is the Single-Vector Lanczos Method,[9] called via the SVDLIBC library.[10]

Let's now continue with the example and perform recommendation with the model. In the last line of listing 3.9, we call `svd.recommend()`, passing in three parameters. The first parameter is the user we're trying to determine recommendations for; in this case, we've randomly chosen user 10. We also pass in two additional parameters: `only_unknowns=True` and `is_row=False`. The first of these tells the method to return ratings only for items that haven't been rated by user 10. The latter is a peculiarity of the library we're using, because `is_row=False` tells the recommendation to occur over columns: that is, users, not items (which are along the rows). Because the model used here is that of matrix factorization, we could just as easily have provided an item ID (movie) and asserted `is_row=True` in order to determine a list of appropriate users for that movie. In contrast to the user-based and item-based methods discussed earlier in this chapter, this method can provide similar functionality to each without a huge amount of change to the code.

Enough of the details—what about the results of the recommendation? Let's take a look. The next listing shows the films that have been recommended.

---

[9] C. Lanczos, "An Iteration Method for the Solution of the Eigenvalue Problem of Linear Differential and Integral Operators," *Journal of Research of the National Bureau of Standards* 45, no. 4 (October 1950), http://mng.bz/cB2d.

[10] Doug Rohde, SVDLIBC, http://tedlab.mit.edu/~dr/SVDLIBC/.

Listing 3.10 Output from model-based recommendation

```
[items_full[str(x[0])].get_data() for x in films]

[{'Genres': 'Action|Adventure\n', 'Title': 'Sanjuro (1962)'},
 {'Genres': 'Crime|Drama\n', 'Title': 'Pulp Fiction (1994)'},
 {'Genres': 'Crime|Thriller\n', 'Title': 'Usual Suspects, The (1995)'},
 {'Genres': 'Comedy|Crime\n', 'Title': 'Some Like It Hot (1959)'},
 {'Genres': 'Drama\n', 'Title': 'World of Apu, The (Apur Sansar) (1959)'},
 {'Genres': 'Documentary\n', 'Title': 'For All Mankind (1989)'},
 {'Genres': 'Animation|Comedy\n', 'Title': 'Creature Comforts (1990)'},
 {'Genres': 'Comedy|Drama|Romance\n', 'Title': 'City Lights (1931)'},
 {'Genres': 'Drama\n', 'Title': 'Pather Panchali (1955)'},
 {'Genres': 'Drama\n',
  'Title': '400 Blows, The (Les Quatre cents coups) (1959)'}]
```

Here you can see that user 10 has been recommended some action/adventure, crime/drama, and crime/thriller. They seem to like a bit of comedy too, as well as some animation. Looks reasonable, but we don't know anything about the user. The following listing digs in to the rating information for user 10 to see what they've watched and rated before.

Listing 3.11 Films rated by user 10

```
get_name_item_reviewed(10,user_full,items_full)

[(2622, "Midsummer Night's Dream, A (1999)", 'Comedy|Fantasy\n', 5.0),
 (3358, 'Defending Your Life (1991)', 'Comedy|Romance\n', 5.0),
 (1682, 'Truman Show, The (1998)', 'Drama\n', 5.0),
 (2125, 'Ever After: A Cinderella Story (1998)', 'Drama|Romance\n', 5.0),
 (1253, 'Day the Earth Stood Still, The (1951)', 'Drama|Sci-Fi\n', 5.0),
 (720,
  'Wallace and Gromit: The Best of Aardman Animation (1996)',
  'Animation\n',
  5.0),
 (3500, 'Mr. Saturday Night (1992)', 'Comedy|Drama\n', 5.0),
 (1257, 'Better Off Dead... (1985)', 'Comedy\n', 5.0),
 (3501, "Murphy's Romance (1985)", 'Comedy|Romance\n', 5.0),
 (1831, 'Lost in Space (1998)', 'Action|Sci-Fi|Thriller\n', 5.0),
 (3363, 'American Graffiti (1973)', 'Comedy|Drama\n', 5.0),
 (587, 'Ghost (1990)', 'Comedy|Romance|Thriller\n', 5.0),
 (150, 'Apollo 13 (1995)', 'Drama\n', 5.0),
 (1, 'Toy Story (1995)', "Animation|Children's|Comedy\n", 5.0),
 (2, 'Jumanji (1995)', "Adventure|Children's|Fantasy\n", 5.0), ...
```

This is only a very small portion of 401 movies rated by this user, but we certainly find some animation/comedy coming through (both *Wallace and Gromit* and *Creature Comforts* are made by the same production company, Aardman Animations). We also see comedy and drama feature in both the rated movies and the recommended movies. Note, however, that the user gave 154 ratings of 5, so this small list isn't completely indicative of this user's interests. Let's dig in a little further and look at the distribution of genres for user 10. Figure 3.3 provides the genres for which the user has rated

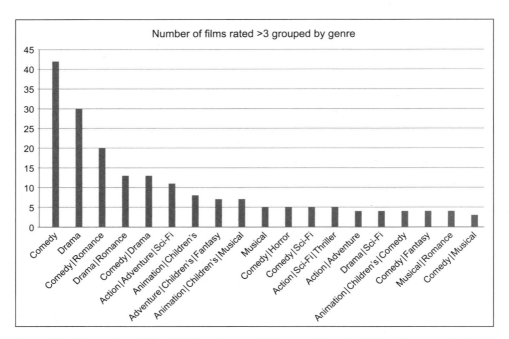

Figure 3.3 The number of films that have been rated by user 10 as 4 or higher. These are broken out by genre, so user 10 has rated more than 40 comedy films with a 4 or a 5. Only the top 19 genres are displayed here.

higher than 3, and figure 3.4 provides the genres for which the user has rated lower than 3. We don't report on films that have been rated with the average score of 3.

This should now start to make more sense. Figure 3.3 shows that this user is clearly interested in comedy and drama films, because they account for the overwhelming majority of positive ratings provided by the user. If you return to our recommendation in listing 3.10, you'll see that this does correlate well. Seven of 10 of these recommendations have either comedy or drama in their genre title. Romance, action/adventure/sci-fi, and animation also feature highly in the user's positive ratings, because they appear in their recommendations. Perhaps surprising is the inclusion of the thriller and crime categories, because these don't feature highly or at all in the existing ratings. These can be explained through the collaborative filtering process at work.

Within the existing dataset, there will be co-occurrence of the user's highly rated films with others films of different genres. This algorithm has found these patterns and is thus returning new and unseen categories for the user to try. This isn't surprising, really, because a recommender algorithm should certainly try to provide recommendations outside the obvious. A little thought might reveal that this correlation isn't unsurprising—viewers of drama may well enjoy crime/thriller films from time to time.

Figure 3.4 provides a histogram of those genres containing films that received low ratings from user 10. At first glance, we see that comedy and action/sci-fi both

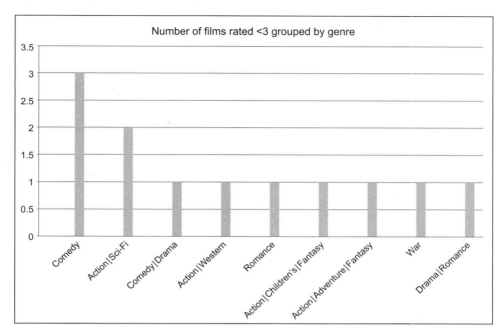

Figure 3.4 **The number of films that have been ranked as lower than 3 by user 10, broken out by genre. In this case, the user has ranked three comedy films and two action/sci-fi films below 3 and has watched several other categories of films and ranked them with a score of 1.**

received two or more low rankings, but we must be careful how we interpret this. Take a look at the scales on both figure 3.3 and figure 3.4. This user clearly has a bias to rate films highly, as well as an interest in comedy movies (and has rated more than 40 positively). There are techniques to tackle rating biases in model-based CF, but rather than discuss them here, we refer you to the literature.[11]

3.5.3 Recommendation using SVD: choosing users for a given movie

We've already provided an example of SVD for recommending movies to users, but because of the flexibility of model-based CF it's equally easy to perform recommendation of users for a given movie: that is, which users we should recommend it to. You could easily imagine such an approach would be useful in the advertising world, should we need to decide which user to promote an item to.

Let's imagine that we are LucasFilm and that we are just promoting the new *Star Wars* film: *Star Wars, Episode 1: The Phantom Menace* (1999). Using SVD and the existing dataset, how might we find the right users to promote this to? The next listing provides the answer.

---

[11] Arkadiusz Paterek, "Improving Regularized Singular Value Decomposition for Collaborative Filtering," *Proceedings of the ACM SIGKDD* (2007), http://mng.bz/TQnD.

Listing 3.12   Investigating user recommendations in model-based CF

```
> items_full[str(2628)].get_data()
{'Genres': 'Action|Adventure|Fantasy|Sci-Fi\n',
 'Title': 'Star Wars: Episode I - The Phantom Menace (1999)'}
> users_for_star_wars = svd.recommend(2628,only_unknowns=True)
> users_for_star_wars
[(446, 4.7741731815492816),
 (3324, 4.7601341930085157),
 (2339, 4.7352608789782398),
 (1131, 4.6541316195384743),
 (5069, 4.6479235651508217),
 (4755, 4.6444117760840502),
 (4634, 4.6308837065012067),
 (4649, 4.619985795550809),
 (1856, 4.5846499038453166),
 (4273, 4.5803152198983419)]
```

We first check to see whether we have the correct film for recommendation. In this case, item ID 2628 does indeed correspond to the *Star Wars* film we're interested in. By calling svd.recommend() with this ID and *without* the option is_row=False, we can perform recommendations across the rows: that is to say, the users. What is returned are the IDs of the top 10 users and the scores that we predict they would give this movie.

Again, let's dig a little further in the next listing to see if these recommendations make intuitive sense.

Listing 3.13   Analyzing the ratings of users recommended *Star Wars: TPM*

```
> movies_reviewed_by_sw_rec =[get_name_item_reviewed(x[0],
user_full,items_full) for x in users_for_star_wars]
> movies_flatten = [movie for movie_list in movies_reviewed_by_sw_rec for
➥movie in movie_list]
> movie_aggregate = movies_by_category(movies_flatten, 3)
> movies_sort = sorted(movie_aggregate,key=lambda x: x[1], reverse=True)
> movies_sort

[['Drama\n', 64],
 ['Comedy\n', 38],
 ['Drama|War\n', 22],
 ['Drama|Romance\n', 16],
 ['Action|Sci-Fi\n', 16],
 ['Action|Adventure|Sci-Fi\n', 14],
 ['Sci-Fi\n', 14],
 ['Action|Sci-Fi|Thriller\n', 13],
 ['Thriller\n', 12],
 ['Comedy|Romance\n', 12],
 ['Comedy|Drama\n', 11],
 ['Action|Drama|War\n', 11],
 ['Drama|Romance|War\n', 10],
 ['Drama|Thriller\n', 9],
 ['Horror|Sci-Fi\n', 9],
 ['Film-Noir|Thriller\n', 8],
 ['Western\n', 8],
```

```
['Comedy|Sci-Fi\n', 8],
['Drama|Sci-Fi\n', 7]…
```

We first get the movies rated by those in the recommended user set, before flattening this list. We need to flatten the list from a list of lists (where each entry contains the list of rated movies for that user) to a list containing all the ratings of the users together. The method `movies_by_category` builds a list that contains the genres of the films with a count giving the number of times the movie was rated in the set of users under consideration. The parameter to this method allows the movies to be filtered based on the value of their rating, so in this case we count only movies that have received a rating of 3 or higher. Finally, we sort the output list so that the genres with the largest number of films appear first.

Essentially, what we've done is to build a list of genres ranked most positively by the set of users to whom we're going to recommend *The Phantom Menace*. Figure 3.5 presents this output in a graphical form.

There are several things to note. First, there is a high prevalence of sci-fi within the categories of films rated highly by this aggregate user set. No fewer than 4 out of 10 of the top-rated categories include sci-fi somewhere in the genre title. Intuitively, this is as expected. The *Star Wars* series is sci-fi, and so it would certainly make sense if others who are interested in sci-fi were recommended this new film. What might be slightly surprising is that the most popular two genres among these users are the drama and

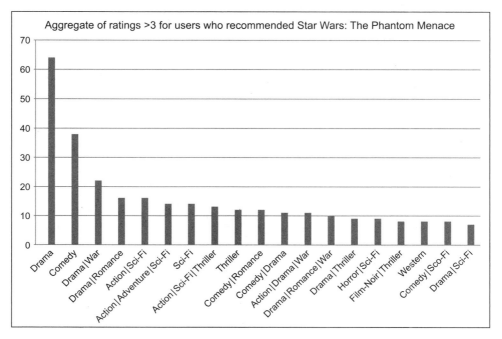

Figure 3.5 Number of ratings >3 aggregated by genre over all users in the set for whom we are to recommend *Star Wars: The Phantom Menace*

comedy categories. At first glance this may seem erroneous, but remember that there are many films in these categories. Also remember that films in these genres may receive high ratings from all users in the dataset, providing us with another example of bias.

In the previous sections, we introduced you to the world of recommender systems and provided specific details of user-based and model-based recommendation engines. We used the MovieLens dataset, a non-commercial dataset consisting of 1 million ratings from 6,000 users over 4,000 movies, to choose both movies for a user and users for a movie.

Although user-based CF has the benefit of being simple to understand and explainable—because it's easy to present to a user *why* they were recommended a given movie (because they're similar to other users who like it)—user-based CF can suffer from performance issues where sparsity increases (that is, there are many movies and users but not much overlap between users in terms of their ratings). Conversely, with model-based CF, it can be difficult to explain a certain recommendation to a user, but such methods can perform better in the presence of sparsity due to their introduction of a latent space through which the users and movies are connected. As always, it's up to the machine-learning practitioner to choose the solution that best matches their requirements.

3.6   *The Netflix Prize*

It's difficult to talk about recommender systems and not mention Netflix in the same breath. The Netflix Prize, which concluded in 2009, was a roaring success and saw more than 41,000 entries from 186 countries[12] compete to obtain the best root-mean-square error (RMSE) score in recommending relevant movies to users given the users' past ratings. Teams were submitting new entries for evaluation against a publically known quiz test set (as opposed to a privately held evaluation set held by Netflix) up until the last minutes before closing—exciting stuff! But the story behind the development of these algorithms is just as compelling.

In the end, the $1 million prize was awarded to team BellKor's Pragmatic Chaos. This was a composite team from three of the top contenders in the competition: Team Pragmatic Theory, Team BellKor, and Team BigChaos. The algorithm provided a 10.06% improvement over Netflix's homegrown Cinematch algorithm, thus securing the prize for the first team to breach the 10% mark. Rather than provide the specifics of the developed algorithm here, we'll talk more generally about the approach and its impact. For those interested in the details, we strongly recommend the following papers: "The BellKor Solution to the Netflix Grand Prize,"[13] "The BellKor 2008 Solution to the Netflix Prize,"[14] and "The Pragmatic Theory Solution to the Netflix Grand

---

[12] Netflix, www.netflixprize.com/leaderboard (2009).

[13] Yehuda Koren, "The BellKor Solution to the Netflix Grand Prize," August 2009, http://mng.bz/TwOD.

[14] Robert M. Bell, Yehuda Koren, and Chris Volinsky, "The BellKor 2008 Solution to the Netflix Prize," http://mng.bz/mW25.

Prize."[15] Collectively these papers provide the full documentation for the prizewinning approach.

The result achieved by the team blended hundreds of individual predictors to achieve results with performance in excess of any individual predictor alone. By blending many algorithms, each of which captured specifics of the interactions between user and item, the team was able to achieve exceptional results. What's interesting about this competition is that the most impressive results came after these three teams pooled their predictors.

You may be surprised to learn that many of the concepts required to understand the winning algorithm have already been introduced in this or previous chapters. We'll look at one of the predictors (from BellKor) and briefly discuss how this predictor was combined with others to reach a recommendation.

Team BellKor introduced a baseline predictor. That is, they modeled the item and user biases that are present in the dataset. To this, they added temporal dynamics. This helped their algorithm understand changes in overall popularity of a film (for example, if films have been re-released, they may garner more attention) as well as the propensities of users to change their rating biases (such as becoming more or less critical). They also added an SVD-like approach, as discussed previously. This had the effect of modeling global patterns, such as those discussed, but such an approach can often miss local patterns in the data. To counter this, they added a neighborhood method, similar to item-based and user-based CF. This helped capture local patterns between users, items, and the surrounding neighborhood within the data. In the end, this was only one of 454 candidate predictors used to select a set whose results were combined using gradient-boosted decision trees (GDBT).[16, 17]

Although this was a truly impressive achievement, Netflix didn't actually implement the final algorithm and instead chose to continue with a simpler, albeit less-accurate algorithm (yielding only an 8.43% improvement versus the winning 10.06%). This algorithm won the first progress prize and was implemented even before the competition concluded. According to Netflix, the company's reasoning was that the additional effort required to scale up the winning algorithm didn't justify the increase in accuracy.

Intelligent-algorithm developers have an important lesson to learn here. We must focus not just on the accuracy of a proposed solution but also its cost. There's another reason Netflix didn't implement the winning algorithm: by the time the competition closed, the business had begun to shift focus. Recommendations were crucial to Netflix back in its DVD rental days, because they allowed for good suggestions to be served to users, such that Netflix could carefully select films for a limited number of mail-order

---

[15] Martin Piotte and Martin Chabbert, "The Pragmatic Theory Solution to the Netflix Grand Prize," August 2009, http://mng.bz/1et7.

[16] Jerome H. Friedman, "Stochastic Gradient Boosting," March 26, 1999, https://statweb.stanford.edu/~jhf/ftp/stobst.pdf.

[17] Jerry Ye, Jyh-Herng Chow, et al., "Stochastic Gradient Boosted Distributed Decision Trees," *Proceedings of the 18th ACM CIKM* (November 2009), http://mng.bz/WiMO.

rental slots. With the focus shifting to online streaming, this became less relevant because the delivery mechansim was amost instantaneous. A user can watch whatever they want, wherever and wherever they want. Herein lies our second important lesson: a reasonably intelligent algorithm delivered quickly can often be worth more than an extremely accurate one delivered at a later date.

3.7   *Evaluating your recommender*

Commercial recommendation systems operate under demanding conditions. The number of users is typically on the order of millions and the number of items on the order of hundreds of thousands. An additional requirement is the capability to provide recommendations in real time (typically, sub-second response times) without sacrificing the quality of the recommendations. This is typically performed with some layer of caching, and the time taken to use SVD for matrix factorization is usually not real-time and depends on many other factors: for example, the amount of memory you have and, more important, the implementation of SVD. It also might depend on how long you're willing to wait for the answer!

As you've seen, by accumulating ratings from each user, it's possible to enhance the accuracy of predictions over time. But in real life, it's imperative that we give excellent recommendations to new users for whom, by definition, we don't have a lot of ratings.

Another stringent requirement for state-of-the-art recommendation systems is the ability to update predictions based on incoming ratings. In large commercial sites, thousands of ratings and purchases may take place in a few hours and perhaps tens of thousands (or more) in the course of a single day. The ability to update the recommendation system with that additional information is important and must happen online—without downtime.

Let's say that you wrote a recommender and you're satisfied with its speed and the amount of data it can handle. Is this a good recommender? It's not useful to have a fast and scalable recommender that produces bad recommendations. So, let's talk about evaluating the accuracy of a recommendation system. If you search the related literature, you'll find dozens of quantitative metrics and several qualitative methods for evaluating the results of recommendation systems. The plethora of metrics and methods reflects the challenges of conducting a meaningful, fair, and accurate evaluation for recommendations. The review article by Herlocker, Konstan, Terveen, and Riedl contains a wealth of information if you're interested in this topic.[18]

We'll demonstrate a measure known as the root-mean-square error (RMSE) of the predicted ratings over the MovieLens dataset. The RMSE is a simple but robust technique of evaluating the accuracy of recommendations. This metric has two main features: it always increases (you don't get kudos for predicting a rating accurately); and by taking the square of the differences, the large differences (>1) are amplified, and it doesn't matter if you undershoot or overshoot the rating.

---

[18] Jonathan L. Herlocker, et al., "Evaluating Collaborative Filtering Recommender Systems," *ACM Transactions on Information Systems* 22, no. 1 (January 2004).

We can argue that the RMSE is probably too naïve. Let's consider two cases. In the first case, we recommend to a user a movie with four stars, and he really doesn't like it (he'd rate it two stars); in the second case, we recommend a movie with three stars, but the user loves it (he'd rate it five stars). In both cases, the contribution to the RMSE is the same, but it's likely that the user's dissatisfaction would probably be larger in the first case than in the second case. You can find the code that calculates the RMSE for our model-based CF solution in the following listing. As we've mentioned, other metrics are available, and we'd encourage you to try those also.

Listing 3.14   Calculating the root-mean-square error for a recommender

```
from recsys.evaluation.prediction import RMSE

err = RMSE()
for rating, item_id, user_id in data.get():
    try:
        prediction = svd.predict(item_id, user_id)
        err.add(rating, prediction)
    except KeyError, k:
        continue

print 'RMSE is ' + str(err.compute())

err = RMSE()
print d
for rating, item_id, user_id in data.get():
    try:
        prediction = svd.predict(item_id, user_id)
        rmse.add(rating, pred_rating)
    except KeyError, k:
        continue

print 'RMSE is ' + err.compute()
```

3.8   Summary

- You've learned about the concepts of distance and similarity between users and items, and you saw that one size doesn't fit all—you need to be careful in your selection of a similarity metric. Similarity formulas must produce results that are consistent with a few basic rules, but otherwise you're free to choose the ones that produce the best results for your purposes.

- There are two broad categories of techniques for creating recommendations: collaborative filtering and the content-based approach. Focusing on the former, we provided three different approaches that you can use to perform recommendation: user-based, item-based, and model-based.

- We performed item and user recommendation, and in each instance we looked at the distribution of ratings over movie genres. Movie genres are an imperfect way to reason about model-based CF but can capture some of the properties of user preference and movie subject.

- In the final pages of this chapter, we looked at the Netflix Prize. Although this competition concluded in 2009, it's still synonymous with the concept of recommendation. We provided a broad overview of the winning approach, but we leave it to you to uncover all the intricacies of this algorithm.

Classification: placing things where they belong

"What is this?" is the question children perhaps ask most frequently. The popularity of that question among children—whose inquisitive nature is as wonderful as it is persistent—shouldn't be surprising. In order to understand the world around us, we organize our perceptions into groups and categories. In the previous chapter, we presented a number of algorithms that can help us determine structure from our data. In this chapter, we'll look at *classification* algorithms that help us assign each data point to an appropriate category or *class* (hence the term *classification*). The act of classification would answer a child's question by providing a statement in the form "This is a boat," "This is a tree," "This is a house," and so on.

We could argue that, as part of our mental processing, determining structure precedes classification. When we tell the child that what she is holding is a boat, we implicitly know that this is a vehicle, that it belongs on the sea (and not in the air or on land), and that it floats! This implicit knowledge comes before our classification of the item as a boat, narrowing the possible selections for us. In a similar way, determining data clusters, or transforming the data points of the original data, can act as a highly beneficial step, uncovering valuable information that can be used for classification.

In the following sections, we'll provide a number of real-world examples where classification is important, before presenting an overview and taxonomy of classifiers in the space. We clearly can't cover in depth all known classifiers in this book, so the overview should help you orient yourself in the related literature. You'll also learn about logistic regression—an approach belonging to a more general class of algorithms known as *generalized linear models*. We'll discuss its use in classifying fraud and determining unusual behavior online and hint at some further work in this field (which we'll cover in much more detail in the next chapter).

How can you tell whether you assigned the most appropriate class to a data point? How can you tell whether classifier A is better than classifier B? If you've ever read brochures of business intelligence tools, you may be familiar with statements such as "Our classifier is 75% accurate." What's the meaning of such a statement? Is it useful? These questions will be addressed in section 4.4. We'll discuss classifying large volumes of data points and doing efficient online classification.

Let's begin by discussing the potential applications of classification and presenting the technical terms that you'll encounter repeatedly along the way. So, what is classification good for, and what practical problems can it solve for us?

4.1   *The need for classification*

Whether we realize it or not, we encounter classification on a daily basis. In our everyday experiences, we can list the food items on a restaurant's menu, which are classified according to menu categories—salads, appetizers, specialties, pastas, seafood, and so on. Similarly, the articles in a newspaper are classified based on their subject—politics, sports, business, world, entertainment, and so on. So we see that classification abounds in our daily lives.

The books in a library carry a *call number,* which consists of two numbers: the *Dewey classification number* and the *Cutter number.* The top categories of that system are things such as generalities, religion, natural science, mathematics, and so forth. The Library of Congress in the United States has its own classification system that was developed in the late 19th and early 20th centuries to organize and arrange its book collections.

Over the course of the 20th century, the Library of Congress system was adopted for use by other libraries as well, especially large academic libraries in the United States. We mention two systems of classifying books because the Library of Congress classification system isn't strictly hierarchical as the Dewey classification system is, where the hierarchical relationships between the topics are reflected in the numbers of the classification.

In medicine, a plethora of classification systems are used to diagnose injuries or diseases. For example, radiologists and orthopedic surgeons use the Schatzker classification system to classify tibial plateau fractures (a complex knee injury). Similarly, there are classification systems for spinal cord injuries; for coma, concussion, and traumatic brain injuries; and so on. You must have heard the term *Homo sapiens*, of which *Homo* is our genus and *sapiens* is our species. This classification can be, and typically is, extended to include other attributes such as *family, order, class, phylum*, and so forth.

Generally speaking, the more attributes you use, the finer the degree of classification is going to be. Having a "large" number of attributes is usually a good thing, but there are caveats to this general principle. One notorious symptom of dealing with many attributes is the *curse of dimensionality*, which was discussed in chapter 2.

As you may recall, the curse of dimensionality refers to the fact that a space becomes more and more homogenous as the number of attributes increases. In other words, the distance between any two points will be roughly the same no matter which points you select and what metric you apply to measure the distances. If that's the case, it becomes increasingly difficult to distinguish which category is "closer" to a given data point, because no matter where you "stand" in your space, everything seems to be the same distance apart!

In general, *flat reference structures* aren't as rich as *hierarchical reference structures*. In turn, the hierarchical reference structures are less rich than those that are hierarchical *and* semantically enriched. A reference structure that's semantically enriched falls under the study of *ontologies*: taxonomies of meaning (usually) hand created in order to encode domain-specific knowledge. For the purposes of this book, an ontology consists of three things: *concepts, instances,* and *attributes.*

Figure 4.1 depicts a small segment of a (rudimentary) general ontology by focusing on the classification of a vehicle. Concepts are depicted as ellipses, instances are depicted as rectangles, and attributes are depicted as rounded rectangles. Note the hereditary property of attribute assignment. If attribute 1 is assigned to the root of the concept tree, then it cascades to the concept leaf nodes. Thus, values for attribute 1 can be assigned to instances of a boat and an automobile. Only an automobile instance can have values for attribute 2. Attribute 1 could be the attribute *Name*, which for practical reasons you always want, whereas attribute 2 could be the attribute *Number of Wheels*. Attributes are defined at the level of the concepts, but only instances have concrete and unique values because only instances represent real things.

Think of concepts as analogous to classes in your favorite object-oriented language. Instances are analogous to concrete instances of a class, and attributes are the variables within these class instances. Clearly, a code base that uses packages to group together classes by functionality or component, that uses inheritance to abstract common structure and behavior, and that properly uses encapsulation is superior to a code base that doesn't have these qualities. In object-oriented programming, when you define a class, you define the data type of the variables, but you don't assign a value to a variable (unless it's a constant). This parallel holds true here; concepts inherit attributes from the concepts above themselves in the tree and don't become instances until their attributes have been assigned. This is a good working definition that'll serve you well 80% to 90% of the time. If you're ever in doubt, you can consult this analogy to obtain some insight into your structure.

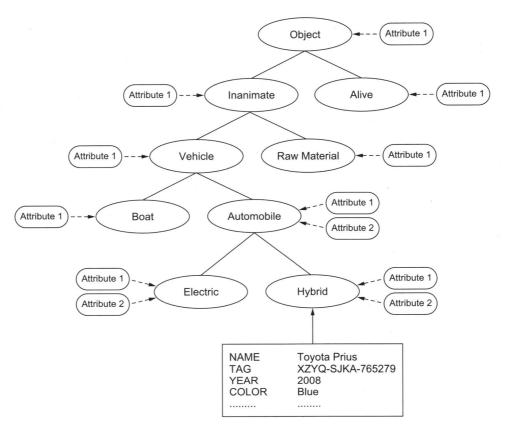

Figure 4.1   The basic elements of a reference structure (a rudimentary ontology). Ellipses denote concepts, whereas rounded rectangles denote attributes. Rectangles denote instances. Concepts inherit attributes from above.

We could obviously go on with more classification systems; they're everywhere. The point is that classifying data is equivalent to organizing it. Classification systems improve communication by reducing errors due to ambiguities. They also help us organize our thoughts and plan our actions. The reference structure, which is used for organizing our data, can be as simple as a set of labels or as advanced as a *semantic ontology*. Have you heard of the *Semantic Web*? At the heart of the Semantic Web lie a number of technologies and formal specifications related to creating, using, and maintaining semantic ontologies. Ontologies are also useful in model-driven architectures,[1] which are a software design initiative of the Object Management Group (OMG, www.omg.org).

Look at your database. Your application could be an online store, an intranet document management system, an internet mashup, or any other kind of web

---

[1] D. Gasevic, D. Djuric, and V. Devedzic, *Model Driven Architecture and Ontology Development* (Springer, 2006).

application. When you think about your data and the ways it could be organized, you'll realize the value of a classification system for your application. Starting with section 4.3, we'll introduce classification mechanisms in web applications in order to demonstrate the use of classification algorithms and the issues that may arise. But first, here's an overview of classification systems. If you want to jump into action quickly, you can skip the next section.

4.2   *An overview of classifiers*

One way that we could view the set of all classification systems is with respect to the reference structure they use. At the top level of such a perspective, we can divide all classification systems into two broad categories: *binary* and *multiclass*. Binary classification systems, as the name suggests, provide a yes/no answer to the question "Does this data point belong to class X?" A medical diagnosis system could answer the question of whether a patient has cancer. An immigration classification system could answer whether a person is a terrorist. Multiclass classification systems assign a data point to a specific class, out of many, such as the assignment of a news article in a news category.

Within the set of multiclass classification systems, we can further group classification systems on the basis of two criteria: whether the multiple classes are discrete or continuous, and whether the multiple classes are "flat" (just a list of labels) or have a hierarchical structure. The Dewey classification scheme and the ICD-10 catalog from the previous section are examples of classification systems that have multiple discrete and finite classes. The result of classification may be a continuous variable, such as when classification is used for predictions, also known as *forecasting*. If you provide the value of a stock on Monday, Tuesday, Wednesday, and Thursday as input and want to find the value of a stock on Friday, you can pose that problem as a multiclass classification that's discrete or continuous. The discrete version could predict whether the stock price will increase, remain unchanged, or decrease on Friday. The continuous version could provide a prediction for the actual stock price.

Categorization of classification systems, with respect to the underlying technique, isn't quite as clear or widely accepted. But we could say that two broad categories have gained a significant level of adoption in the industry. The first category includes *statistical algorithms* and the second *structural algorithms*, as shown in figure 4.2.

Statistical algorithms come in three flavors. Regression algorithms are particularly good at forecasting—predicting the value of a continuous variable. Regression algorithms are based on the assumption that it's sufficient to fit our data to a particular model; often that model is a linear function of the variables at hand, although not always, as you'll see in section 4.3. Another kind of statistical classification algorithms stems from the Bayes theorem. A fairly successful and modern statistical approach combines the Bayes theorem with a probabilistic network structure that depicts the dependency between the various attributes of the classification problem.

Structural algorithms have three main branches: *rule-based* algorithms, which include if-then rules and decision trees; *distance-based* algorithms, which are generally

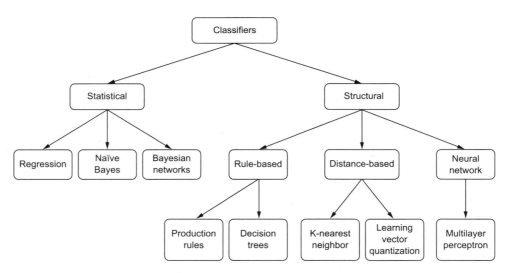

Figure 4.2   An overview of classification algorithms based on their design

separated into functional and nearest neighbor schemes; and *neural networks (NN)*. Neural networks form a category of their own—although we should mention that equivalency between certain neural networks and some advanced statistical algorithms (such as Gaussian processes) has been established and studied extensively. In the following subsections, we'll give a more detailed summary of both structural and statistical classification algorithms.

4.2.1 Structural classification algorithms

As shown in figure 4.2, the branch of rule-based structural algorithms consists of *production rules* (if-then clauses) and decision tree (DT)–based algorithms. The production rules can be collected manually by human experts or deduced by decision trees. Rule-based algorithms are typically implemented as *forward-chaining* production systems—a frightening term, if you ask us! The best algorithm in this category is called *Rete*;[2] *rete* translates to "network" in Latin. It's the basis for well-known libraries such as CLIPS, Jess, and Soar.

Decision tree–based algorithms are based on a simple but powerful idea. Did you ever read Charles Dickens' *A Christmas Carol*? In that book, Dickens describes a game (*Yes and No*) in which Scrooge's nephew had to think of something and the other players had to figure out what it was; he would answer only yes or no, depending on their questions. Versions of this game exist in many cultures—it's fairly popular in Spanish-speaking countries among children, where it's known as *veo, veo*. Similar to these familiar games, the idea behind most DT algorithms is to ask questions whose answers

---

[2] Charles Forgy, "Rete: A Fast Algorithm for the Many Pattern/Many Object Pattern Match Problem," *Artificial Intelligence* 19 (1982): 17–37.

will eliminate as many candidates as possible based on the provided information. Decision-tree algorithms have several advantages, such as ease of use and computational efficiency. Their disadvantages are usually prominent when we deal with continuous variables, because we're forced to perform a discretization—the continuum of the values must be divided into a finite number of bins in order to construct the tree. In general, decision-tree algorithms don't have good generalization properties, and thus they don't perform well with unseen data. A commonly used algorithm in this category is C5.0 (on Unix machines) or See5 (on Microsoft Windows machines). It can be found in a number of commercial products, such as Clementine, now IBM SPSS Modeler,[3] and RuleQuest.[4]

The second branch of structural algorithms is composed of distance-based algorithms. In the previous chapters, we introduced and extensively used the notions of similarity measure and generalized distance. These algorithms are fairly intuitive, but it's easy to misuse them and end up with bad classification results because many of the data-point attributes aren't directly related to each other. A single similarity measure can't expediently capture the differences in the way the attributes should be measured; careful normalization and analysis of the attribute space are crucial to the success of distance-based algorithms. Nevertheless, in many low-dimensional cases, with low complexity, these algorithms perform well and are fairly simple to implement. We can further divide distance-based algorithms into functional and nearest neighbor–type algorithms.

Functional classifiers approximate the data by function, as the name suggests. This is similar to regression, but we differentiate between them on the basis of the rationale behind the use of the function. In regression, we use a function as a model of the probability distribution; in the case of functional classifiers, we're merely interested in the numerical approximation of the data. In practice, it's hard (and perhaps pointless) to distinguish between linear regression and linear approximation through the minimization of the squared error.

Nearest-neighbor algorithms attempt to find the nearest class for each data point. By using the same formulas you've seen earlier about generalized distances, you can calculate the distance of each data point from each available class. The class that's closest to the object is assigned to that object. Perhaps the most common classification algorithm of that type is k-nearest neighbors (kNN), although another algorithm known as learning vector quantization (LVQ) is also well studied and broadly adopted.

Neural network (NN) algorithms belong in a subcategory of structural algorithms by themselves. These algorithms require a good deal of mathematical background to be presented properly. We'll do our best to present them in chapter 6 from a computational perspective without being overly heavy on the mathematics. The main idea behind this family of classification algorithms is the construction of an artificial

---

[3] Tom Khabaza, *The Story of Clementine* (Internal Report, Integral Solutions Limited, 1999).
[4] Ross Quinlan, RuleQuest Research: Data Mining Tools, www.rulequest.com.

network of computational nodes that's analogous to the biological structure of the human brain, which is basically made of *neurons* and *synapses* that connect them.

NN algorithms have been shown to perform well on a variety of problems. There are two major disadvantages of neural networks: we don't have a design methodology that would be applicable in a large number of problems, and it's difficult to interpret the results of neural network classification; the classifier may commit few errors, but we're unable to understand why. This is why we consider neural networks to be a "black box" technique, as opposed to a decision tree or a rule-based algorithm—where the result of a classification for a particular data point can be easily interpreted.

4.2.2   *Statistical classification algorithms*

Regression algorithms are based on the idea of finding the best fit of the data to a formula; the most common formula is a linear function of the input values.[5] Regression algorithms are usually employed when the data points are inherently numerical variables (such as the dimensions of an object, the weight of a person, or the temperature in the atmosphere); but unlike Bayesian algorithms, they're not very good for categorical data (such as employee status or credit score description). In addition, if the model about the data is linear, then it's not easy to justify the adjective *statistical*; in essence, linear regression is no different from the good-old high school exercise of fitting a line to a bunch of x,y points.

Things get more interesting and obtain the flavor of a statistical approach in the case of so-called *logistic regression*. In this case, the model (the logistic function) predicts values between 0 and 1, which can be interpreted as the probability of class membership; this works well in the case of binary classification if we threshold the probability. This model is widely used in industry and will be the focus of the next section. Here we'll address its use to classify online fraud, an especially difficult task because these events occur so rarely in comparison to non-fraud events.

Many of the techniques in the statistical algorithms category use a probability theorem known as the *Bayes rule* or *Bayes theorem*.[6] In this kind of statistical classification algorithm, the least common denominator is the assumption that the attributes of the problem are independent of each other, in a fairly quantitatively explicit form. The fascinating aspect of Bayesian algorithms is that they seem to work well even when that independence assumption is clearly violated!

Bayesian networks are a relatively modern approach to machine learning that attempts to combine the power of the Bayes theorem with the advantages of structural approaches, such as decision trees. Naïve Bayes classifiers and their siblings can represent simple probability distributions but fall short in capturing the probabilistic structure of the data, if there is one. By using the powerful representation of *directed acyclic graphs* (DAG), the probabilistic relations of the attributes can be depicted graphically.

---

[5] Trevor Hastie, Robert Tibshirani, and Jerome Friedman, *The Elements of Statistical Learning: Data Mining, Inference and Prediction*, 2nd. ed. (Springer-Verlag, 2009).
[6] Kevin Murphy, *Machine Learning: A Probabilistic Perspective* (MIT Press, 2012).

We won't cover Bayesian networks in this book; if you're interested in learning more about this subject, then you should look at *Learning Bayesian Networks.*[7]

4.2.3 *The lifecycle of a classifier*

No matter what type of classifier you choose for your application, the lifecycle of your classifier will fit in the general diagram of figure 4.3. There are three stages in the lifecycle of a classifier: *training, validation* (also known as *testing*), and *production.*

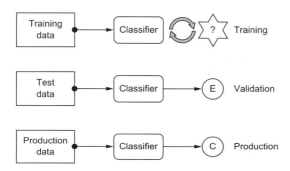

Figure 4.3   The lifecycle of a classifier: training, validation (or testing), and use in production

In the training stage, we provide the classifier with data points for which we've already assigned an appropriate class. Every classifier contains a number of parameters that must be determined before it's used. The purpose of that stage is to determine the various parameters; we used a question mark inside a star to indicate that the primary goal is determining these parameters. In the validation stage, we want to validate the classifier and ensure that before we roll it out to a production system, we've achieved a certain level of credibility for our results. We've used an *E* in a circle to indicate that the primary goal is determining the classification error, but the quality standard can and should be measured by various metrics (see section 4.4 for a discussion on the credibility and cost of classification). The data that we use in the validation stage (test data) must be different than the data that we used in the training stage (training data).

The training and validation stages may be repeated many times before the classifier transitions into the production stage, because there may be configuration parameters that aren't identified by the training process but are given as input during the design of a classifier. This important point means we can write software that wraps the classifier and its configuration parameters for the purpose of automatically testing and validating a large number of classifier designs. Even classifiers that are fundamentally different in nature, such as naïve Bayes, neural network, and decision trees, could participate in the testing. We can either pick the best classifier, as determined by the quality metrics of the validation stages, or combine all the classifiers into what could be called a *metaclassifier* scheme. This approach is gaining ground in the industry and has provided consistently better results in a wide range of applications. Recall that

---

[7]   R. E. Neapolitan, *Learning Bayesian Networks* (Prentice-Hall, 2003).

combining intelligent algorithms was also discussed in the context of recommender systems in chapter 3.

In the production stage, we're using our classifier in a live system to produce classifications on the fly. Typically, the parameters of the classifier don't change during the production stage. But it's possible to enhance the results of the classifier by embedding (into the production stage) a short-lived training stage that's based on human-in-the-loop feedback. These three steps are repeated as we get more data from our production system and as we come up with better ideas for our classifier. You've now seen the big picture about classification algorithms. In the literature, you can find many different overviews of classification algorithms.[8]

In order to provide you with a sufficiently in-depth and applicable example, for the remainder of this chapter we'll concentrate on statistical algorithms and, in particular, a method of classification using logistic regression. We choose this approach because the method is so widely applied in industrial web applications. The example we'll provide classifies online financial transactions as either fraudulent or legitimate.

4.3   Fraud detection with logistic regression

In this section, we'll concentrate on the use of a technique known as *logistic regression*: a statistical classification algorithm that takes as its input a number of features and a target variable and maps this to a likelihood number between 0.0 and 1.0. For the purposes of fraud detection, these features could be the properties of a transaction, amount, time, day of week, and so on, with the target variable being equal to ground truth data: that is, whether the transaction was eventually considered fraudulent. You might have noticed that the output of this algorithm is continuous, but our goal is to provide a binary output (for example, 1 for fraud, 0 for genuine). We achieve this final mapping by assigning a 1 if the likelihood of fraud is greater than 0.5 and 0 otherwise.

Before we get stuck in the details of logistic regression, we'll first provide a brief primer on linear regression, because logistic regression can be seen as a simple extension of it. Both approaches share most of the same concepts, so it will provide a good way to warm up before delving into more complex mathematics.

4.3.1   A linear-regression primer

Before you can understand logistic regression, you must first understand linear regression. If you think back to your early career in mathematics, you may remember the equation for a straight line in Euclidean space, namely

$$y = mx + c$$

where (x,y) represents the coordinates of a data point in the space, m represents the gradient or relationship between the two axes, and c is an offset or a starting point. In simple terms, the gradient m relates the rate of change of x with the rate of change in

---

[8]   L. Holmström, P. Koistinen, J. Laaksonen, and E. Oja, "Neural and Statistical Classifiers—Taxonomy and Two Case Studies," *IEEE Transactions on Neural Networks* 8, no. 1 (1997): 5–17.

y. If x changes by δx, then y also changes by $m \times \delta x$. The offset, or starting point, denotes *the value of y when x is equal to zero*.

We call this a *linear relationship*. If we're trying to model two variables using the linear equation, we must first be sure the underlying relationship we're trying to model is reasonably approximated by such. Failure to do so may result in a poor model that fails to generalize the phenomena under investigation. Figure 4.4 provides a graphical representation of a straight-line (linear) model using some illustrative data that appears to have a linear relationship. We solve the linear equation given previously and plot the straight line overlaid on our data.

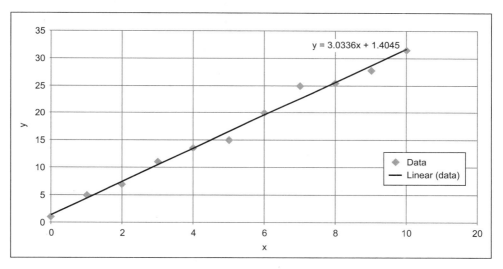

Figure 4.4 Graphical illustration of a linear model. The data points provide a clear linear relationship between *x* and *y*. The linear line provides the line of best fit modeled by *y=mx+c*.

You'll notice that the data isn't perfect. In the real world, more often than not the data you collect won't exactly follow some predicted pattern but is subject to bias and noise, as we discussed in chapter 2. Consequently, the best we can do is to solve for the line of best fit. This line of best fit is given by minimizing the residuals—or the error between the model and the actual data itself. Figure 4.5 illustrates this concept.

Now you can see that the line of best fit has been given by modifying our model parameters (of which there are only two: the gradient, *m*, and the offset, *c*) until the sum of the square of the residuals is minimized. We use the square of the residuals, because this is invariant to the direction of error: that is, whether the data point is

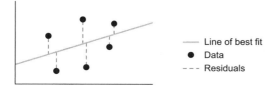

Line of best fit
● Data
--- Residuals

Figure 4.5 Calculating the residuals, or the distance between the model and the data. In this illustration, we use the vertical distance in y as a measurement of the error, but other methods are available.

above or below the model line. This is known as *model training*. In general, our straight-line model isn't restricted to only a single variable, *x*, and can be generalized into *n*+1 dimensions by using the following form:

$$y = m_1 x_1 + m_2 x_2 + \dots + m_{n-1} x_{n-1} + m_n x_n + c$$

In this case, our approach to modeling is exactly the same; all that has changed is the residual function and the details of training. Each has to take into account the increased number of dimensions, so the training algorithm has to update m_i for all *i*=1, ... ,*n* as well as *c*.

What we've described here is a concept that's universal throughout machine learning: models must be trained in order to best generalize the data we've collected. Such an approach is the same regardless of the model type (linear or otherwise), so you'll see this pattern again and again in your work.

You might now be asking why we don't just use linear regression to detect fraud. It would indeed be possible to do this, but there are many reasons we shouldn't. In the following section, we'll provide the details behind logistic regression and why it's a much more appropriate solution to determining fraud.

4.3.2   *From linear to logistic regression*

In the previous section, we covered the basics of regression, specifically linear regression. Unfortunately, we'd encounter several problems if we attempted to perform fraud detection using a linear model. The first problem would be around the output (known as the *codomain*) of the model. In a linear model, *y* may range from negative infinity to positive infinity. This isn't appropriate for our fraud-detection algorithm, because we'd much prefer to have the output fixed in a certain range: 0.0 for highly unlikely to be a fraud and 1.0 for highly likely to be fraud. We would then have a threshold such that values above 0.5 would be classified as fraud, whereas values below this would be considered genuine.

The second problem concerns the linearity of the model. If we considered a simple linear fraud-detection model with a model in two dimensions—that is, a single feature (so *y* providing the probability of fraud, and *x* a continuous feature of the transaction)—then a single-unit change in *x* would have a linear response in *y*. But if we think about it, this might not always be suitable!

Let's run a little thought experiment to see if we can figure out why. If we imagine that this continuous variable *x* corresponds to the value of a transaction, then we might imagine that high values point to fraudulent transactions. Consider a change in *x* of £100. If the linear model provides a given probability of fraud at £50, then the difference in this probability at £150 is given by $m \times 100$. Now, if we consider the probability of fraud at £250,000 and £250,100, the change in probability is exactly the same: $m \times 100$! In general, this doesn't make sense for our application.

Ideally we'd like a response in likelihood of fraud that grows quickly as the value of *x* goes up and then slows for higher values. Similarly, as the value of *x* decreases, we'd like a response that decreases quickly and then slows for smaller values. The effect of this would be a larger difference in the classifier's output between £100 and £5,000 than between £5,000 and £10,000. Intuitively, this makes sense because moving into the thousands may mean more for the likelihood of fraud than adding thousands to an already-large number. What if we could use something other than a straight line—a curve, perhaps—that better models the previous behavior? Luckily, we can; we use the logistic curve! Figure 4.6 demonstrates the response of *y* with *x* for such a curve.

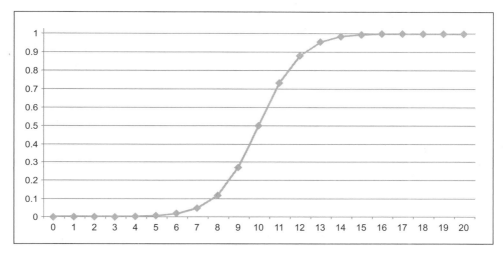

Figure 4.6   The response of *y* with *x* for a logistic curve. This particular curve is centered on *x*=10 and has been plotted using 20 samples uniformly distributed on *x*. Note the larger differences in *y* for values of *x* around 10 and much smaller differences in *y* around *x*=0 and *x*=20.

Notice that the response in *y* is much larger around *x*=10 than it is around *x*=0 and *x*=20. This is exactly the response we stated as ideal for our likelihood predictor. The following equation provides the general form for the logistic curve:

$$y = \frac{L}{1 + e^{-k(x - x_0)}}$$

Note that in the case of figure 4.6, the parameters have been set to *k*=1, *L*=1, and x_0=10, where *L* determines the maximum value of the curve and x_0 the offset of the curve on the x-axis. In general, and from now on, we'll set *L*=1 because we always want the maximum value of our curve to be equal to 1.

This form can easily be extended to handle multiple variables through the inclusion of additional variables in the exponent of *e*, giving rise to the following form:

$$y = \frac{1}{1 + e^{-(\beta_0 + \beta_1 x_1 + \dots + \beta_n x_n)}}$$

So far, so good. We've managed to create a model in which response is nonlinear and that can handle multiple input variables, but what does it all mean? Let's do some basic manipulation of this equation to see where we get. If we set $t=\beta_0+\beta_1 x_1+\ldots+\beta_n x_n$ and then multiply through top and bottom by e^t, we obtain the following form:

$$y = \frac{e^t}{1 + e^t}$$

The next step is somewhat a leap of faith. We know that y is equivalent to the probability of the event occurring with the features given in the exponent of e, so now we rearrange the equation to express $y/(1-y)$—the probability of the event occurring divided by the probability of the event not occurring. This is known as the *odds* of the event. Let's first calculate $1-y$ and substitute this back into our equation afterward:

$$1 - y = 1 - \frac{e^t}{1 + e^t}$$

$$1 - y = \frac{1 + e^t - e^t}{1 + e^t}$$

$$1 - y = \frac{1}{1 + e^t}$$

Now that we have the equation for $1-y$, the modeled probability of the negative event, let's express the odds using our initial definition of y:

$$\frac{y}{1 - y} = \frac{e^t}{1 + e^t} \bigg/ \frac{1}{1 + e^t}$$

$$\frac{y}{1 - y} = e^t$$

Substituting back in for t and taking the natural logarithm on both sides, we end up with our final equation:

$$ln\left(\frac{y}{1-y}\right) = \beta_0 + \beta_1 x_1 + \ldots + \beta_n x_n$$

Compare this with the original equation from section 4.3.1, and what do you notice? That's correct; they're both linear models, but where our original model expressed probability as a linear combination of the input variables, our new logistic regression model expresses the *log-odds* as a linear combination of input variables. Training can occur in a way much similar to the linear model: we update the values of β in order to best fit the data (to minimize loss). To define *fit* and minimize error, we can use maximum likelihood estimation: that is, find the set of parameters that maximize the likelihood function, or the probability of the data given the model. In practice, this means running through the data (once or many times) and updating the values of β to positively reinforce features that are present during a fraudulent transaction, while negatively reinforcing features that are present during genuine transactions.

As a final note before we start to get into the code, the final equation reveals something important about how we should interpret the parameters of logistic regression. Let's imagine that we've trained our model, and we now hold all of our features constant, with the exception of x_1. For every unit of x_1 the log-odds of the model increase by β_1. Raising e to this will give the increase of odds for the same increase in x_1. Thus, a unit change in x_1 increases the odds of the target by e^{β_1}, holding all other features constant.

4.3.3 *Implementing fraud detection*

In the previous sections, we provided you with the basic theory behind the powerful method of logistic regression. But enough with the theory! You're probably itching to implement a solution using this method. This section will show you how.

We'll start with a basic dataset[9] consisting of several features of a financial transaction, along with a human-labeled ground truth: whether the transaction was considered fraudulent or genuine. Figure 4.7 provides this data.

IsFraud	Amount	Country	TimeOfTransaction	BusinessType	NumberOfTransactionsAtThisShop	DayOfWeek
0	10	DK	13	2	0	1
0	100	LT	18	1	3	4
0	49.99	AT	11	4	3	0
0	12	AUS	9	6	4	3
0	250	UK	12	1	5	6
0	149.99	UK	17	2	2	5
0	10	UK	16	8	1	4
0	49.99	DK	12	9	4	3
0	18	UK	14	2	3	6
0	27	DK	10	1	5	5
0	40	DK	11	1	6	2
0	2	UK	10	2	7	4
0	34.99	UK	9	4	8	3
0	2	UK	8	9	9	0
1	18000	LT	13	9	0	0
1	20000	LT	14	9	0	0
1	19000	LT	13	9	0	0
1	6000	LT	13	9	1	4
1	9000	LT	12	9	0	4
1	5000	LT	12	9	0	4
1	20000	LT	12	9	0	0
1	10000	LT	12	9	0	6
1	20000.01	UK	13	1	0	0
1	21000	LT	13	9	0	0
1	11000	LT	13	9	1	6
1	210000	UK	14	1	0	0
1	22000	UK	12	1	1	0
1	280000	LT	12	9	0	0
1	15000	LT	12	9	0	6

Figure 4.7 Data for fraud detection

---

[9] This dataset has been hand crafted to demonstrate logistic regression. In subsequent chapters, we'll apply our approach to real-world data.

In figure 4.7, the columns describe whether the transaction is genuine or fraudulent, the amount of the transaction, the country of the transaction, the type of business where the transaction occurred, the number of previous transactions at this establishment, and the day of the week when the transaction took place. It's our goal in this section to use the logistic-regression implementation of scikit-learn to effectively predict and label fraudulent transactions.

Before we go any further, what do you notice about the data? Can you see any patterns between the features of the data and the IsFraud label? At first glance, it looks like a higher-value transaction placed by a first-time shopper correlates quite highly with the IsFraud label. It will be interesting to see if our model captures this information. Let's now load in the relevant libraries and import the data in order to achieve our task, as shown in the following listing.

Listing 4.1   Importing the libraries and dataset

```
import csv
import numpy as np
from sklearn.preprocessing import OneHotEncoder, LabelEncoder
from sklearn import linear_model, datasets, cross_validation
import matplotlib.pyplot as plt

dataset = []
f = open('./fraud_data_3.csv', 'rU')
try:
    reader = csv.reader(f,delimiter=',')
    next(reader, None)              Skips the headers in
    for row in reader:              the first line of data
        dataset.append(row)
finally:
    f.close()
```

This is the easy part! We load several standard Python libraries along with several from scikit-learn that will be discussed as we continue the exercise. In the process of loading in the data, we skip the first line, which contains the headers for the dataset.

The next step relates to how we use the data in the dataset. If you recall, there are two types of feature data: categorical and continuous. In the former, the feature is considered to belong to one of a number of distinct categories, so in this example BusinessType is a good example of a categorical feature. Although it's encoded as an integer, the ordering of these business types is meaningless; just the membership in the business category is interesting for the purposes of classification. For continuous features, the data is considered drawn from a continuous distribution. The number can take any valid value, and the ordering of two values is meaningful. A good example of this is the Amount column, in which two numbers are comparable; £50 is considered to be greater than £1. We'll create a mask to define which of our feature values are categorical and which aren't. The next listing illustrates this, along with the next step in which we start to extract the continuous and categorical features so that we can treat them differently.

Listing 4.2   Masking categorical features

```
target = np.array([x[0] for x in dataset])
data = np.array([x[1:] for x in dataset])
# Amount, Country, TimeOfTransaction, BusinessType,
# NumberOfTransactionsAtThisShop, DayOfWeek
categorical_mask = [False,True,True,True,False,True]
enc = LabelEncoder()

for i in range(0,data.shape[1]):
    if(categorical_mask[i]):
        label_encoder = enc.fit(data[:,i])
        print "Categorical classes:", label_encoder.classes_
        integer_classes = label_encoder.transform(label_encoder.classes_)
        print "Integer classes:", integer_classes
        t = label_encoder.transform(data[:, i])
        data[:, i] = t
```

Several important things are happening in listing 4.2. First, we're creating two new arrays, target and data. These contain the classification label: that is, whether the transaction is considered a fraud and all the features in the dataset, respectively. Then we modify the data array in place so that all the categorical data has new labels. This is good practice, because it can encode any data type into a distinct set of integers; for example, if the business type was recorded as a string, this would be mapped to a set of integers that could be understood during training of the model.

In the next step, shown in the following listing, we separate the categorical and the non-categorical data. We do this because we're going to encode the categorical data in a special way, in a form known as *one-hot-encoding*.[10]

Listing 4.3   Splitting out and encoding categorical features

```
mask = np.ones(data.shape, dtype=bool)              ◁─── Creates a mask object full of "True"

for i in range(0,data.shape[1]):                    ◁─┐  Fills the columns with 0s where
    if(categorical_mask[i]):                          │  the data is of categorical type
        mask[:,i]=False                             ──┘

                                                         Extracts the non-
                                                         categorical data
data_non_categoricals = data[:, np.all(mask, axis=0)]   ◁─┘
data_categoricals = data[:,~np.all(mask,axis=0)]    ◁─── Extracts the categorical data

hotenc = OneHotEncoder()
hot_encoder = hotenc.fit(data_categoricals)         ◁─── Encodes only the categorical data
encoded_hot = hot_encoder.transform(data_categoricals)
```

---

[10] Kevin Murphy, *Machine Learning: A Probabilistic Perspective* (MIT Press, 2012).

One-hot-encoding

In the example, we discuss the use of one-hot-encoding for categorical features. But what is this, and why should we bother with it? For logistic regression, all features are eventually encoded as a number, and this is where we can experience problems if we're not careful to deal with categorical variables correctly.

Let's take a simple example to illustrate the approach. In our dataset, we've included a field that specifies the country in which the transaction takes place. This has to be encoded to a number, and we use the scikit-learn LabelEncoder to do this. For illustrative purposes, let's say that UK=1, DK=2, and LT=3.

If we were to express this as a single variable within logistic regression, then we would learn a single coefficient, β, which encodes how a change in the country will impact the change in log-odds of a fraud. But what does it mean for the country to change from UK (1) to DK (2)? What about from UK (1) to LT (3)? What if LT and the UK have the same performance characteristics and should be grouped together?

Because there's no ordering of these features, it doesn't make sense to treat them this way. Instead, we encode them using one-hot-encoding. In lieu of a single feature, we create three, of which only a single feature can be active (or *hot*) at any given time. For example, UK may be encoded as 100, LT as 010, and DK as 001. Now three parameters are learned, one for each feature. This sidesteps the need for ordering because three features are treated independently although only a single feature can be active at any given time.

The code in listing 4.3 splits out the features into two arrays: `data_non_categoricals`, which contains the continuous features, and `data_categoricals`, which contains the categorical features. We then encode the latter using one-hot-encoding to ensure that the value each categorical variable can take is encoded independently and that the ordering of any feature encoding doesn't impact the end results.

Let's first look at the performance of a simple model using only the continuous features, shown in the next listing.

Listing 4.4   Simple model using continuous features only

```
new_data=data_non_categoricals
new_data=new_data.astype(np.float)

X_train, X_test, y_train, y_test =
➥cross_validation.train_test_split(new_data,
                                    target,
                                    test_size=0.4,

        random_state=0,dtype=float)

logreg = linear_model.LogisticRegression(tol=1e-10)
logreg.fit(X_train,y_train)
log_output = logreg.predict_log_proba(X_test)

print("Odds: "+ str(np.exp(logreg.coef_)))
```

Trains the logistic regression model

Creates a train and test set by splitting the data 60/40

Obtains the output of the LR model for the test set

```
print("Odds intercept" + str(np.exp(logreg.intercept_)))
print("Likelihood Intercept:" +
    str(np.exp(logreg.intercept_)/(1+np.exp(logreg.intercept_))))

f, (ax1, ax2) = plt.subplots(1, 2, sharey=True)
plt.setp((ax1,ax2),xticks=[])

ax1.scatter(range(0,
            len(log_output[:,1]),1),
            log_output[:,1],
            s=100,
            label='Log Prob.',color='Blue',alpha=0.5)

ax1.scatter(range(0,len(y_test),1),
            y_test,
            label='Labels',
            s=250,
            color='Green',alpha=0.5)

ax1.legend(bbox_to_anchor=(0., 1.02, 1., 0.102),
           ncol=2,
           loc=3,
           mode="expand",
           borderaxespad=0.)

ax1.set_xlabel('Test Instances')
ax1.set_ylabel('Binary Ground Truth Labels /  Model Log. Prob.')

prob_output = [np.exp(x) for x in log_output[:,1]]
ax2.scatter(range(0,len(prob_output),1),
            prob_output,
            s=100,
            label='Prob.',
            color='Blue',
            alpha=0.5)

ax2.scatter(range(0,len(y_test),1),
            y_test,
            label='Labels',
            s=250,
            color='Green',
            alpha=0.5)

ax2.legend(bbox_to_anchor=(0., 1.02, 1., 0.102),
           ncol=2,
           loc=3,
           mode="expand",
           borderaxespad=0.)

ax2.set_xlabel('Test Instances')
ax2.set_ylabel('Binary Ground Truth Labels / Model Prob.')

plt.show()
```

Running this listing should return several things. First you should see the values of e^β for the learned parameters, next e^{β_0}, and finally the likelihood intercept (the value of y when all values of x are equal to 0):

```
Odds: [[ 1.00137002  0.47029208]]
Odds intercept[ 0.50889666]
Likelihood Intercept:[ 0.33726409]
```

This tells us several things. The first line indicates that, holding all other features constant, a unit increase in the transaction amount increases the odds of fraud by 1.00137002. Looking at the data, this intuitively makes sense. We do see that in our dataset, fraudulent transactions tend to have a higher transaction value.

The second value is the β parameter relating to our second continuous variable, the number of transactions that have taken place at this location. We see that a unit increase in this feature results in a decrease in the odds of fraud by 0.47; thus the odds of fraud are approximately halved for every additional transaction that user has had in that establishment. Put simply, fraud is likely to occur at new retailers with respect to the user, not at existing ones.

The odds intercept is the value of e^{β_0}: that is, the odds where all other values are set to 0. From the odds intercept, we've also calculated the likelihood, which gives us an indication of the likelihood of fraud with price and transaction number set to zero. We note that this number is less than the prior probability of fraud without conditioning on any variables (approximately 50%), but this can be explained by the tendency of frauds to have high transaction values. The intercept encodes the likelihood where all x_i are equal to zero, and this would include a theoretical transaction value of zero. This drags down the probability of fraud because no fraudulent transactions have been seen at low transaction amounts.

The final output from this code is a graph that plots the output of the model versus the ground truth (figure 4.8). The output is presented in two forms. On the left is the log-probability against the label values, and on the right are the exponentiated values and the labels. In both cases, each unit on the x-axis relates to a single test instance.

In figure 4.8, data labels may only take values 1 or 0 indicating fraud and not fraud, respectively. At graph right, model output lies in the range 1.0 to 0.0 and represents the output from our trained logistic regression model. In general, we'd like to see no difference between these plots, such that non-fraud data (label 0) is assigned a probability of 0.0 by the model, whereas fraud data is assigned a probability of 1.0 (corresponding to a data item with label 1). The plot indicates that our model is fairly good, but data points 9 and 11 (read from the left) have been assigned a slightly higher probability of fraud than zero.

So far, we've used only two of the possible six variables available to us to model fraudulent transactions. Let's now add in our four hot-encoded categorical variables in listing 4.5 and see how this changes model performance.

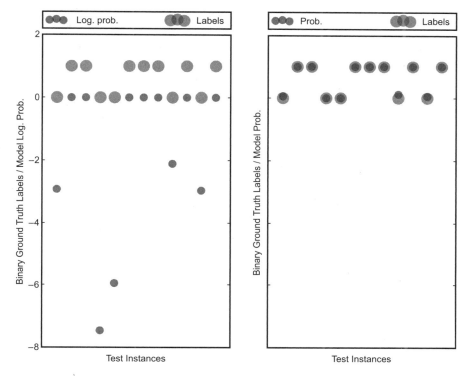

Figure 4.8 **Output of the model plotted against the test data ground truth. Values for the data labels may only take values of 1 or 0, indicating fraud and not fraud, respectively. Log-probability may take values between 0.0 and −∞ (graph left). Exponentiation of the log-probability provides our estimated probability of fraud. This lies in the range 1.0 to 0.0. We note that most cases are well classified; the probability of fraud output from the model (right) is near to the value of the label (where fraud is given by a label of 1).**

Listing 4.5   Using both categorical and non categorical variables with LR

```
new_data = np.append(data_non_categoricals,encoded_hot.todense(),1)
new_data=new_data.astype(np.float)

X_train, X_test, y_train, y_test =
➥cross_validation.train_test_split(new_data, target, test_size=0.4,
➥random_state=0,dtype=float)

logreg = linear_model.LogisticRegression(tol=1e-10)
logreg.fit(X_train,y_train)
log_output = logreg.predict_log_proba(X_test)

print("Odds: "+ str(np.exp(logreg.coef_)))
print("Odds intercept" + str(np.exp(logreg.intercept_)))
print("Likelihood Intercept:" +\
      str(np.exp(logreg.intercept_)/(1+np.exp(logreg.intercept_))))
```

```
f, (ax1, ax2) = plt.subplots(1, 2, sharey=True)
plt.setp((ax1,ax2),xticks=[])

ax1.scatter(range(0,len(log_output[:,1])),1),
            log_output[:,1],
            s=100,
            label='Log Prob.',color='Blue',alpha=0.5)

ax1.scatter(range(0,
            len(y_test),1),
            y_test,
            label='Labels',
            s=250,
            color='Green',
            alpha=0.5)

ax1.legend(bbox_to_anchor=(0., 1.02, 1., 0.102),
            ncol=2,
            loc=3,
            mode="expand",
            borderaxespad=0.)

ax1.set_xlabel('Test Instances')
ax1.set_ylabel('Binary Ground Truth Labels /  Model Log. Prob.')
prob_output = [np.exp(x) for x in log_output[:,1]]

ax2.scatter(range(0,len(prob_output),1),
            prob_output,
            s=100,
            label='Prob.',
            color='Blue',
            alpha=0.5)

ax2.scatter(range(0,len(y_test),1),
            y_test,
            label='Labels',
            s=250,
            color='Green',
            alpha=0.5)

ax2.legend(bbox_to_anchor=(0., 1.02, 1., 0.102),
            ncol=2,
            loc=3,
            mode="expand", borderaxespad=0.)

ax2.set_xlabel('Test Instances')
ax2.set_ylabel('Binary Ground Truth Labels / Model Prob.')
plt.show()
```

The code in listing 4.5 differs from listing 4.4 only in that we now construct our array new_data from both the non-categorical data and the one-hot-encoded categorical data. Everything else should be exactly the same. But note that the output obtained is significantly different. You should see something similar to the following in the first instance, before a similar graph to the one in figure 4.8 is returned:

```
Odds: [[ 1.00142244  0.48843238  1.          0.97071389
         0.77855355  0.95091843  0.85321151  0.98791223
         0.99385787  0.95983606  0.81406157  1.
         0.869761    1.          0.94819493  1.
         0.96913702  0.91475145  0.81320387  0.99837556
         0.97071389  0.869761    0.9778946   1.
         0.81320387  0.99385787  0.94499953  0.82707014
         0.98791223  0.98257044]]
Odds intercept[ 0.61316832]
Likelihood Intercept:[ 0.38010188]
```

Given the two graphs returned from each version of our experiment, we might conclude that these additional features have had very little impact on the classifier's performance. We'll discuss more about performance in the next section, but before we do that, you should understand why the model parameters have such a different form in this experiment compared to the last.

You'll note that there are a total of 30 model parameters in this version. Why is this, given that there are only six features? This is a consequence of our encoding method. For each possible value of a categorical variable, a feature is created and is set to 1 only when that value is observed. This means that only one of the values can be "hot" at any given time, leading to the name. Analysis of the parameters of the learned model shows that the first two features remain relatively unchanged from the previous experiment and that most of the other features have a value of 1 or below, leading us to believe that non-zero values of these encoded features lead to a decrease in the likelihood of fraud. Not so much, however, that they have changed the eventual classification of the data between the two experiments.

As an aside, these experiments should be considered to be illustrative rather than definitive. Model training with so few data points is never recommended, and the results that we may obtain with many more features would almost certainly be different than those we've obtained here.

Let's now take this opportunity to summarize what we've accomplished in this section. We started out with the most humble linear model—that is, drawing a straight line through our data points—and we extended this to a model that is linear in the log-odds of the target variable. This powerful technique allows for a change in an attribute to provide a nonlinear change in the odds (although linear in the log odds). We showed how this can then be applied to a real-world problem, where we need to determine whether an online financial transaction is fraudulent, and we provided the code to do so. In subsequent chapters, we'll return to logistic regression, but for now we'll leave the application of fraud detection behind.

4.4   Are your results credible?

Let's say you've built your classifier based on logistic regression, a neural network, or something else. How do you know whether you did a good job? How do you know that you're ready to use your intelligent algorithm in production and reap the awe of your colleagues and the accolades of your boss? Evaluating your classifier is as important as building it. In the field (and particularly at sales meetings!) you're going to hear things that range from exaggerations to outright nonsense. The goal of this section is to help you evaluate your own classifier, if you're a developer, and help you understand the legitimacy (or otherwise) of third-party products, whether you're a developer or a product manager.

We'll start by stating that no single classifier will perform classification well on every problem and every dataset. Think of it as the computational version of "nobody knows everything" and "everybody makes mistakes." The learning techniques we discussed in the context of classification belong to the category of supervised learning. The learning is "supervised" because the classifier undergoes a process of training, based on known classifications, and through supervision it attempts to learn the information contained in the training dataset. As you can imagine, the relation of the training data to the actual data in your deployment will be crucial for the success of classification.

For the purpose of clarity, we'll introduce a few terms and reconnect with some of the concepts first introduced in section 1.6. To make things simple, we'll consider a standard binary classification problem such as identifying email spam or fraud. For example, let's pretend that we're trying to discern whether a particular email message should be characterized as spam. A basic tool in assessing the credibility of a classifier, and typically the starting point of such an investigation, is the *confusion matrix*. It's a simple matrix where the rows refer to the category that the classifier assigns a particular instance and the columns refer to the category that an instance of a description belongs to. In the case of binary classification, there are only four cells in that matrix. The general case (multiclass classification) doesn't differ conceptually from the binary case, but it results in more complicated analysis.

Table 4.1 presents the confusion matrix for a binary classification such as email spam filtering or fraud detection. The table captures the possible outcomes of binary classification. If the classification assigns a particular email message to the spam category, then we say that the classification is *positive*.

Table 4.1 A typical confusion matrix for a simple binary classification problem

	Positive	Negative
True	True positive (TP)	True negative (TN)
False	False positive (FP)	False negative (FN)

Otherwise, we say that the classification is *negative*. Of course, the classification itself could be correct (true) or incorrect (false). Thus, the matrix contains four possible outcomes—the possible combinations between positive/negative and true/false. This also leads to the realization that there are two types of error. The first type of error consists of false positive classifications; an error of this type is called a *type I error*. The other type of error consists of false negative classifications; an error of this type is called *type II error*. In plain terms, when you commit a type I error, you convict the innocent, and when you commit a type II error, you free the guilty! This analogy is particularly good in pointing out the importance of *classification cost*. Voltaire would prefer to release 100 guilty people than convict 1 innocent person; that sensitivity remains in the European courts. The moral of this anecdote is that decisions have consequences, and the degree of the consequences isn't uniform. This is particularly true in the case of multiclass classification. Consider the following definitions, some of which were introduced in section 1.6:

- *FP rate = FP/ N, where N = TN + FP*
- *Specificity = 1 − FP rate = TN/ N*
- *Recall = TP/ P, where P = TP + FN*
- *Precision = TP/ (TP + FP)*
- *Accuracy = (TP + TN)/ (P + N)*
- *F-score = Precision × Recall*

Suppose we find out about a classifier whose accuracy, as defined earlier, is 75%. How close to the true accuracy of the classifier is our estimate? In other words, if we repeat the classification task with different data, how likely is it that our accuracy will be 75%? To answer that question, we'll resort to something that's known in statistics as a *Bernoulli process*. This is described as a sequence of independent events whose outcome is considered either as success or as failure. That's an excellent example for our fraud-detection use case, and in general for any binary classification. If we denote the true accuracy as A* and the measured accuracy as A, then we want to know if A is a good estimate of A*.

You may recall from your statistics courses the notion of a *confidence interval*. That's a measure for the certainty that we assign to a specific statement. If our accuracy is 75% in a set of 100 email messages, our confidence may not be very high. But if our accuracy is 75% in a set of 100,000 email messages, our confidence will probably be much higher. Intuitively, we understand that as the size of the set increases, the confidence interval must become smaller, and we feel more certain about our results. In particular, it can be shown that for a Bernoulli process with 100 samples, the true accuracy is located between 69.1% and 80.1%, with 80% confidence.[11] If we increase the size of the set that we use to measure the accuracy of the classifier 10 times, then the new interval ranges from 73.2% to 76.7% for the same confidence level (80%). Every good statistics textbook has formulas for calculating these intervals. In theory, these results are valid when your sample size is greater than 30 instances. In practice, you should use as many instances as you can.

Unfortunately, in practice, you may not have as many instances as you would like. To face that challenge, machine-learning folks have devised a number of techniques that can help us evaluate the credibility of classification results when data are scarce. The standard method of evaluation is called *10-fold cross-validation*. This is a simple procedure that's best illustrated by an example. Let's say we have 1,000 emails that we've already classified manually. In order to evaluate our classifier, we need to use

---

[11] Ian Witten and Eibe Frank, *Data Mining* (Morgan Kaufmann, 2005).

some of them as a training set and some as the testing set. The 10-fold cross-validation tells us to divide the 1,000 emails into 10 groups of 100 emails; each batch of 100 emails should contain roughly the same proportion of legitimate to spam emails as the 1,000 emails set does. Subsequently, we take nine of these groups of emails, and we train the classifier. Once the training is completed, we test the classifier against the group of 100 emails that we didn't include in our training. We can measure metrics, some of which we mentioned earlier, and typically people will measure the accuracy of the classifier. This is repeated 10 times, and each time we leave out a different group of 100 emails. At the end of these trials, we have 10 values of accuracy that we can now use to obtain an average value of accuracy.

You may wonder whether the accuracy will change if you divide your original set into 8 or 12 parts. Yes, of course, it's unlikely that you'll obtain an identical answer. Nevertheless, the new averaged value of accuracy should be close enough to what you obtained before. Results from a large number of tests, on various datasets and with many different classifiers, suggest that the 10-fold cross-validation will produce fairly representative measurements for a classifier.

Taking the 10-fold cross-validation to its extreme case, we can always use as a training set all the email instances except for one and use the one that we left out for testing. Naturally, this technique is called *leave-one-out*. It has certain theoretical advantages, but on real datasets (with hundreds of thousands, if not millions, of instances) the computational cost is often prohibitive. We could opt to leave one instance out but not do it for all instances in the dataset. This leads to a technique called *bootstrap*. The basic idea of bootstrap is that we can create a training set by sampling the original dataset with replacements. In other words, we can use an instance from the original dataset more than once and create a training set of 1,000 emails in which a particular email instance may appear more than once. If we do that, we'll end up with a testing set of about 368 email instances that weren't used in the training set. The size of the training set remains equal to 1,000 email instances because some of the remaining 632 email instances are repeated in the training set; for more mathematical explanation of these numbers, see Witten and Frank, *Data Mining*.

It's been found that plotting the TP rate (TPR) versus the FP rate (FPR) can be useful in analyzing the credibility of a classifier. As you saw in chapter 1, these plots are called *ROC curves* and originated in signal-detection theory in the 1970s. In recent years, there's been a large amount of work in machine learning that uses ROC graphs for analyzing the performance of one or more classifiers. The basic idea is that the ROC curve should be as far away from the diagonal of a TPR/FPR plot as possible.

In the real world, classification systems are used often as decision support systems; mistakes of classification can lead to wrong decisions. In some cases, making wrong decisions, although undesirable, can be relatively harmless. But in other cases, it may be the difference between life and death; think of a physician who misses a cancer diagnosis or an emergency situation for an astronaut in deep space relying on the result of your classifier. The evaluation of classification systems should examine both the degree of credibility and the associated cost of making classifications. In the case of binary classification, the idea is to assign a *cost function* that's a function of the FP and FN rates.

In summary, one of the most important aspects of a classifier is the credibility of its results. In this section, we described a number of metrics that can help evaluate the credibility of classifiers, such as precision, accuracy, recall, and specificity. Combinations of these metrics can yield new metrics, such as the F-score. We also discussed the idea of cross-validating the results by splitting the training set in different ways and looking at the variation of these classifier metrics as the datasets change. In the following section, we'll discuss a number of issues related to large datasets.

4.5 Classification with very large datasets

Many datasets used for academic and research purposes are quite small when compared to real-world implementations. Transactional datasets of large corporations are anywhere between 10 million and 100 million records, if not larger; insurance claims, telecommunications log files, recordings of stock prices, click trace logs, audit logs, and so on (the list is long) are on the same order of magnitude. So, dealing with large datasets is the rule rather than the exception in production applications, regardless of whether they're web-based. The classification of very large datasets deserves special attention for at least three reasons: the proper representation of the dataset in the training set, the computational complexity of the training phase, and the runtime performance of the classifier on a very large dataset.

Regardless of the specific domain of your application and the functionality that your classifier supports, you must ensure that your training data is representative of the data that will be seen in production. You shouldn't expect that a classifier will perform as well as the validation-stage measurements suggest, unless your training data is very representative of your production data. We repeat ourselves to stress that point! In many cases, early excitement quickly turns to disappointment because this condition isn't met. So, you wonder, in that case, how can you ensure that your training data is representative?

The case of binary classification is easier to address because there are only two classes—an email message either is spam or isn't, a transaction is fraudulent or it isn't, and so on. In that case, assuming that you have a reasonable number of training instances from both classes, your focus should be on the coverage of the attribute values among the training instances. Your assessment can be purely empirical ("Yeah, that's good enough. We have enough values; let's roll it to production!"), utterly scientific (sampling your data over time and testing whether the samples come from the same statistical distribution as the training data), or somewhere in between these extremes. In practice, the latter scenario is more likely; we could call it the semi-empirical approach to supervised learning. The empirical aspect of it is that along the way to assessing the completeness of your training set, you make a number of reasonable assumptions that reflect your understanding and experience of the data that your application is using. The scientific aspect of it is that you should collect some basic statistical information about your data, such as minimum and maximum values, mean values, median values, valid outliers, percentage of missing data in attribute values, and so on. You can use that information to sample previously unseen data from your application and include it in your training set.

The case of multiclass classification is similar in principle to the case of binary classification. But in addition to the guidelines that we mentioned previously, we're now faced with an additional complexity. Our new challenge is that we need to select our training instances so that all classes are represented equivalently in the training set. Discriminating among 1,000 different classes is a much harder problem to solve compared to binary selection. The case of multidimensional (many attributes), multiclass classification has the additional drawbacks that result from the curse of dimensionality (see chapter 2).

If your database contains 100 million records, you'll naturally want to take advantage of all the data and use the information contained there. In the design phase of your classifier, you should consider the scaling characteristics of the training and validation stages for your classifier. If you double the size of your training data, then ask yourself:

- How much longer does it take me to train the classifier?
- What's the accuracy of my classifier on the new (larger) set?

You probably want to include more quality metrics than just accuracy, and you probably want to take a few more data sizes (four times the original size, eight times the original, and so on), but you get the idea. It's possible that your classifier works great (it's trained quickly and provides good accuracy) in a small sample dataset, but its performance degrades significantly when it's trained over a substantially larger dataset. This is important because time to market is always important, and the "intelligent" modules of your application should obey the same production rules as the other parts of your software.

The same principle holds for the runtime performance of the classifier during the third stage of its lifecycle—in production. It's possible that your classifier was trained quickly and provides good accuracy, but it's all for naught if it doesn't scale well in production! In the validation stage of the classifier, you should measure its performance and its dependency on the size of the data. Let's say that you use a classifier whose dependence on the size of the data is quadratic—if the data doubles in size, then the time that it takes to process the data is four times larger. Let's further assume that your intelligent module will use the classifier in the background to detect fraudulent transactions. If you used 10,000 records for your validation and all records were classified in 10 minutes, then you'd process 10 million records in about 10 million minutes! You probably wouldn't have that much time available, so you should either pick a different classifier or improve the performance of the one you have. Frequently, in production systems, people have to trade classifier accuracy for speed; if a classifier is extremely accurate and extremely slow, it's most likely useless!

Pay attention to the idiosyncrasies of your classification system. If you use a rule-based system, you may encounter what's known as the *utility problem*. The learning process—the accumulation of rules—can result in the overall slowdown of the system in production. There are ways to avoid or at least mitigate the utility problem,[12] but you need to be aware of them and ensure that your implementation is compatible with these techniques. Of course, the degradation of performance isn't the only problem in that case. You'd also need to provide ways to manage and organize these rules, which is an engineering problem with a solution that'll depend strongly on the specific domain of your application. In general, the more complicated the classifier implementation, the more careful you should be to understand the performance characteristics (both speed and quality) of your classifier.

4.6 *Summary*

- We provided a taxonomy of this broad field covering both statistical and structural algorithms. Statistical algorithms focus on the fit of a particular function to some data, often using algorithmic approaches to find the maximum likelihood of the data given the model. Conversely, structural algorithms look at features such as distance between points or a set of rules to subdivide the feature space in order to find patterns between the features and the target.

- We concentrated on a specific instance of a statistical algorithm known as logistic regression and provided intuition behind this by illustrating its relationship to a linear (straight-line) model. Logistic regression is actually linear in the log-odds of target variable and provides a powerful way to estimate the probability of an event with many features. We demonstrated this using a small dataset containing both legitimate and fraudulent financial transactions.

- We concluded by looking at several metrics for measuring the performance of an algorithm and discussing large-scale implementation issues that relate to classification.

- In the world of big data, classification algorithms are often deployed over massive datasets, sometimes even operating in real time. This comes with its own set of challenges, which we've only touched on here. To scale up training to deal with large datasets requires an intimate knowledge of both the domain under investigation and the employed machine-learning approaches. Theory alone is not enough; a huge amount of development and resources go into keeping production-grade decisioning systems up and running.

---

[12] R. B. Doorenbos, *Production Matching for Large Learning Systems*, PhD thesis, Carnegie Mellon (CMU, 1995).

Case study: click prediction for online advertising

This chapter covers

- A real, large-scale intelligent system
- Targeting users with web-browsing data
- Ranking users' propensity to interact using logistic regression

Online click prediction is a specific problem in the world of advertising and is an excellent example of a high-velocity, high-throughput problem where decisions must be made with a very low latency. In general, this class of problems has a large number of applications. Online trading, website optimization, social media, the Internet of Things, sensor arrays, and online gaming all generate high-velocity data and can benefit from fast processes that make decisions in light of the most recent information possible.

Every time you open a browser and navigate to a web page, thousands if not millions of decisions are made in order to determine what ads to put in front of you. These decisions are made by communicating across many data stores and by understanding whether a specific ad will have a positive impact on the user. This has to happen quickly, because decisions must be made before the page can finish loading.

From an advertiser's standpoint, we can only proxy a positive impact through interaction with an ad. So, we try to predict the likelihood of interaction with an ad on a web page, based on all of the information surrounding a user and the context. Due to the volume and velocity of data generated on the web and the requirement for a rapid answer, this isn't a simple problem.

The solutions presented here should be equally applicable to different applications. For example, if we consider a smart city, where all cars are enabled with sensors to determine the speed, velocity, and chosen route, low-latency decisions could be used to open/close contraflow lanes or reroute traffic to keep it moving. This application follows a similar problem pattern. Can we take a huge amount of data that's arriving with high velocity and build models around this to perform decisioning quickly? Luckily, the answer is yes! In order to properly explore this solution, we're going to have to delve a little into the specifics of online advertising. For maximum generality, we'll try to keep advertising specifics to a minimum and focus on the intelligent algorithms, drawing parallels with other applications as much possible.

5.1 History and background

Opinions regarding the practice of online advertising are polarized among web users. Despite this, it does look like online advertising is here to stay. Spending has seen year on year increases of around 5%, set to reach $189.38 billion US in 2015, increasing steadily year on year to 2018, where total spend will hit a massive $220.55 billion US.[1] As more money moves from traditional media channels such as print and TV to the digital world, and advertisers begin to use the new ways in which we interact with media and our devices, technology will play an even more prevalent role.

The initial growth of online advertising was at least in part due to the increased opportunity for performance measurement.[2] Advertisers could for the first time measure exactly how many users they had reached and, more important, their subsequent behavior. This was a boon for the industry, because with traditional media channels the efficacy of advertising could only be measured through the indirect effect it had on aggregate sales. It was possible to determine whether a particular user bought a product and their exact behavior leading up to the purchase. It also became possible to test the effectiveness of ads in place. Advertisers could now test many different ads, images, and copy in real time, discounting those that did not perform well and increasing budgets in those that did. In general, optimization problems such as this one have many applications outside advertising.

Ultimately, what was witnessed was a drive toward data-driven decisioning. More and more data could be captured and used in order to better target users. This in turn led to the development of a whole new ecosystem that was created to service both buyers and sellers in this environment. In this chapter, we'll introduce the concept of

---

[1] "Total US Ad Spending to See Largest Increase Since 2004," *eMarketer*, July 2, 2014, http://mng.bz/An1G.
[2] Bill Gurley, The End of CPM," *Above the Crowd*, July 10, 2000, http://mng.bz/Vq6D.

the *exchange* and the *demand-side platform*. We'll further develop these concepts in this chapter, and you'll learn how you can use the information collected about a user to increase the odds of interaction with an ad.

Figure 5.1 provides a graphical overview of the ecosystem. You can see that the exchange is the medium through which publishers (websites such as theguardian .com, huffingtonpost.com, and more) can sell advertising space (slots and spaces of a predefined size) to individual advertisers (think companies like Nike, Adidas, O2, and Vodafone). Advertisers often buy through what's known in the industry as a *demand-side platform* (DSP).

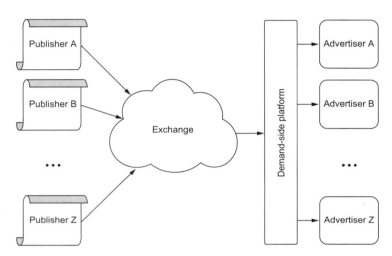

Figure 5.1   The online advertising ecosystem. Publishers make their content (advertising slots) available through an exchange that allows access programmatically—that is, through an intelligent algorithm. A demand-side platform aggregates demand for content from advertisers and buys on their behalf.

A DSP acts on behalf of multiple advertisers and combines buying power to reach the very best publishers on the web. There are many examples of DSPs on the web, such as Turn (www.turn.com), MediaMath (www.mediamath.com), and DataXu (www.dataxu.com). These platforms are a conduit through which it's possible to buy advertising. We can easily draw parallels with the world of equity trading. Not everybody is allowed on the trading floor, so representatives act on behalf of many individuals who wish to buy. In this parallel, the DSP is equivalent to the trader, where the advertising exchange is equivalent to the stock exchange. In the first case, the DSP aggregates demand, just as an individual trader does. In the second case, both exchanges act as a platform for assets to be bought and sold.

In both the advertising and equity markets, an intelligent algorithm now more often performs trading than a human. In the world of finance, this is often referred to as *high-frequency trading*. In the advertising world, this is known as *programmatic buying*, because advertising space is bought through the use of a computer program (an intelligent algorithm) as opposed to in person.

An intelligent algorithm is used to determine the quality of the user and ad available for purchase, and this ultimately impacts the price that's bid (and subsequently paid) to place an ad in front of that user. In the following sections, we'll look at a specific algorithm used to determine quality, but you first need to know a bit more about the process by which an exchange makes media available for trading. We'll then provide some real data and discuss some of the specific complications that arise when training large quantities of data. Without further ado, let's jump in!

5.2 The exchange

Figure 5.1 presented a high-level overview of how ad placements (the space in which an ad is placed on a website) are bought and sold. The *exchange* cloud hides a high degree of complexity. In this section, we'll lift the lid on this complexity and provide a stripped-back version that illustrates the process involved blow by blow. Figure 5.2 provides a graphical overview of this process.

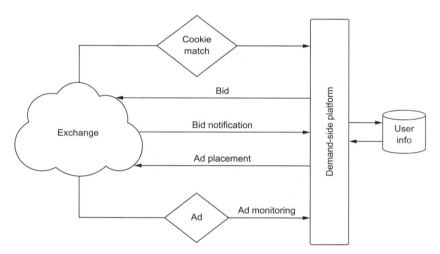

Figure 5.2 A graphical overview of the steps involved in buying ad placements on an exchange. Events should be read from top to bottom. First, a cookie match occurs. This can be performed either exchange side or DSP side. Once the DSP has a unique identifier that it can use, it uses this to look up additional information about the user and construct a bid price (the subject of section 5.4.5 onward). If the bid is successful, bid notification is returned for logging by the DSP. The next stage is for the DSP to specify the ad to be served. Physically, this can be served by the exchange itself or by the DSP. Events in the ad are fired directly back to the DSP regardless of where the ad is hosted.

5.2.1 Cookie matching

This is the first step that occurs every time a page that contains ads is loaded. A *cookie* is a unique identifier for a user for each domain (or website/web service) that's held in the browser. It's guaranteed to be unique, but it lasts for only a specific lifetime or until a user flushes their browser cookie cache. Because of strict security enforced by the browser, web services can't share each other's cookies; if an exchange wants to provide an individual's reference to a DSP so they can make a decision about whether they should place an ad in front of the user, one of two things must happen.

EXCHANGE-SIDE COOKIE MATCHING

The first option relies on a unique mapping of DSP cookies to the exchange's cookies to be hosted by the exchange itself. In this scenario, whenever a page is loaded, the exchange is contacted and looks up the appropriate cookie ID for the DSP. The details of the ad placement are then returned to the DSP, along with that DSP's unique identifier. It's then up to the DSP to look up further information about this user from its stores and decide what to do with this opportunity. The benefit of this setup is that you don't need to host a service yourself to do the cookie translation; but the service will more than likely cost you extra with the exchange.

DSP-SIDE COOKIE MATCHING

The second option relies on the DSPs themselves hosting this service. Whenever a page is loaded, the exchange contacts the DSP with its cookie ID (and additional information about the ad placement), and you perform the lookup. This obviously adds extra complexity to your decisioning stack due to the time-critical nature of lookups (exchange responses must occur within milliseconds). It might cost you less in the short term, but the service must be developed and maintained.

In either case, the result is exactly the same for the DSP. Every time a page is loaded for which there's an opportunity through the exchange, the DSP obtains a unique identifier for the user that can be used to look up further information. The DSP also obtains specific information about the ad placement that's available. What the DSP does with it gets to the heart of the intelligent algorithm presented in this chapter. In order to perform well against the other DSPs in the space, it's imperative that it uses all of its historical information to predict the future behavior of this user. This allows the DSP to pay the right price for this user, maximizing its chances of serving an ad and minimizing the chances of wasting money.

5.2.2 Bid

Given a unique identifier for the user and some general information about ad placement under offer, the DSP has to now decide two things: first, whether to place an ad in this placement; and second, if it does, how much is it willing to pay for the ad?

This seemingly simple question hides a raft of complexity. If a DSP is paid on a cost-per-click basis, then you might wish to bid based on the expectation of a click (and therefore monetary return). This basic approach is the subject of section 5.4.4, but it's possible there are other objectives to meet. Advertising campaigns of different sizes have different budgets, and it may be important to those advertisers to meet their budget or to pace their budget evenly throughout the running time of the campaign. Campaigns may also be in contention with each other for the same space on certain publishers. They may not be interested in clicks at all but perhaps conversions (that a user then clicks and subsequently buys something). So, you see, what appears at first to be simple is actually a difficult multi-objective optimization problem!

5.2.3 Bid win (or loss) notification

Once a DSP has decided if it will bid and by how much, subsequently placing the bid, the next thing that occurs is a notification from the exchange specifying whether the DSP was successful. In the event of failure, no further action is taken. Because the DSP didn't win the placement, the failure will be logged, and that will be the end of communication for this particular opportunity.

If the DSP was successful in securing the ad placement, then the cost of this placement is returned to the DSP. The majority of exchanges use what is known as a *second price*, or *Vickrey*, auction[3] in that the winner (highest bidder) of the auction pays only the price of the second-highest bid. Consequently, this final price must be returned to the DSP for logging before the next phase proceeds.

5.2.4 Ad placement

Ad placement is the most straightforward of all of the phases; once an ad placement has been won, the ad must then be rendered in it. All exchanges use a defined set of ad sizes[4] for which each advertiser and each campaign has a pre-prepared set of ads (known sometimes as *creatives*). Some exchanges go as far as to have these creatives preapproved, so that the exchange can check these for quality and brand safety before a bid is even made.

As with cookie matching, ads can be served by DSPs themselves or by the exchange. The latter has clear safety benefits for the exchange but will come with cost implications for the DSP.

5.2.5 Ad monitoring

The final stage of the auction sequence allows us to gather data on the ad that was eventually shown. This information is invaluable for several reasons. The first is that advertisers need to know whether an ad has been interacted with—that is, if it has been clicked, watched, or shared. Without this, we'd have no metric by which the clients can measure success, nor could we generate an invoice based on these metrics! The second is that this information is crucial to us as a DSP. If we know what interests a user, then we can build and target ads that lead to more positive responses for that user and to users similar to this one. Monitoring is both an ongoing requirement and the means to operate effectively as a business.

---

[3] Vijay Krishna, *Auction Theory,* 2nd ed. (Academic Press, 2009).
[4] Internet Advertising Bureau, "IAB Standard Ad Unit Portfolio," www.iab.com/guidelines/iab-standard-ad-unit-portfolio.

5.3   *What is a bidder?*

Understanding the process of bidding is the first step toward understanding the context in which an intelligent algorithm must operate. So far, we've only provided a high-level overview of how we buy ads on an exchange. All we know is that we're given some information by the exchange and that we must return a bid price in order to secure this user and this placement. In practice, a bidder that follows loosely the design presented in figure 5.3 achieves this.

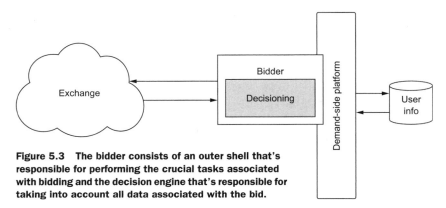

Figure 5.3   The bidder consists of an outer shell that's responsible for performing the crucial tasks associated with bidding and the decision engine that's responsible for taking into account all data associated with the bid.

The bidder is made up of an outer shell and an inner core. The outer shell is responsible for performing the crucial tasks associated with bidding, such as retrieving user information and responding to the exchange in a timely manner. At the inner core of the bidder is the decision engine, responsible for taking into account all user, placement, and context data and returning an estimate of click probability. In the rest of this section, we'll look at some requirements for a bidder (the outer shell) before delving further into the details of the decision engine (the inner shell) in section 5.4.

5.3.1   *Requirements of a bidder*

In general, we can evaluate a bidder against its performance in the following categories. Although the list isn't exhaustive, the items on it are of upmost importance for high-velocity, low-latency applications. We discuss the ramifications of these and their possible tradeoffs here:

- *Speed*—This is arguably the most important of these categories. A bidder *must* be fast. All exchanges place an extremely tight time requirement for response on their partners. From initial page load to the auction occurring and ad placement being filled, the typical duration is somewhere in the region of 100 milliseconds. Failing to meet this time requirement consistently can lead to missed opportunities and, in the worst case, to being barred from the exchange! The exchange has a reputation to uphold with its publishers and can't risk the possibility of empty ad slots that not only look unsightly on the publisher's page but also represent missed revenue for them.

- *Simplicity*—One way to achieve speed is through adopting a simple design. The bidder should perform only one function and should be easy to debug and maintain. Remember, once your bidder is live and participating in auctions, then every moment it's offline represents a loss of revenue for both you and your advertisers.

- *Accuracy*—Exchanges contain a lot of inventory. Part of the difficulty of participating in an exchange is that it's easy to buy lots of poor inventory and to buy it very quickly! For this reason it's extremely important that your bidder be accurate. Over time, you should be able to determine a positive correlation with the price that you bid and the performance of these ads.

- *Extensibility*—There are many exchanges available through which inventory can be bought. Some inventory is available through only one exchange, whereas others are available on many. In order to maximize your reach as a DSP, you'll want to integrate with as many exchanges as possible. For this reason, extending your bidder should be easy. Don't be tempted to tightly couple your bidder with the first exchange that you integrate with, but keep your solution as generic as possible.

- *Evaluation*—Once your bidder is in place and performing reasonably well, you'll want to start improving your decisioning to try to obtain the best users at the lowest cost. Every change to your bidder and its associated decisioning must be monitored to ensure that changes have the right effect. Often the results of a change can only be seen over days and weeks, not minutes and hours.

5.4 What is a decisioning engine?

In the previous sections, we introduced the basics of the problem of buying ad placements online through an exchange and how this is performed in practice through the use of a bidder. In this section, we're going to concentrate on a specific aspect of the bidder. We'll uncover how to take the raw data provided by the exchange and convert this into a value you're willing to pay to deliver an ad. Let's look at the types of information you can use to generate these probabilities.

5.4.1 Information about the user

In reality, the only information provided about a user is a cookie identifier. It's up to the DSP to record and store such information. When someone is seen for the first time, no information is available about them whatsoever! If they interact with an ad they're shown, this will be stored, as will any other interaction that occurs in the scope of a DSP's advertising: for example, if the user starts a video or cancels a full-screen advertisement. These small interactions are stored away and looked up each time this user is seen in the wild. This allows a DSP to build up a picture of user behaviors that are synonymous with the likelihood to click, as well as those that aren't.

5.4.2 Information about the placement

Quite separate from information about the user, information about the ad placement can be predictive of a click. Independent of the user, certain sizes of ads tend to perform well, as do certain publishers. For example, ads on premium news sites such as theguardian.co.uk may have a higher click-through rate (CTR) than those on small business retail outlets.

5.4.3 Contextual information

Finally, there are sources of information that don't fall into either *user* or *placement* groups. Such information is typically harder to use but is no less valuable. For example, we know that long weekends such as Black Friday[5] and Cyber Monday[6] typically lift CTR across the board and that sunnier days tend to yield fewer clicks than rainy days, when people may venture out and shop at brick-and-mortar stores rather than stay in and buy online!

5.4.4 Data preparation

The first step in building a decisioning engine is to prepare your data. Given that the measurement of success is the user clicking the ad, essentially you have two outcomes: a positive one, where the use clicks the ad, and a negative one, where the user doesn't. Thus, you require training instances for each. Because the volume of data received is very large, this might be problematic, not just from the point of storage but also from the point of model training. You need a way to reduce the size of this data without losing the patterns contained within. This is achieved by down-sampling—that is, randomly selecting a smaller subset of the data.

You generate a new, down-sampled dataset in the following way. First, you keep all ad impressions that resulted in a click. These precious data points can't be down-sampled, but because they represent only a small fraction of all impressions shown (an industry average click-through rate is much less than 1%), you don't need to. Instead, you can heavily down-sample the impressions that didn't lead to a click, leaving a dataset of a much more manageable size. This also has the effect of rebalancing your dataset. So, instead of having a very large dataset with very few positive impressions (which few classification or regression techniques will manage well), you now have a much more balanced dataset in which the positive instances represent a larger proportion of the total. We'll discuss the importance of balancing your dataset further in section 5.5.2.

5.4.5 Decisioning engine model

In chapter 4, we introduced logistic regression and used this to perform fraud detection on a very small dataset. This same approach has been used successfully in many

[5] BBC News, "Black Friday: Online Spending Surge in UK and US," November 27, 2015, www.bbc.co.uk/news/business-34931837.
[6] BBC News, "Cyber Monday Adds to Online Sales Surge," November 30, 2015, www.bbc.co.uk/news/business-34961959.

DSPs to calculate the probability of a user interacting with an ad. In the previous chapter, we placed a hard threshold on the output of the logistic regression model in order to create a classifier; but in this chapter, we'll use the output of the logistic regression model as is, taking the output probability as the likelihood of a click. Recall that the general form of the logistic regression model is given as follows

$$\ln\left(\frac{y}{1-y}\right) = \beta_0 + \beta_1 x_1 + \dots + \beta_n x_n$$

where y is the probability of the event under investigation, $1-y$ the inverse probability, β_i for $i>0$ represents the feature coefficients, and β_0 represents the threshold. Thus, in order to determine the log odds of the likelihood of clicking, we'll train a model using the data prepared as per section 5.4.4 and calculate the log odds (and subsequently the probability) of a click at the time of bid request by substitution into the previous equation.

5.4.6 Mapping predicted click-through rate to bid price

Assuming that we have a trained model as given previously and that we've just received a bid request from the exchange, mapping the output of our model to a bid value is a fairly straightforward process. We'll define a few terms first to make this easier:

- *CPI*—Cost per impression
- *CPM*—Cost per 1,000 impressions
- *CTR*—Click-through rate (Σ clicks / Σ impressions)
- *CPC*—Cost per click

In general, exchanges accept bids on a CPM basis. Rather than specify how much we're willing to pay for a single request, we return how much we'd pay for 1,000 such requests. Assuming a client provides us with a CPC target (how much they're willing to pay for a click), we have a well-defined problem:

$$Bid\ CPM = CPC \times E(CTR) \times 1,000$$
$$Bid\ CPM = CPC \times y \times 1,000$$

That is, our returned bid should be proportional to the probability of a click (given the information known about the placement and the user) multiplied by the cost of a single click, multiplied by 1,000.

5.4.7 Feature engineering

Sections 5.4.1 through 5.4.4 described the basic features that may be available at the time of a bid request, but these aren't always used in their basic form. Such features are used to generate several hundred more features, many of which then become binary indicators of a particular user status. For example, we could cross the domains visited with an ad-size feature to gain an individual feature for every particular combination. This removes the assumption that the domain and placement ad size are independent predictors of a click and allows the model to pick out excellent-performing ad placements on a site-by-site basis. Many DSPs and algorithm designers in this space will be understandably guarded about such details because these represent their secret sauce! Data science teams are constantly striving to improve the performance of their algorithms through feature engineering.

5.4.8 Model training

Because of the large volume of training data available, it's important to be able to perform out-of-core learning. Although Python with scikit-learn is great for data exploration and applications with a modest amount of data, it's not suitable at all when the amount of this data increases dramatically. This is because the implementations in scikit-learn require that all data being operated over must reside in memory. Consequently, we chose to adopt John Langford's open source Vowpal Wabbit (VW, https://github.com/JohnLangford/vowpal_wabbit). VW is currently receiving a high degree of interest and is being actively developed by many in the machine-learning community. We'll provide a brief primer on its use so that you can evaluate some exchange data, but we encourage you to read the documentation on GitHub.[7, 8]

5.5 Click prediction with Vowpal Wabbit

As just mentioned, Vowpal Wabbit is a fast machine-learning library that's able to train models without reading all data into memory. In general, VW supports a class of algorithms known as *linear supervised learning* (although VW does now provide some support for nonlinear algorithms). They're *supervised* in the sense that the classes that are to be learned are provided and *linear* in the sense that the general form of the model is linear, as you saw earlier.

In this section, we'll use the power of VW and use some real-world data generated by Criteo, a leading DSP. Criteo has made the data available in order to spur research in this area, but it comes with a catch. The data is absent of any semantics, so we don't know what each field refers to or the meaning of the values contained within. Download the full dataset (4.5 GB),[9] and we'll outline the steps to get the classifier up and running and navigate around some of the pitfalls that might beset the would-be practitioner.

First you'll need to install VW; you can find detailed instructions for this on the GitHub page[10] as well as in the prerequisites file accompanying this book. Because VW is an active research project, documentation can sometimes lag behind the most recent version of the code. Thus the most up-to-date information can often be found on the mailing list, where you'll also be able to interact with the developers of VW.

VW is accessed from the command line and is controlled, in the most part, via command-line switches. It's an extremely powerful platform, and we'll touch on only

---

[7] John Langford, "Vowpal Wabbit command-line arguments," http://mng.bz/YTlo.
[8] John Langford, Vowpal Wabbit tutorial, http://mng.bz/Gl40.
[9] Criteo, "Kaggle Display Advertising Challenge Dataset," http://mng.bz/75iS.
[10] John Langford, Vowpal Wabbit wiki, http://mng.bz/xt7H.

some of its features here. As ever, the GitHub page and mailing list will have the most detailed information, and I strongly urge you to keep checking there if you're going to develop further applications with VW.

5.5.1 *Vowpal Wabbit data format*

Vowpal Wabbit uses a specific file format that is very flexible but can be difficult to understand at first. Before we get started, we need to convert the file provided to us by Criteo into one that Vowpal Wabbit can understand. A sample of the raw data provided by Criteo is given in figure 5.4.

Class	Integer 1	Integer 2		Integer 12	Integer 13	Categorical 1	Categorical 2		Categorical 25	Categorical 26
0	1	7		5	0	68fd1e64	80e26c9b		7b4723c4	25c83c98
0	2	35	...	44	1	68fd1e64	f0cf0024	...	41274cd7	25c83c98
1	2	3		1	14	287e684f	0a519c5c		c18be181	25c83c98

Did the user interact?

These columns show 13 properties expressed as integers; likely to be event counts relating to user.

The next columns are 26 categorical properties associated with the bid request.

Figure 5.4 Overview of the raw data provided by Criteo. The first field relates to the event we're trying to predict. This relates to the user performing some event, such as clicking the ad. The next 13 columns are integer properties with count semantics; a higher number means some event has been performed more times than if a lower number is seen. The next 26 features are categorical and most likely represent some property of the bid request: for example, the site from which the bid request was made.

Criteo provides 13 features, each taking an integer value and 26 categorical features. The data is presented such that for a single log line, all integer features occur first, followed by the categorical features.

According to the "readme" file provided with the data, the integer features consist of mostly count information (for example, the number of times a user has performed something), whereas the values of the categorical features have been hashed into 32 bits. This means although integer values have integer semantics (a higher number means an event has been performed more than a lower number), we can't prescribe any such semantics to the categorical values. We might imagine that each categorical value represents some property: for example, which site the user is on at the time of the bid request. Note that hashing ensures consistency across bid requests—that is, the same hashed value implies the same non-hashed value. So although we don't know the meaning of a particular hash, the meaning is consistent every time we see that hashed value.

To be compatible with the VW file format, we first need to change the class labels. VW refers to positive instances with a 1 and negative instances with a -1. More important, we must change the format of each log line to use the pipe (|) to separate features and specify to VW which features are categorical and which are continuous. This latter point is extremely important, because if we don't distinguish between the two, our model won't use the count semantics just mentioned. Each unique count value will be treated as a label, and the model will lose the ability to understand that all the count values are related through integer semantics: for example, that 2 is greater than 1, 3 is greater than 2, and so on. If you look in the accompanying folder for this chapter, you'll find that we've already written this code for you!

In order to proceed with the example in this chapter, you'll need to download dac.tar.gz from Criteo,[11] untar/gz the file, and extract the train.txt data file from the dac subdirectory. Next, run the included Python script against the training file using the following command:

```
python ch5-criteo-process.py </path/to/train.txt>
```

This will create two files called train_vw_file and test_vw_file. These are created in the current directory of the aforementioned script. Note that if you wish, you can change the output files from this script by providing two additional parameters:

```
python ch5-criteo-process.py </path/to/train.txt> </path/to/train_vw_file>
➡</path/to/test_vw_file>
```

Each resulting file contains data in the following format:

```
-1 |i1 c:1 |i2 c:1 |i3 c:5 |i4 c:0 |i5 c:1382 |i6 c:4 |i7 c:15 |i8 c:2 |i9
➡c:181 |i10 c:1 |i11 c:2 |i13 c:2 |c1 68fd1e64 |c2 80e26c9b |c3 fb936136
➡|c4 7b4723c4 |c5 25c83c98 |c6 7e0ccccf |c7 de7995b8 |c8 1f89b562 |c9
➡a73ee510 |c10 a8cd5504 |c11 b2cb9c98 |c12 37c9c164 |c13 2824a5f6 |c14
➡1adce6ef |c15 8ba8b39a |c16 891b62e7 |c17 e5ba7672 |c18 f54016b9 |c19
➡21ddcdc9 |c20 b1252a9d |c21 07b5194c |c23 3a171ecb |c24 c5c50484 |c25
➡e8b83407 |c26 9727dd16
```

Let's look at this in detail. In general, attributes of this data point are separated by the pipe, or vertical bar (|). Note that the first entry is -1. This is the target class for this datum. This data was extracted from an ad that didn't end up receiving a click from the user it was targeted at; positive 1 would denote that a click did occur.

Notice the human-readable tags: i1, i2, i3, and so on. These are called *namespaces*. We've chosen namespaces beginning with i to denote integer features and those beginning with c to denote categorical features. Namespaces in VW are an advanced feature that allows you to experiment with the combination of different spaces. This would allow you, for example, to generate model coefficients for derived features with a simple command-line switch: if you knew that namespace c1 represented the site that the bid request was seen on and namespace c2 represented the ad unit size, you could easily include "ad size per site" as a new feature in the model. Also notice that some namespaces include an additional piece of information, denoted by c:. This is the name of the feature in the namespace. Where no name is specified, its name is implied by the value. This allows you to express the difference between categorical variables and continuous ones. Let's take a concrete example to ensure that you understand this.

---

[11] Criteo, http://mng.bz/75iS.

The `c1` namespace in the previous example contains the feature `68fd1e64`. Implicit to this is a value, 1, that denotes that feature `68fd1e64` is present; thus, it's categorical. We could equivalently write this as `68fd1e64:1`. In the example of `i1`, the namespace has a feature, `c`. This has associated with it a continuous variable, 1, denoting the count on the number of events (of name `c`) relating to `i1` that have occurred. In practice, this distinction is important because it means the difference between training a single coefficient for a continuous variable (the correct way to proceed for integer semantics) or a coefficient for every seen value of the variable (incorrect!). We won't go further into this here, but I encourage you to read the associated documentation on namespaces on the project wiki.[12]

> ### How features are represented in VW
>
> VW uses a bit vector of a specified size called a *feature table*, and each feature is represented by hashing into this vector. Weights are learned, not per feature, but per entry within the vector.
>
> This has a few benefits, including a reduced fixed-size learning space, but it means collisions can occur (where two different features trigger the same bit). In general, provided an appropriate vector size is chosen, the impact of this on the accuracy of the trained classifier is negligible. It also means that to uncover the impact of a feature (analyze its learned weights), we need to hash into the bit vector and perform the dot product of the vector and the weights. We'll encounter this later.

We mentioned earlier that you need to create two files. You create these files directly from the Criteo training data (train.txt). Because the Criteo data was originally compiled for a competition, the test data file (test.txt) that comes with the package doesn't contain any labels. This would make it impossible for us to discuss the efficacy of our classifier without submitting it to the competition. In order to create our own test set, we further split the train.txt set into two files at the rate of 70/30: 70% of the training data is placed in a new training dataset file (train_vw_file), whereas we hold the remaining 30% in a test file (test_vw_file) to evaluate our solution. Now that you understand the format of the data that we're working with and its internal representation in VW, and you have both a training set and a testing set, let's proceed with data preparation.

5.5.2   Preparing the dataset

First, we'd like to understand how balanced the data is. By *balanced,* we mean is the proportion of positive samples roughly equal to the proportion of negative samples? This is an important step because the training algorithm we'll use is sensitive to such properties of the data. Without a balanced dataset, the coefficients of the logistic model will be updated to reflect the negative samples more often than the positive

---

[12] John Langford, Vowpal Wabbit input format, http://mng.bz/2v6f.

samples. Put another way, the negative samples will have more importance than the positive ones. This isn't ideal and can be best tackled by forcing the data to be balanced before training.

We can ensure that this is true with a bit of command-line manipulation. A word to the wise: these files are large, and editing them in your favorite text editor may cause your memory to fill up and your application to crash! Take a look at the following listing for an appropriately safe method to do this.

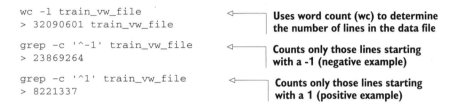

Listing 5.1   Determining how balanced the data is

```
wc -l train_vw_file
> 32090601 train_vw_file
```
⊲ Uses word count (wc) to determine the number of lines in the data file

```
grep -c '^-1' train_vw_file
> 23869264
```
⊲ Counts only those lines starting with a -1 (negative example)

```
grep -c '^1' train_vw_file
> 8221337
```
⊲ Counts only those lines starting with a 1 (positive example)

Here we use some simple command-line utilities to determine the number of positive and negative examples in the training set. Because every training example is on its own line in the data file, the first line tells us how many training points are available in the training set. The second and third lines use grep to select and count only those lines starting with negative and positive outcomes, respectively. We see that there are approximately three times more negative examples than positive ones. Note that this isn't representative of the general click-through rate. Clickers generally represent a much smaller proportion of the population; we believe this dataset has previously been down-sampled by Criteo an undisclosed amount.

We'll also need to shuffle our data. Why? VW performs what is known as *online learning*. Remember, it's out of core, in that the whole dataset doesn't need to be in memory. In order to learn effectively on a line-by-line basis, data must be drawn randomly from the underlying distribution. The simplest way to do this is by shuffling the input data before running over this line by line. For more information on stochastic gradient descent (SGD), the online method we'll use to train our model, the following papers will be useful: Bottou, "Online Learning and Stochastic Approximations,"[13] and Bottou, "Stochastic Gradient Tricks."[14]

To balance and shuffle our dataset for training, we'll continue to work at the command line. The next listing provides the command to extract, shuffle, and create the dataset.

---

[13] Leon Bottou, "Online Learning and Stochastic Approximations," in *Online Learning and Neural Networks*, by David Saad (Cambridge University Press, 1998).

[14] Leon Bottou, "Stochastic Gradient Tricks," in *Neural Networks: Tricks of the Trade*, ed. Gregoire Montavon, (Springer-Verlag, 2012): 421–36.

Listing 5.2   Balancing, shuffling, and creating the training dataset

Extracts negative samples, shuffles, and places in the negative_examples.dat file

Extracts positive samples, shuffles, and places in the positive_examples.dat file

```
grep '^-1' train_vw_file | sort -R > negative_examples.dat

grep '^1' train_vw_file | sort -R > positive_examples.dat
awk 'NR % 3 == 0' negative_examples.dat > \
        negative_examples_downsampled.dat

cat negative_examples_downsampled.dat > all_examples.dat

cat positive_examples.dat >> all_examples.dat

cat all_examples.dat | sort -R > all_examples_shuffled.dat
awk 'NR % 10 == 0' all_examples_shuffled.dat > \
        all_examples_shuffled_down.dat
```

Uses awk to take every third example from negative_examples.dat file

Places the down-sampled negative examples into all_examples.dat

Appends the positive examples to the negative ones

Down-samples the training set

Shuffles the balanced training set

This listing uses several more command-line tools to down-sample and shuffle our data, creating a balanced dataset. As in listing 5.1, we use `grep` to select those lines of the training file that we're interested in (positive or negative samples) before using `sort` to shuffle the data into an output file. We use `awk` to pick every third line from the negative examples and rely on redirection to move data between files. Listing 5.2 is heavily annotated for those interested in the precise details, but the result of running this code snippet is the creation of a balanced and shuffled training set called all_examples_shuffled.dat; this training set is then further down-sampled by 10 to create a more manageable dataset, all_examples_shuffled_down.dat. Both of these datasets are balanced, but one is a (smaller) subset of the other. The rest of this chapter uses the more aggressively down-sampled dataset, because it will return a trained model much more quickly. But we must note that because VW is out of core, you should have no problem training on either dataset; the only difference will be the time taken to complete, and possibly the size of the feature table required (discussed shortly). I'll leave it you to re-create the training and testing steps using the larger training set.

With our data shuffled and ready to train, we can now proceed to call VW. The next listing provides the code to train and to create a human-readable view of our model.

Listing 5.3   Training a logistic regression model using VW

```
vw all_examples_shuffled_down.dat \
    --loss_function=logistic \
    -c \
    -b 22 \
    --passes=3 \
    -f model.vw

vw all_examples_shuffled_down.dat \
    -t \
    -i model.vw \
    --invert_hash readable.model

cat readable.model | awk 'NR > 9 {print}' | \
    sort -r -g -k 3 -t : | head -1000 > readable_model_sorted_top
```

> **Trains a logistic regression model using a cache (-c) , a feature table of size 22 (-b 22),[15] and three passes over the dataset. Saves the model to the model.vw file.**

> **Runs vw in test-only mode (-t) over the same data using the previously trained model. The purpose of this isn't to test on the same data but to run through the data once and create the inverse hash lookup.**

> **Sorts the readable model by the learned parameter, and keeps the top 1,000**

The first line trains our model using VW. Several command-line switches perform specific functions, and more information regarding these can be found in Langford, "Vowpal Wabbit command-line arguments," cited previously. In order to perform logistic regression, we need to tell VW to use the logistic loss function to calculate the difference between the desired output and the prediction. This will allow SGD to modify the coefficients to converge on a solution whereby the linear combination of the coefficients and the features approaches the log-odds of the target variable. The -c tells VW to use a cache. This stores the input data in a format that's native to VW, making subsequent passes over the data much faster. The -b switch tells VW to use 22 bits for the feature vector, which is appropriate for our dataset. The -f switch tells VW to store the resultant model (essentially the coefficients of the model) in a file called model.vw.

If you recall from the previous chapter, the basics of model training are simple to understand—to update the coefficients to minimize the error in prediction—that is, the loss function. To do this effectively, VW stores the features in a hashed format. So, every feature, *f*, is represented by an associated bitmask given by its hash: $h(f)$. Thus, it's quick to look up a feature to change its coefficients on each learning pass. This has an associated advantage known as the *hashing trick*,[16] which allows for very large feature spaces to be stored using a fixed-size representation. This has the effect that learning cost is capped without too much impact to the predictive power of the data.

Essentially, model.vw contains a vector of learned weights; but, unfortunately, to human eyes it doesn't make much sense, because we don't know how the human-readable features relate to this vector. As machine-learning practitioners, we're interested in the

---

[15] This has been chosen because on analysis of the dataset used here, there are more than 2.1 million individual features. To be able to represent these uniquely, you'd require a binary feature vector of size at least $\log_2(2.1 \times 10^6)$, which, rounded up to the nearest integer, is 22. Note that when using the full, non-downsampled data, this number may have to be revised. You can easily count the number of features in this case by running a full pass of listing 5.3 over your new dataset and performing a line count on readable.model.

[16] Olivier Chapelle, Eren Manavoglu, and Romer Rosales, "Simple and Scalable Response Prediction for Display Advertising," *ACM Transactions on Intelligent Systems and Technology* 5, no. 4 (2015): 61.

human-readable features so we can gain some intuition as to what features the model thinks are important. This is the focus of the second line of listing 5.3. We call vw again in test mode (-t) using the model we've already trained. In general, you should never test on the same data you train on, but in this case we're not interested in the results! By running through the train data in test mode a single time with the -invert_hash option set, we build a table that links the human-readable feature name to the effective impact on the classifier, through the weights associated with the hashed feature value.

Because there are so many learned values, and they're written out to the readable .model file in no particular order, before we can analyze the coefficients we must sort this file. We do this using the command-line tools awk, sort, and head. Essentially, we throw away the first nine rows (which include header information and preamble) and then sort the remaining rows on the third column, telling sort that the columns are denoted by the colon (:). The final output is sent to readable_model_sorted_top, and we reproduce the top 20 coefficients in the listing that follows. The features you see here are those that, if set (holding all other features constant), cause the greatest increase to log odds.

Listing 5.4   Human-readable output from VW

```
c24^e5c2573e:395946:3.420166
c3^6dd570f4:3211833:1.561701
c12^d29f3d52:2216996:1.523759
c12^977d7916:2216996:1.523759
c13^61537f27:2291896:1.373842
c12^d27ed0ed:2291896:1.373842
c12^b4ae013a:2291896:1.373842
c16^9c91bbc5:1155379:1.297896
c3^f25ae70a:64455:1.258160
c26^ee268cbb:64455:1.258160
c21^cfa6d1ae:64455:1.258160
c26^06016427:3795516:1.243104
c15^2d65361c:506605:1.240656
c12^13972841:506605:1.240656
c3^e2f2a6c7:3316053:1.234188
c18^eafb2187:3316053:1.234188
c18^fe74f288:3396459:1.218989
c3^8d935e77:2404744:1.214586
c4^f9a7e394:966724:1.212140
c3^811ddf6f:966724:1.212140
```

 **① Most important features**

Listing 5.4 presents a snippet of the human-readable output. Values after the ^ character are the values of feature in the raw data; the second and third columns present the hash value and the coefficient, respectively. We've presented only the top 20 coefficients here (there are over 2 million in the down-sampled set, probably because domain is used in the dataset and every domain is encoded singularly), but we can already see some interesting trends. The most important feature appears to be c24, followed by a c3, and then a c12 ①. So in general, each of these three features causes the largest increase in log odds if set (in the order presented), assuming all other features are held constant. Note that none of the features with integer semantics appear here.

You may also notice a repetition of weight values for some of the features in this list. This is because those features activate the same bits of the feature vector after they're hashed (hash collision). You can see this: the number after the first colon is the same for several lines of listing 5.4. Consequently, their impact is unified into the single same value when the dot product between the feature vector and the learned weights is performed.

In reality, this isn't ideal, although it might not be so bad—the impact is averaged by the learner. In essence, if either of these features is present, a net positive or negative effect is added to the log likelihood of the event that is to be predicted.[17]

Unfortunately, because Criteo anonymized the data, we're unable to decipher what these features relate to. If we could, though, it would be great from an analytics point of view and would make a wonderful story! What we're really interested in determining is how well our model performs, and (luckily!) we can do this without decoding the features. Recall that in a previous chapter we introduced the AUC, or the area under the receiver operating characteristic (ROC) curve, whereby a value close to 1 represents a perfect classifier. We'll now apply this methodology to an unseen test set, but first we must use VW and our previously trained model to obtain some predictions from our test data.

5.5.3   *Testing the model*

The following listing provides the code to evaluate a test set against a trained model and to generate both the probabilities and ground truth that will be used in the next step to create a ROC curve.

Listing 5.5   Testing against a trained model in VW

```
vw -d test_vw_file \
    -t \
    -i model.vw \
    --loss_function=logistic \
    -r predictions.out
~/dev/vowpal_wabbit/utl/logistic -0 predictions.out > \
    probabilities.out | cut -d ' ' -f 1 test_vw_file | \
    sed -e 's/^-1/0/' > ground_truth.dat
```

The first command uses the -d option to specify the data file, along with the -t option for testing (no learning). The -i option loads the previously trained model into memory, and we specify the -r switch to output the raw predictions. The next line uses a helper function to transform these raw predictions (which are of the form $\beta_0 + \sum_i \beta_i x_i$) into their associated probability, as specified by y in section 5.4.5. Note that you'll most likely need to change the path to the helper function on your system. The logistic script can be found under the utl subdirectory of the VW repository (http://mng.bz/pu5U) originally checked out as per the book's prerequisites/requirements file.

---

[17] More information about feature hashing and collision avoidance can be found at http://mng.bz/WQi7.

These resulting probabilities are stored in the probabilities.out file. The final line of listing 5.5 separates the columns of the training file by splitting on white space and selecting the first column, which contains the ground-truth class data. This is then piped to sed, which replaces any occurrences of -1 (how VW deals with negative classes in logistic regression) with 0. The output is sent to the ground_truth.dat file.

We're now finally at the position where we can evaluate the efficacy of our model against the test data. The next listing shows the scikit-learn code that's required to generate the AUC and a graph of the ROC curve, shown in figure 5.5.

Listing 5.6 Generating the ROC curve with scikit-learn

```
import numpy as np
import pylab as pl
from sklearn import svm, datasets
from sklearn.utils import shuffle
from sklearn.metrics import roc_curve, auc

ground_truth_file_name = './ground_truth.dat'
probability_file_name = './probabilities.out'

ground_truth_file = open(ground_truth_file_name,'r')
probability_file = open(probability_file_name,'r')

ground_truth = np.array(map(int,ground_truth_file))
probabilities = np.array(map(float,probability_file))

ground_truth_file.close()
probability_file.close()

#from: http://scikitlearn.org/stable/
#        auto_examples/model_selection/plot_roc.html
fpr, tpr, thresholds = roc_curve(ground_truth, probabilities)
roc_auc = auc(fpr, tpr)
print "Area under the ROC curve : %f" % roc_auc

pl.clf()
pl.plot(fpr, tpr, label='ROC curve (area = %0.2f)' % roc_auc)
pl.plot([0, 1], [0, 1], 'k--')
pl.xlim([0.0, 1.0])
pl.ylim([0.0, 1.0])
pl.xlabel('False Positive Rate')
pl.ylabel('True Positive Rate')
pl.title('Receiver operating characteristic')
pl.legend(loc="lower right")
pl.show()
```

Generates the false positive and true positive rates (and their associated thresholds) using scikit-learn

After the imports, the first 11 lines here are essentially preamble, reading in the ground truth and the probabilities required in order to generate the ROC curve. The data for the ROC curve is extracted in a single line. The rest of the code generates the graph and has been taken from the scikit-learn documentation.[18] Figure 5.5 shows the output from this code.

---

[18] scikit-learn, "Receiver Operating Characteristic (ROC), http://mng.bz/9jBY.

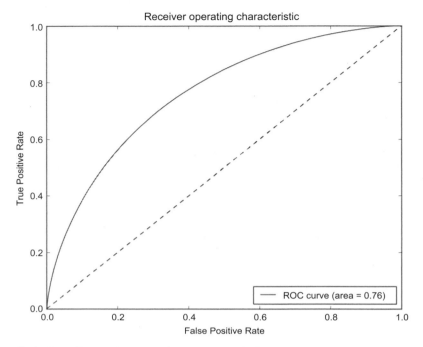

Figure 5.5   The receiver operating characteristic for our model based on the supplied test data. The area under the curve is given as 0.76.

The results show a value of 0.76 for the area under the curve based on our trained model and held-out test data. To translate this into a more intuitive number, if we chose a threshold corresponding to the point on the ROC curve closest to the top-left corner of figure 5.5 and used this threshold as a hard classifier to choose between clickers and non-clickers, we'd have a true positive rate of about 0.7 (that is, when the model predicted a click, it was right 70% of the time) and a false positive rate of about 0.3 (that is, 30% of non-clickers were incorrectly identified as clickers). To obtain these numbers, find the point closest to the upper-left corner on the upper curve in the figure, and read off the values on the x- and y-axes, respectively. In reality, however, models such as these are used not to classify impressions that will be clicked but to determine how much money should be paid to show an ad, as per the methodology in section 5.4.6.

5.5.4   *Model calibration*

In the previous section, we alluded to the fact that we don't use the output of our trained model to create a classifer per se; rather, we use the output of the logistic regression model to estimate the probability of the click occurring. But if you remember, to achieve efficient model training, we changed the frequency of the positive events in the data such that the positive and negative events represented an even proportion of the training data. Thus, in order to obtain outputs from the model that are representative of the underlying probabilities of a click, we must *calibrate* the model.

The method we use here is taken from the paper by Olivier Chapelle et al.[19] and is based on some simple observations. First, recall that, in our model, the log odds of the positive event occurring are linearly related to the input data via the learned weights

$$\frac{\Pr(y = 1|\mathbf{x}, \boldsymbol{\beta})}{\Pr(y = -1|\mathbf{x}, \boldsymbol{\beta})} = \beta_0 + \beta_1 x_1 + \ldots + \beta_n x_n$$

where we now use the model probability in the numerator and denominator of this equation. Consider now only the distribution of the data. If we apply Bayes' rule to the top and bottom of the odds and simplify, we obtain the following relationship:

$$\frac{\Pr(y = 1|\mathbf{x})}{\Pr(y = -1|\mathbf{x})} = \frac{\Pr(\mathbf{x}|y = 1)\Pr(y = 1)}{\Pr(\mathbf{x}|y = -1)\Pr(y = -1)}$$

Using the fact that only negative instances of a click are down-sampled and, as in Chapelle's paper, using Pr′ to denote the resultant probability distribution after sampling the data down, then this may be equivalently written as follows

$$\frac{\Pr(y = 1|\mathbf{x})}{\Pr(y = -1|\mathbf{x})} = \frac{\Pr'(\mathbf{x}|y = 1)\Pr'(y = 1)}{\Pr'(\mathbf{x}|y = -1)\Pr'(y = -1)/r}$$

where r is the rate by which the negative samples have been down-sampled.[20] This leads us to the relationship between the odds in the original dataset versus those in the down-sampled dataset:

$$\frac{\Pr(y = 1|\mathbf{x})}{\Pr(y = -1|\mathbf{x})} = r\frac{\Pr'(y = 1|\mathbf{x})}{\Pr'(y = -1|\mathbf{x})}$$

Thus, we return to our original model equation,

$$\ln\left(r\frac{Pr'(y = 1|\mathbf{x}, \boldsymbol{\beta})}{Pr'(y = -1|\mathbf{x}, \boldsymbol{\beta})}\right) = \beta_0 + \beta_1 x_1 + \ldots + \beta_n x_n$$

or equivalently

$$\ln\left(\frac{Pr'(y = 1|\mathbf{x}, \boldsymbol{\beta})}{Pr'(y = -1|\mathbf{x}, \boldsymbol{\beta})}\right) = (\beta_0 - \ln(r)) + \beta_1 x_1 + \ldots + \beta_n x_n$$

---

[19] Chapelle et al., "Simple and Scalable Response Prediction for Display Advertising," *ACM Transactions on Intelligent Systems and Technology* 5, no. 4 (January 2014): 1–34.

[20] For example, starting with a dataset of 1,000 positive examples and 9,000 negative examples, if you were to sample the negative examples to 1,000 and create a balanced dataset, then you would have employed a value of $r = 1/9$.

You can train on a down-sampled dataset, removing only negative training instances; but if you wish to obtain output from the model that reflects the probability of the positive event accurately, you must complete a further step.

As you can see, the trained model will have an intercept that's $\ln(r)$ lower than that which would be obtained if you didn't used a down-sampled set. So if you wish to correct for this, you must add $\ln(r)$ to the resultant score. Don't forget, though, that although we've down-sampled the data, it was also down-sampled by an unknown amount by Criteo! Consequently, we're unable to calibrate the model fully without additional information.

In this section, we covered a great deal and discussed the basics of performing online ad-click prediction. Note that there's a lot more to this problem than building a good model! In general, you must consider the competing needs of many different advertisers, their metrics for success, and your profit margins. Building an effective model is only the start, and many advertising-tech companies have entire teams of data scientists working on these problems. In the next section, we'll cover just a few of the complexities you'd encounter when deploying a model such as this.

5.6 *Complexities of building a decisioning engine*

As the idiom says, the devil is the details. In order to build an effective click-prediction engine, we must address various issues and answer various questions. In this section, we'll pose some open questions for you to think about—these are very much still open research questions that are being addressed by the ad-tech machine-learning community at the time of writing. In the following paragraphs, we'll often frame from an advertising perspective, but these problems are equally applicable to models in any domain.

First, let's touch on the issue of training intervals and frequency. How often do we train a model, and how long does it remain valid? You might wish to build a model on day n and apply it to day $n+1$, but what if today's model isn't representative of tomorrow? You might train the model for a week or build specific models for particular days of the week that could provide better performance on a day-to-day basis, but they might not. You need a way to track or monitor the performance over time.

This leads us to the question of *drift*. If you build a model on day n and apply this to subsequent days, $n+1, n+2$, and so on, you'll most likely see that the model drifts. In other words, the performance of the model decreases over time. This is because the underlying behavior of the population is changing. In the advertising world, publishers change their content, certain sites become unavailable, and even the weather changes! Ultimately, unless you're learning in real time and updating your model with every data point as you see it, the model is out of date the moment it's trained, and it will become increasingly out of date the longer it's used.

This brings us to the question of a training pipeline. Remember, data is constantly flowing into our systems from millions of interactions on the web. As this happens, we need to capture, direct, store, preprocess, and process continuously, generating training datasets every single moment, hour, day, and week. This is a complex task, and it requires significant engineering effort. If you consider this book's appendix, you should see that collecting and massaging your data is the first step in a *pipeline* of steps that make up a larger intelligent application. This pipeline may contain a data-ingestion step, a data-cleansing step, a down-sampling step, a training step, and a release step, each stage firing after the completion of the last and running over a fixed amount of data (say, an hour of data at a time).

5.7 The future of real-time prediction

In this chapter, we provided an example of a real-world problem that requires you to make decisions in real time from a huge amount of data. Click prediction is a specific problem in the world of advertising, but many of its solutions are easily applicable to other domains. I believe the future of real-time prediction will be improved in two important areas: through real-time data acquisition and processing and through adaptive and responsive models.

Taking the first in hand, we've already discussed the importance of a data pipeline—a way of acquiring, shaping, and processing data to get it ready for model training and deployment. To date, many systems built to achieve this task are based on batches of data moving from one step to the next. The reason for this is that most data-processing systems have been built in this manner! Only recently have stream-processing engines such as Storm, Storm Trident, and Spark Streaming become available, not to mention the exciting work on Millwheel[21] and FlumeJava[22] at Google. These systems have the potential to change the game for prediction by lowering the latency between an event being captured and a model being trained to incorporate this behavior. This low latency can be achieved because each data point can flow through the system without having to wait for the batch in which it's contained completing.

This leads us to our second area of importance, adaptive and responsive modeling. By reducing the latency of data flowing around the system, data can be delivered to the model-training step much earlier. If we can then reduce the latency between this data point and a model reflecting this data point, we can act on events before we were otherwise able to. This might lead us away from batch-training methods to truly online learning—not just in the sense that models are updated sequentially in an out-of-core fashion, but in that they're updated sequentially *as the data arrives*.

---

[21] Tyler Akidau et al., "MillWheel: Fault-Tolerant Stream Processing at Internet Scale," The 39th International Conference on Very Large Data Bases (VLDB, 2013): 734–46.

[22] Craig Chambers et al., "FlumeJava: Easy, Efficient Data-Parallel Pipelines," ACM SIGPLAN Conference on Programming Language Design and Implementation (ACM, 2010): 363–75.

5.8   Summary

- We've built an intelligent algorithm for online click prediction.
- We provided a complete introduction to a very important application on the intelligent web. Very few applications have received such attention from the ML community and continue to do so at this level.
- You learned about the use of an out-of-core machine-learning library called Vowpal Wabbit that allows training to occur without reading all the data into memory.
- We discussed the future of real-time click prediction on the web.

Deep learning and neural networks

This chapter covers

- Neural network basics
- An introduction to deep learning
- Digit recognition using restricted Boltzmann machines

There is much discussion about deep learning at the moment, and it's widely seen to be the next big advance in machine learning and artificial intelligence. In this chapter, we'd like to cut through the rhetoric to provide you with the facts. At the end of this chapter, you should understand the basic building block of any deep learning network, the *perceptron*, and understand how these fit together in a deep network. Neural networks heralded the introduction of the perceptron, so we'll discuss these before exploring deeper, more expressive networks. These deeper networks come with significant challenges in representation and training, so we need to ensure a good foundational knowledge before leaping in.

Before we do all of this, we'll discuss the nature of deep learning and the kinds of problems deep learning has been applied to and what makes these successful. This should give you a foundational motivation for deep learning and a frame on which to hang some of the more complicated theoretical concepts later in the chapter. Remember that this is a still a vibrant and active area of research in the community, so I recommend that you keep abreast of the latest advances by following the literature. Startup.ML[1] and KDNuggets[2] are just a couple of the resources that can provide you with an up-to-date summary of what's happening in the community. But I urge you to do your own research and come up with your own conclusions!

6.1   *An intuitive approach to deep learning*

In order to understand deep learning, let's choose the application of image recognition; namely, given a picture or a video, how do we build classifiers that will recognize objects? Such an application has potentially wide-reaching applications. With the advent of the quantified self[3, 4] and Google Glass, we could imagine applications that recognize objects visible to the user and provide augmented visuals through their glasses.

Let's take the example of recognizing a car. Deep learning builds up layers of understanding, with each layer utilizing the previous one. Figure 6.1 shows some of the possible layers of understanding for a deep network trained to recognize cars. Both this example and some of the images that follow have been reproduced from Andrew Ng's lecture on the subject.[5]

At the bottom of figure 6.1, you can see a number of stock images of cars. We'll consider these our training set. The question is, how do we use deep learning to recognize the

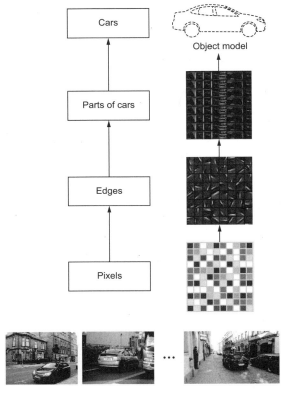

Figure 6.1   Visualizing a deep network for recognizing cars. Some graphical content reproduced from Andrew Ng's talk on the subject, cited previously. A base training set of pictures is used to create a basis of edges. These edges can be combined to detect parts of cars, and these parts of cars can be combined to detect an object type, which is in this case a car.

[1] Startup.ML, "Deep Learning News," June 30, 2015, http://news.startup.ml.

[2] KDNuggets, "Deep Learning," www.kdnuggets.com/tag/deep-learning.

[3] Gina Neff and Dawn Nafus, *The Quantified Self* (MIT Press, 2016).

[4] Deborah Lupton, *The Quantified Self* (Polity Press, 2016).

[5] Andrew Ng, "Bay Area Vision Meeting: Unsupervised Feature Learning and Deep Learning," YouTube, March 7, 2011, http://mng.bz/2cR9.

similarities between these images: that is, that they all contain a car, possibly without any hand-labeled ground truth? The algorithm isn't told that the scene contains a car.

As you'll see, deep learning relies on progressively higher-concept abstractions built directly from lower-level abstractions. In the case of our image-recognition problem, we start out with the smallest element of information in our pictures: the pixel. The entire image set is used to construct a basis of features—think back to chapter 2, where we discussed extracting structure from data—that can be used in composite to detect a slightly higher level of abstraction such as lines and curves. In the next-highest level, these lines are curves that are combined to create parts of cars that have been seen in the training set, and these parts are further combined to create object detectors for a whole car.

There are two important concepts to note here. First, no explicit feature engineering has been performed. If you remember, in the last chapter, we talked about the importance of creating a good representation of your data. We discussed this in the context of click prediction for advertising and noted that experts in the space typically perform this manually. But in this example, unsupervised feature learning has been performed; that is, representations of the data have been learned without any explicit interaction from the user. This may parallel how we as humans may perform recognition—and we're very good at pattern recognition indeed!

The second important fact to note is that the concept of a car hasn't been made explicit. Given sufficient variance in the input set of pictures, the highest-level car detectors should do sufficiently well on any car presented. Before we get ahead of ourselves, though, let's clear up some of the basics around neural networks.

6.2 *Neural networks*

Neural networks aren't a new technology by any means and have been around since the 1940s. They're a biologically inspired concept whereby an output neuron is activated based on the input from several connected input neurons. Neural networks are sometimes known as *artificial* neural networks, because they achieve artificially a functionality similar to that of a human neuron. Jeubin Huang[6] provides an introduction to the biology of the human brain. Although many aspects of the functionality of the human brain are still a mystery, we're able to understand the basic building blocks of operation—but how this gives rise to consciousness is another matter.

Neurons in the brain use a number of dendrites to collect both positive (*excitative*) and negative (*inhibitory*) output information from other neurons and encode this electrically, sending it down an axon. This axon splits and reaches hundreds or thousands of dendrites attached to other neurons. A small gap exists between the axon and the input dendrites of the next neuron, and this gap is known as a *synapse*. Electrical information is converted into chemical output that then excites the dendrite of the

---

[6] Jeubin Huang, "Overview of Cerebral Function," Merck Manual, September 1, 2015, http://mng.bz/128W.

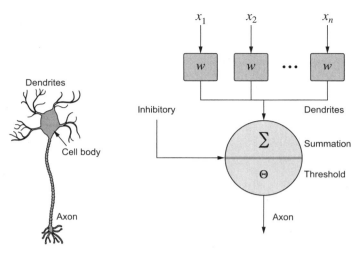

Figure 6.2   On the left, we provide a schematic of a human biological neuron. To the right, we show a human-inspired neural network implemented using weighted summation, an inhibitory input, and a threshold.

next neuron. In this scenario, learning is encoded by the neuron itself. Neurons send messages down their axon only if their overall excitation is large enough.

Figure 6.2 shows the schematic of a human biological neuron and an artificial neuron developed by McCulloch and Pitts, the so-called *MCP model*.[7] The artificial neuron is built using a simple summation and threshold value and works as follows. Logic inputs, positive only, are received from the dendrite equivalents, and a weighted summation is performed. If this output exceeds a certain threshold and no inhibitory input is observed, a positive value is emitted. If an inhibitory input is observed, the output is inhibited. This output may then be fed onward to the input of other such neurons through their dendrites' equivalent inputs. A little thought will reveal that this is—ignoring the inhibitory input—a linear model in n-dimensional space, with linked coefficients, where n is the number of inputs to the neuron. Note that in this case, we assume that all dendrite inputs are from different sources; but in theory, the same source can be attached multiple times if we wish for it to be considered more important. This is equivalent to increasing the weight of that input.

Figure 6.3 illustrates the behavior of this model for $n=1$. In this illustration, we use a simple hand-built neuron with a unit weight ($w=1$). The input to the neuron is allowed to vary from –10 to 10, and the summation of the weighted input values is provided on the y-axis. Choosing a threshold of 0, the neuron will fire if the input is greater than 0 but not otherwise.

---

[7]   Warren S. McCulloch and Walter H. Pitts, "A Logical Calculus of the Ideas Immanent in Nervous Activity," *Bulletin of Mathematical Biophysics* 5 (1943): 115–33.

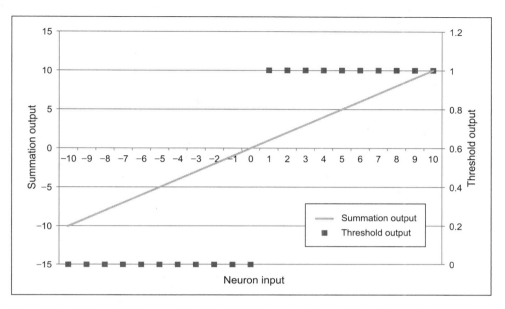

Figure 6.3   MCP as a 2-D linear model without inhibitory input. The weights of the model correspond to the coefficients of a linear model. In this case, our neuron supports only a single input, and the weight has been set to 1 for illustration. Given a threshold of 0, all inputs with a value less than or equal to 0 would inhibit the neuron from firing, whereas all inputs with a value greater than 0 would cause the neuron to fire.

6.3   *The perceptron*

In the previous section, we introduced the MCP neuron. With this basic approach, it turns out that it's possible to learn and to generalize training data, but in a very limited fashion. But we can do better, and thus the perceptron was born. The perceptron builds on the MCP model in three important ways:[8, 9]

- A *threshold bias* was added as an input to the summation. This serves several equivalent purposes. First, it allows bias to be captured from the input neurons. Second, it means output thresholds can be standardized around a single value, such as zero, without loss of generality.

- The perceptron allows input weights to be independent and negative. This has two important effects. First, a neuron doesn't need to be connected to an input multiple times to have a greater impact. Second, any dendrite input can be considered inhibitory (although not completely so) if it has a negative weight.

- The development of the perceptron heralded the development of an algorithm to learn the best weights given a set of input and output data.

---

[8] Frank Rosenblatt, *The Perceptron—A Perceiving and Recognizing Automaton* (Cornell Aeronautical Laboratory, 1957).

[9] Rosenblatt, "The Perceptron: A Probabilistic Model for Information Storage and Organization in the Brain," *Psychological Review* 65, no. 6 (November 1958): 386–408.

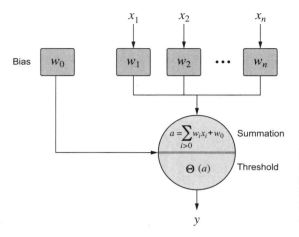

Figure 6.4   The perceptron. Inputs x_1 through x_n are received and multiplied by their associated weight, with perceptron bias, w_0, being added in afterward. This output, given by a, is then passed through a threshold function to obtain the output.

Figure 6.4 provides a graphical overview of this new extended model. As before, an intermediate value is created using the weighted summation of the inputs, but we now notice the inclusion of a bias value, w_0. This is learned along with the input weights during the training step; more about this in the following sections. The intermediate value, denoted by a here, is then passed through a threshold function to obtain the final result, y.

6.3.1   Training

Now that you know that a neural network consists of many more basic elements called perceptrons, let's look at how to train a perceptron in isolation. What does it mean to *train* a perceptron? Let's take a more concrete example using the logical AND function. We'll consider a perceptron of two binary inputs with a binary threshold activation function around 0. How do we learn the weights, such that the output of the perceptron is 1, if and only if the two inputs are both equal to 1? Put another way, can we choose continuous valued weights such that the weighted sum of the inputs is greater than 0 when the two inputs are both 1, with the output being less than 0 otherwise? Let's formalize this problem. We give $\mathbf{x}$ as our vector of binary input values and $\mathbf{w}$ as our vector of continuous input weights:

$$\mathbf{x} = (x_1, x_2), \quad \mathbf{w} = (w_1, w_2)$$

Thus, we need to learn weights such that the following restrictions hold true for combinations of binary inputs x_1, x_2:

$$\mathbf{x} \cdot \mathbf{w} = \begin{cases} > 0, & \text{if } x_1 = x_2 = 1 \\ \leq 0, & \text{otherwise} \end{cases}$$

Unfortunately for us, there are no solutions if we pose the problem like this! There are two options to make this problem tractable. Either we allow the threshold to move, defining it as a value not equal to 0, or we introduce an offset; both are equivalent. We'll opt for the latter in this text, providing these new vectors:

$$\mathbf{x} = (1, x_1, x_2), \quad \mathbf{w} = (w_0, w_1, w_2)$$

Our existing equalities remain the same. You can now see that with careful weight selection, we can create the AND function. Consider the case where $w_1 = 1$, $w_2 = 1$, and $w_0 = -1.5$. Table 6.1 provides the output from our perceptron and the output from the AND function.

Table 6.1 Comparing the output of our perceptron with the output of the logical AND function, which returns 1 if both inputs are equal to 1. Results provided are for the case where $w_1 = 1$, $w_2 = 1$, and $w_0 = -1.5$.

x_1	x_2	w_0	Weighted sum	Sign of weighted sum	x_1 AND x_2
1	0	−1.5	−0.5	Negative	0
0	1	−1.5	−0.5	Negative	0
0	0	−1.5	−1.5	Negative	0
1	1	−1.5	0.5	Positive	1

Now that we understand that it's indeed possible to represent a logical AND using a perceptron, we must develop a systematic way to learn our weights in a supervised manner. Put another way, given a dataset consisting of inputs and outputs, related linearly in this case, how do we learn the weights of our perceptron? We can achieve this using the perceptron algorithm developed by Rosenblatt.[10, 11] The following listing presents the pseudo code used for learning.

Listing 6.1 The perceptron learning algorithm

```
Initialize w to contain random small numbers

For each item in training set:
    Calculate the current output of the perceptron for the item.
    For each weight, update, depending upon output correctness.
```

So far, so good. Looks easy, right? We start with some small random values for our weights and then iterate over our data points and update the weights depending on the correctness of our perceptron. In fact, we update the weights only if we get the output wrong; otherwise, we leave the weights alone. Furthermore, we update the weights such that they become more like their input vectors in magnitude but with the corresponding sign of the output value. Let's write this down more formally, as shown in the next listing.

---

[10] Rosenblatt, "The Perceptron: A Probabilistic Model for Information Storage and Organization in the Brain."
[11] Rosenblatt, *Principles of Neurodynamics; Perceptrons and the Theory of Brain Mechanisms* (Spartan Books, 1962).

Listing 6.2   The perceptron learning algorithm (2)

```
Initialize w to contain random small numbers
For each example j:
```
$$y_j(t) = \sum_k w_k(t) \cdot x_{j,\,k}$$ ← Calculates the output of the perceptron given the current weights (time t)

```
    For each feature weight k:
```
$$w_k(t+1) = w_k(t) + \eta(d_j - y_j(t)) \cdot x_{j,\,k}$$ ← Updates the features. Note this is often done as a vector operation rather than a for loop.

Features are updated only if the expected output d_j and the actual output differ. If they do, we move the weight in the sign of the correct answer but a magnitude given by the corresponding input and scaled by η. η represents the speed at which the weights are updated in the algorithm.

Provided the input data is linearly separable, such an algorithm is guaranteed to converge to a solution.[12]

6.3.2   *Training a perceptron in scikit-learn*

Previously, we presented the simplest form of a neural network, the perceptron; we also discussed how this algorithm is trained. Let's now move to scikit-learn and explore how we can train a perceptron using some data. The next listing provides the code to perform the necessary imports and create a NumPy array of data points.

Listing 6.3   Creating data for perceptron learning

```
import numpy as np
import matplotlib.pyplot as plt
import random
from sklearn.linear_model import perceptron

data = np.array([[0,1],[0,0],[1,0],[1,1]])
target = np.array([0,0,0,1])
```

Creates four data points in a NumPy array.

Specifies the classes of these data points. In this example, only data point x=1, y=1 has a target class of 1; other data points have been assigned a class of 0.

In listing 6.3, we perform the necessary imports for the single-perceptron example and create a very small dataset with only four data points. This dataset is contained within a NumPy array called `data`. Each data point is assigned to either the class 0 or the class 1, with these classes being stored within the `target` array. Figure 6.5 provides a graphical overview of this data.

In the figure, the only data point with a positive class (with a label of 1) is found at coordinate (1,1) and represented by a round dot. All other data points are associated with the negative class. The following listing provides the sample code to train our simple perceptron and to return the coefficients (w_1, w_2 relating to x_1 and x_2, respectively) along with the bias w_0.

---

[12] Brian Ripley, *Pattern Recognition and Neural Networks* (Cambridge University Press, 1996).

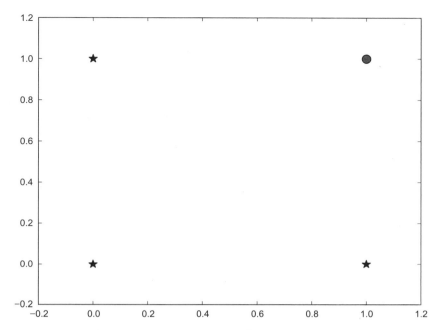

Figure 6.5 Graphical overview of the data for a single perceptron. Data with class label 1 is represented by a round dot, whereas data with class label 0 is represented by a star. It's the aim of the perceptron to separate these points.

Listing 6.4 Training a single perceptron

Creates a single perceptron. n_iter specifies the number of times the training data should be iterated through when training.

```
p = perceptron.Perceptron(n_iter=100)
p_out = p.fit(data,target)
print p_out
msg = ("Coefficients: %s, Intercept: %s")
print msg % (str(p.coef_),str(p.intercept_))
```

Trains the perceptron using the data and the associated target classes

Prints out the coefficients and the bias of the perceptron

The output is similar to the following:

```
Perceptron(alpha=0.0001, class_weight=None, eta0=1.0, fit_intercept=True,
    n_iter=100, n_jobs=1, penalty=None, random_state=0, shuffle=False,
    verbose=0, warm_start=False)
Coefficients: [[ 3.  2.]] ,Intercept: [-4.]
```

The first line provides the parameters under which the perceptron was trained; the second provides the output weights and bias of the perceptron. Don't worry if the coefficients and the intercept are slightly different when you run this. There are many solutions to this problem, and the learning algorithm can return any of them. For a greater understanding of the parameters, I encourage you to read the associated scikit-learn documentation.[13]

6.3.3   *A geometric interpretation of the perceptron for two inputs*

In our example, we've successfully trained a single perceptron and returned the weights and bias of the final perceptron. Great! But how do we interpret these weights in an intuitive way? Luckily, this is easily possible in 2-D space, and we can extend this intuition into higher-dimensional spaces also.

Let's consider the perceptron for two input values only. From figure 6.4 we have

$$y = w_0 + w_1 x_1 + w_2 x_2$$

This should look familiar to you as the equation of a plane (three dimensions) in x_1, x_2, and y. If they're not equivalent, this plane intersects with the viewing plane of figure 6.5, and you're left with a line. When viewed from the point of reference of figure 6.5, points to one side of the line correspond to values of $\mathbf{x} \cdot \mathbf{w} > 0$, whereas points on the other side of the line correspond to values of $\mathbf{x} \cdot \mathbf{w} < 0$. Points on the line correspond to $\mathbf{x} \cdot \mathbf{w} = 0$. Let's take the concrete example from earlier and visualize this. Using the coefficients just learned, we have the equation of a plane given by

$$y = -4 + 3x_1 + 2x_2$$

The value of y is at 90 degrees to the (x_1, x_2) plane and thus can be thought of as along a line following the eyes of the viewer, straight through the viewing plane. The value of y on the viewing plane is given by 0, so we can find the line of intersection by substituting the value of $y = 0$ in the previous equation:

$$0 = -4 + 3x_1 + 2x_2$$

$$4 - 3x_1 = 2x_2$$

$$x_2 = \frac{4}{2} - \frac{3}{2} x_1$$

This last line follows the standard form of a straight line; now all we need to do is plot this to see how the perceptron has separated our training data. The next listing provides the associated code, and figure 6.6 shows the output.

Listing 6.5   Plotting the output of the perceptron

```
colors = np.array(['k','r'])
markers = np.array(['*','o'])

for data,target in zip(data,target):
plt.scatter(data[0],data[1],s=100,
    c=colors[target],marker=markers[target])
```

Sets up a color array, and plots the data points: black star for class zero, red dot for class 1

---

[13] scikit-learn, "Perceptron," http://mng.bz/U20J.

```
grad = -p.coef_[0][0]/p.coef_[0][1]
intercept = -p.intercept_/p.coef_[0][1]

x_vals = np.linspace(0,1)
y_vals = grad*x_vals + intercept
plt.plot(x_vals,y_vals)
plt.show()
```

Calculates the parameters of the straight line (intersection of two planes)

Creates the data points, and plots the line of intersection between the two planes

We plot our four data points along with the projection of the separating plane learned by the perceptron onto the viewing plane. This provides us with a separation as per figure 6.6. In general, for a larger number of input variables, you can think of these as existing in n dimensional space, with the perceptron separating these using a hyperplane in $n + 1$ dimensions. You should now be able to see that the basic linear form of the perceptron—that is, with a threshold activation—is equivalent to separation using a hyperplane. Consequently, such models are of use only where data is linearly separable and will be unable to separate positive and negative classes otherwise.

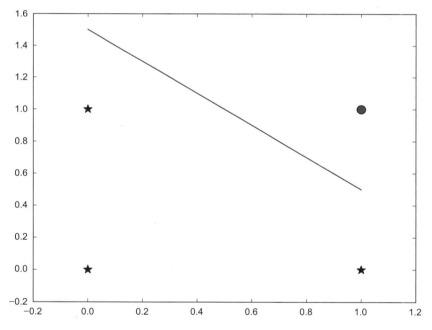

Figure 6.6 **The projection of our separating plane onto the viewing plane ($y = 0$). All points to the top right of the figure satisfy the constraint w · x > 0, whereas points to the bottom left of the line satisfy the constraint w · x < 0.**

6.4   *Multilayer perceptrons*

In the previous sections, we looked at deep learning from a very high level, and you started to understand the basics of neural networks: specifically, a single unit of a neural network known as a perceptron. We also showed that the basic form of the perceptron is equivalent to a linear model.

In order to perform nonlinear separation, we can keep the simple threshold activation function and increase the complexity of the network architecture to create so-called *multilayer feed-forward networks*. These are networks where perceptrons are organized in layers, with the input of a layer being provided by a previous layer and the output of this layer acting as an input to the next. *Feed-forward* comes from the fact that data flows only from the inputs to the outputs of the network and not in the opposite direction—that is, no cycles. Figure 6.7 provides a graphical summary of this concept, extending the notation used in figure 6.3.

In the spirit of demonstrating nonlinearity, let's consider a very small example that would fail if we presented it to a perceptron: the XOR function. This example is taken from Minsky and Papert's 1969 book, *Perceptrons: An Introduction to Computational Geometry.*[14] We'll then consider how a two-layer perceptron can be used to approximate this function and discuss the back-propagation algorithm used to train such a network. Observe the XOR function as shown in table 6.2.

x_1	x_2	Output
0	0	0
0	1	1
1	0	1
1	1	0

Table 6.2   Input and output values for the XOR function. It outputs a 1 if either x_1 or x_2 is set to 1 but a 0 of they're both set to 1 (or both to set to 0).

If we consider the XOR function graphically, using the same conventions as in figure 6.5, we obtain figure 6.8. As you can see, the output from the XOR function isn't linearly separable in two-dimensional space; there exists no single hyperplane that can separate positive and negative classes perfectly. Try to draw a line anywhere on this graph with all positive classes on one side of the line and all negative classes on the opposite side of the line, and you'll fail! We could, however, separate these data points if we had

---

[14] Marvin Minsky and Seymour Papert, *Perceptrons: An Introduction to Computational Geometry* (MIT Press, 1969). A book with an interesting and controversial history, often credited with stymying the progress of multilayer perceptrons for many years. This was due to Minsky and Papert's suspicions that multilayer perceptrons lacked any computational potential above a low-order perceptron (and, by implication, because low-order perceptrons can't represent certain classes of functions, such as XORs, then neither could multilayer perceptrons). This may have caused researchers to abandon them for many years. This controversy is addressed in later editions of the book.

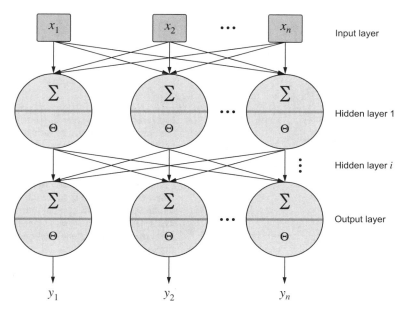

Figure 6.7   A multilayer perceptron. Read from top to bottom, it consists of an input layer (vector of values x), a number of hidden layers, and an output layer that returns the vector y.

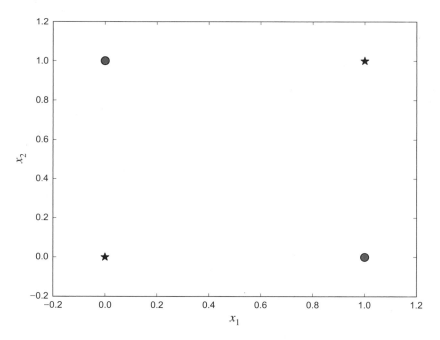

Figure 6.8   Graphical representation of the XOR function. Positive classes are specified with circles, whereas negative classes are specified with stars. No single hyperplane can separate these data points into two sets, so we say that the dataset isn't linearly separable.

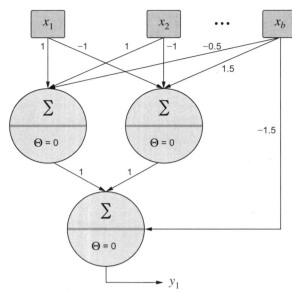

Figure 6.9   **A two-layer perceptron can separate a nonlinearly separable function (XOR). Values on the connections demonstrate the weight of those connections. The introduction of the bias term ensures correct operation with an activation threshold of 0. Conceptually, the two hidden neurons correspond to two hyperplanes. The final combining perceptron is equivalent to a logical AND on the output of the two hidden neurons. This can be thought of as picking out the areas of the (x_1, x_2) plane for which the two hidden neurons activate together.**

more than one hyperplane and a way to combine them. So let's do that! This is equivalent to creating a network with a single hidden layer and a final, combined-output layer. Consider figure 6.9, which shows such a network graphically.

What you see here is a two-layer hidden network with two inputs and a single output. Connected to each hidden node and the output node is a bias term. Remember from earlier that the bias itself will always equal 1; only the weights will change. This allows both the activation profiles and the offsets of the nodes to be learned during training. Spend a little time convincing yourself that this does indeed work.

Each hidden node creates a single hyperplane, as with our single-perceptron case from figure 6.6, and these are brought together with a final perceptron. This final perceptron is an AND gate when two conditions are observed. The first is that the input in x_1, x_2 space is above the bottom line shown in figure 6.10. The second is that the input is below the top line, also shown in figure 6.10. As such, this two-layer perceptron carves out the diagonal across the space that includes both positive examples from the training data but none of the negative examples. It has successfully separated a nonlinearly separable dataset.

In this section, we investigated the application of neural networks to nonlinearly separable datasets. Using the XOR function as an example, we showed that it's possible to create a neural network by hand that separates a nonlinearly separable set and provide intuition as to how this works geometrically. We're missing an important step, however! It's important to be able to automatically learn the weights for a network given a training dataset. These weights can then be used to classify and predict data beyond the original inputs. This is in the subject of the next section.

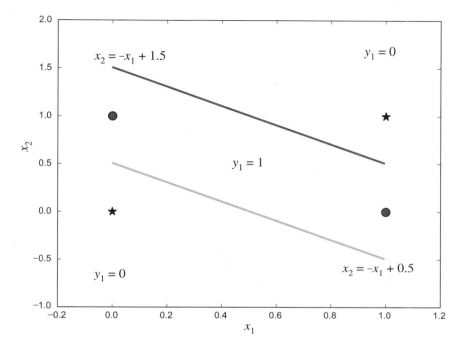

Figure 6.10 Separating a nonlinearly separable dataset using the neural network given in figure 6.9. You should notice that the neuron to the left of figure 6.9 when intersecting with the viewing plane creates the bottom line, whereas the rightmost neuron creates the top line. The leftmost neuron fires an output 1 only when the input is above the bottom line, whereas the rightmost neuron fires an output 1 only when the input is below the top line. The final combining neuron fires $y_1=1$ only when both of these constraints are satisfied. Thus, the network outputs 1 only when the data points are in the narrow corridor between the bottom and top lines.

6.4.1 Training using backpropagation

In the previous examples, we used the step function as our neuron-activation function—that is, a single threshold value over which the neuron is able to fire. Unfortunately, coming up with an automated method to train such a network is difficult. This is because the step function doesn't allow us to encode uncertainly in any form—the thresholds are hard.

It would be more appropriate if we could use a function that approximates the step function but is more gradual. In this way, a small change to one of the weights within the network would make a small change to the operation of the entire network. This is indeed what we'll do. Instead of using the step function, we'll now replace this with a more general activation function. In the next section, we'll briefly introduce common activation functions before explaining how the choice of activation function will help us derive a training algorithm.

6.4.2   Activation functions

Let's take a few moments to look at some possible activation functions for our perceptron. We've already seen the simplest case—a hard threshold around 0. With an offset of zero, this yields the output profile as given by figure 6.3. But what else could we do? Figure 6.11 shows the activation profiles of several other functions. Their definitions follow:

- *Square root*—Defined as $y = \sqrt{x}$, domain [0,inf], range [0,inf].
- *Logistic*—Defined as $1/(1 + e^{-x})$, domain defined for [–inf ,inf], range [0,1].
- *Negative exponential*—Given by e^{-x}, domain [-inf,inf] range [0,inf].
- *Hyperbolic (tanh)*—Defined as $(e^x - e^{-x})/(e^x + e^{-x})$. Note that this is equivalent to logistic with its output transformed to a different range, domain [-inf,inf] range [-1,1].

In general, the use of such activation functions enables us to create and train multilayer neural networks that approximate a much larger class of functions. The most important property of the activation function is that it's differentiable. You'll see why in the following section. For the remainder of this chapter, we'll use the logistic function that you first encountered in chapter 4. Its domain and range are appropriate, and it has been frequently adopted for this purpose in the literature.

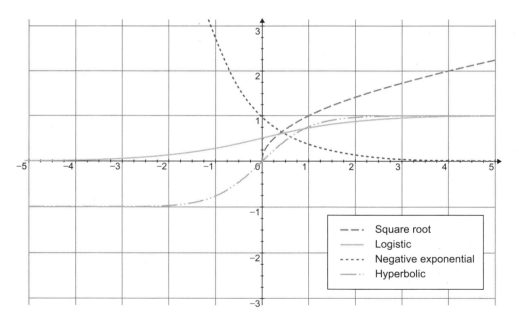

Figure 6.11   Output profiles for several activation functions over the same range as provided in figure 6.3. Activation profiles demonstrated are square root, logistic, negative exponential, and hyperbolic.

Logistic regression, the perceptron, and the generalized linear model

Think back to chapter 4, where we introduced the concept of logistic regression. There we identified that a linear response model would be unsuitable for probability estimation and instead modified the logistic response to curve to create a more appropriate response. From this starting point, we derived that the log-odds are linear in the combination of weights and input variables and applied this to a classification problem.

In this chapter, we started from a basic biological concept and built a computational formalism that captures this. We haven't discussed probability at all but started from a standpoint of activation within a neuron. Intuitively, we've extended this into a more general concept and reached the same equation:

$$y = \frac{1}{1 + e^{-(w_0 + w_1 x_1 + \ldots + w_n x_n)}}$$

In fact, what we've encountered here is a more general class of problem known as *generalized linear models* (GLM).[a] In this class of models, a linear model $(w_0 + w_1 x_1 + \ldots + w_n x_n)$ is related to the output variable, y, by a link function, which in this case is the logistic function $1/(1 + e^{-x})$.

This equivalence of algorithms and concepts is common in machine learning, and you've seen it already in this book. Just think back to section 2.5, where we discussed the equivalence of expectation maximization (EM) with a Gaussian mixture model with tied and coupled covariance, and the vanilla k-means algorithm. The usual reason for this is that multiple researchers have started from different points within the research and discovered equivalence through the extension of basic building blocks.

a. Peter McCullagh and John A. Nelder, *Generalized Linear Models* (Chapman and Hall/CRC, 1989).

6.4.3 *Intuition behind backpropagation*

To provide the intuition behind backpropagation, we're going to work with the same example as previously, the XOR function, but we'll try to learn the weights rather than specify them by hand. Note also that from now on, the activation function will be assumed to be sigmoid (logistic). Figure 6.12 shows the graphical overview of our new network.

Our job is to learn $w(a,b) \ \forall a,b$ using a specified training dataset. More specifically, can we come up with an algorithm that minimizes the error (squared difference between the expected and actual values of y_1) over that dataset, when that dataset's inputs are applied to the network?

One way to do this is through an algorithm known as *backpropagation*. This algorithm operates broadly as follows. First, we initialize all the weights to random values, and then we pass a single training data item throughout the network. We calculate the

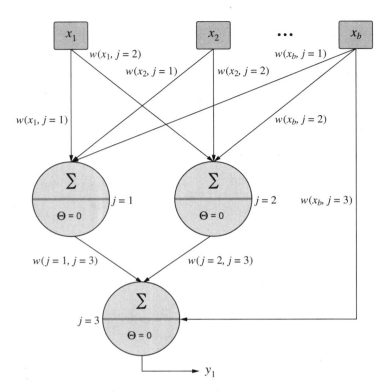

Figure 6.12   Overview of the backpropagation example. Given a set of inputs x_1, x_2 and target variable y_1 that follow the XOR function over x_1 and x_2, can we learn the values of w that minimize the squared difference between the training values and the network output? In this example, we use the logistic activation function: $\theta = 1/(1 + e^{-(w_0 + \sum_j w_j x_j)})$.

error at the output and *backpropagate* this error through the network—hence the name! Each weight in the network is changed in a direction that corresponds to that which minimizes the error of network. This continues until a termination condition is met: for example, a number of iterations are hit or the network has converged.

6.4.4   *Backpropagation theory*

To ease understanding, the update rule for backpropagation can be considered in two parts: updating the weights leading to output neurons and updating the weights leading to hidden neurons. Both are logically identical, but the mathematics for the latter is a little trickier. Because of this, we'll discuss only the former here to give you a taste of backpropagation. See the seminal *Nature* paper[15] if you want to understand the full form.

---

[15] David E. Rumelhart, Geoffrey E. Hinton, and Ronald J. Williams, "Learning Representations by Back-Propagating Errors," *Nature* 323 (October 1986): 533–36.

The first thing to note about training is that we're interested in how the error at the output changes with respect to the change in a single weight value. Only through this value can we move the weight in a direction that minimizes the output error. Let's start by working out the *partial* derivative of the error with respect to a particular input weight in the layer below. That is, we assume that all other weights remain constant. To do this, we'll use the chain rule:

$$\frac{\delta E}{\delta w(i, j)} =$$ **Rate of change of error given change in weight**

$$\frac{\delta E}{\delta o(j)} \times$$ ❶ **Error given the output of the activation function**

$$\frac{\delta o(j)}{\delta n(j)} \times$$ ❷ **Output of the activation function given the weighted sum of its inputs**

$$\frac{\delta n(j)}{\delta w(i, j)}$$ ❸ **Weighted sum of its inputs and an individual weight**

In plain terms, the rate of change of output error is linked to the weight through the rate of change of ❶, ❷, and ❸.

If you remember from earlier, the logistic activation function is used because it makes training tractable. The main reason for this is that the function is differentiable. You should now understand why this is a requirement. Term ❷ of the equation is equivalent to the derivative of the activation function. This can be written as follows:

$$\frac{\delta o(j)}{\delta n(j)} = \frac{\delta}{\delta n(j)} \theta(n(j)) = \theta(n(j))(1 - \theta(n_j))$$

That is, the rate of change of output of our activation function can be written in terms of the activation function itself! If we can compute ❶ and ❸, we'll know the direction in which to move any particular weight to minimize the error in the output. It turns out that this is indeed possible. Term ❸ can be differentiated directly as

$$\frac{\delta n(j)}{\delta w(i, j)} = x_i$$

That is, the rate of change of the input to the activation function with respect to a particular weight linking i and j is given only by the value of x_i. Because we looked only at the output layer, determining the differential of the error given the output ❶ is easy if we can just draw on the concept of error directly:

$$\frac{\delta E}{\delta o(j)} = \frac{\delta}{\delta o(j)} (o_{expected} - o(j))^2 = 2(o(j) - o_{expected})$$

We can now express a complete weight-update rule for a weight leading to an output node:

$$-\alpha x_i 2(o(j) - o_{expected})\theta n(j)(1 - \theta(n_j))$$

Thus, we update the weight depending on the entering value corresponding to that weight, the difference in the output and the expected value, and output of the derivative of the activation function given all input and weights. Note that we add a negative sign and an alpha term. The former ensures that we move in the direction of negative error, and the latter specifies how fast we move in that direction.

This should give you a feeling for how the weights are updated feeding into the output layer, and the inner layer update functions follow much the same logic. But we must use the chain rule to find out the contribution of the output value at that inner node to the overall error of the network: that is, we must know the rate of change of inputs/outputs on the path leading from the node in question to an output node. Only then can the rate of change of output error be assessed for a delta change in the weight of an inner node. This gives rise to the full form of backpropagation.[16]

6.4.5   *MLNN in scikit-learn*

Given that you now understand the multilayer perceptron and the theory behind training using backpropagation, let's return to Python to code up an example. Because there's no implementation of MLPs in scikit-learn, we're going to use PyBrain.[17] PyBrain focuses specifically on building and training neural networks. The following listing provides you with the first snippet of code required to build a neural network equivalent to the one presented in figure 6.12. Please refer to the full code that is available at this book's website for the associated imports required to run this code.

> **Listing 6.6   Building a multilayer perceptron using PyBrain**

```
#Create network modules
net = FeedForwardNetwork()
inl = LinearLayer(2)
hidl = SigmoidLayer(2)
outl = LinearLayer(1)
b = BiasUnit()
```

We first create a `FeedForwardNetwork` object. We also create an input layer (`inl`), an output layer (`outl`), and a hidden layer (`hidl`) of neurons. Note that the input and output layers use the vanilla activation function (threshold at 0), whereas the hidden layer uses the sigmoid activation function for reasons of training, as we discussed earlier. Finally, we create a bias unit. We don't quite have a neural network yet, because we haven't connected the layers. That's what we do in the next listing.

---

[16] Rumelhart et al., "Learning Representations by Back-Propagating Errors," 533–36.
[17] Tom Schaul et al., "PyBrain," *Journal of Machine Learning Research* 11 (2010): 743–46.

Listing 6.7   Building a multilayer perceptron using PyBrain (2)

```
#Create connections
in_to_h = FullConnection(inl, hidl)
h_to_out = FullConnection(hidl, outl)
bias_to_h = FullConnection(b,hidl)
bias_to_out = FullConnection(b,outl)

#Add modules to net
net.addInputModule(inl)
net.addModule(hidl);
net.addModule(b)
net.addOutputModule(outl)

#Add connections to net and sort
net.addConnection(in_to_h)
net.addConnection(h_to_out)
net.addConnection(bias_to_h)
net.addConnection(bias_to_out)
net.sortModules()
```

We now create connection objects and add the previously created neurons (modules) and their connections to the `FeedForwardNetwork` object. Calling `sortModules()` completes the instantiation of the network.

Before continuing, let's take a moment to delve into the `FullConnection` object. Here we create four instances of the object to pass to the network object. The signature of these constructors takes two layers, and internally the object creates a connection between every neuron in the layer of the first parameters and every neuron in the layer of the second. The final method sorts the modules within the `FeedForward-Network` object and performs some internal initialization.

Now that we have a neural network equivalent to figure 6.12, we need to learn its weights! To do this, we need some data. The next listing provides the code to do this, and much of it is reproduced from the PyBrain documentation.[18]

Listing 6.8   Training our neural network

```
d = [(0,0),                      ◁──── Creates a dataset and
     (0,1),                            associated targets that
     (1,0),                            reflect the XOR function
     (1,1)]

#target class                                        Creates an empty
c = [0,1,1,0]                                         PyBrain
                                                     SupervisedDataSet
data_set = SupervisedDataSet(2, 1) # 2 inputs, 1 output  ◁──┘

random.seed()                                ◁──── Randomly samples the four
for i in xrange(1000):                             data points 1,000 times and
    r = random.randint(0,3)                        adds to the training set
    data_set.addSample(d[r],c[r])
```

---

[18] PyBrain Quickstart, http://pybrain.org/docs/index.html#quickstart.

```
backprop_trainer = \
BackpropTrainer(net, data_set,
        learningrate=0.1)

for i in xrange(50):
    err = backprop_trainer.train()
    print "Iter. %d, err.: %.5f" % (i, err)
```

Creates a new backpropagation trainer object with the network, dataset, and learning rate

Performs backpropagation 50 times using the same 1,000 data points. Prints the error after every iteration.

As you now know from section 6.4.4, backpropagation traverses the weight space in order to reach a minima in the error between the output terms and the expected output. Every call to `train()` causes the weights to be updated so that the neural network better represents the function generating the data. This means we're probably going to need a reasonable amount of data (for our XOR example, four data points isn't going to cut it!) for each call to `train()`. To address this problem, we'll generate many data points drawn from the XOR distribution and use these to train our network using backpropagation. As you'll see, subsequent calls to `train()` successfully decrease the error between the network output and the specified target. The exact number of iterations required to find the global minima will depend on many factors, one of which is the learning rate. This controls how quickly the weights are updated at each training interval. Smaller rates will take longer to converge—that is, find the global minima—or they may get stuck in local optima if your optimization surface is non-convex. Larger rates may be quicker, but they also risk overshooting the global minima. Let's take a quick look at the output generated by listing 6.8 and use it to illustrate this concept:

```
Iteration 0, error: 0.1824
Iteration 1, error: 0.1399
Iteration 2, error: 0.1384
Iteration 3, error: 0.1406
Iteration 4, error: 0.1264
Iteration 5, error: 0.1333
Iteration 6, error: 0.1398
Iteration 7, error: 0.1374
Iteration 8, error: 0.1317
Iteration 9, error: 0.1332
...
```

As you see, successive calls reduce the error of the network. We know that at least one solution does exist, but backpropagation isn't guaranteed to find this. Under certain circumstances, the error will decrease and won't be able to improve any further. This can occur if your learning rate is too low and the error surface is non-convex (that is, has local minima). Alternatively, if the learning rate is too large, it may bounce around the global solution—or even outside this region of the error space and into a local minima, or it may bounce between suboptimal (or local) solutions. In both of these cases, the result is the same: the global minima is not found.

Because this outcome depends on the starting values of the weights, we're not able to say if your example will converge quickly, so try running this a few times. Also try experimenting with the learning rate from listing 6.8. How big can you make the rate before the algorithm gets caught in local solutions most of the time? In practice, the choice of training rate is always a trade-off between finding suboptimal solutions and speed, so you want to choose the largest rate that gives you the correct answer. Experiment with this until you're left with a network that has converged with an error of zero.

6.4.6 A learned MLP

In the previous example, we created an MLP using the PyBrain package and trained a multilayer perceptron to mimic the XOR function. Provided your error in the previous output reached zero, you should be able to follow this section with your own model! First, let's interrogate our model to obtain the weights of the network, corresponding to figure 6.12. The following code shows you how.

Listing 6.9 Obtaining the weights of your trained neural network

```
#print net.params
print "[w(x_1,j=1),w(x_2,j=1),w(x_1,j=2),w(x_2,j=2)]: " + str(in_to_h.params)
print "[w(j=1,j=3),w(j=2,j=3)]: "+str(h_to_out.params)
print "[w(x_b,j=1),w(x_b,j=2)]: "+str(bias_to_h.params)
print "[w(x_b,j=3)]:" +str(bias_to_out.params)

> [w(x_1,j=1),w(x_2,j=1),w(x_1,j=2),w(x_2,j=2)]: [-2.32590226  2.25416963 -
     2.74926055  2.64570441]
> [w(j=1,j=3),w(j=2,j=3)]: [-2.57370943  2.66864851]
> [w(x_b,j=1),w(x_b,j=2)]: [ 1.29021983 -1.82249033]
> [w(x_b,j=3)]:[ 1.6469595]
```

The output resulting from executing listing 6.9 provides our trained output for a neuron. Your results may vary, however. The important thing is that the behavior of the network is correct. You can check this by activating the network with input and checking that the output is as expected. Look at the next listing.

Listing 6.10 Activating your neural network

```
print "Activating 0,0. Output: " + str(net.activate([0,0]))
print "Activating 0,1. Output: " + str(net.activate([0,1]))
print "Activating 1,0. Output: " + str(net.activate([1,0]))
print "Activating 1,1. Output: " + str(net.activate([1,1]))

> Activating 0,0. Output: [ -1.33226763e-15]
> Activating 0,1. Output: [ 1.]
> Activating 1,0. Output: [ 1.]
> Activating 1,1. Output: [  1.55431223e-15]
```

You can see that the output of our trained network is very close to 1 for those patterns that should result in a positive value. Conversely, the output is very close to 0 for those patterns that should result in a negative output. In general, positive testing samples should have outputs greater than 0.5, and negative testing samples should provide outputs less than 0.5. In order to ensure that you fully understand this network, try modifying the input values and tracing them through the network in the supporting content spreadsheet available with this book's resources.

6.5 *Going deeper: from multilayer neural networks to deep learning*

In many areas of research, progress is made in fits and starts. Areas can go stale for a period and then experience a rapid rush, usually sparked by a particular advance or discovery. This pattern is no different in the field of neural networks, and we're lucky to be right in middle of some really exciting advances, most of which have been grouped under the umbrella of deep learning. I'd like to share a few of these with you now before delving into the simplest example of a deep network that we can. Why did neural networks become hot again? Well, it's a bit of a perfect storm.

First, there's more data available than ever before. The big internet giants have access to a huge repository of image data that can be used to do interesting things. One example you may have heard of is Google's 2012 paper that trained a nine-layer network with 10 million images downloaded from the internet[19] to recognize intermediate representations without labeling, the most publicized being a cat face! This lends some weight to the hypothesis that more data beats a cleverer algorithm.[20] Such an achievement wouldn't have been possible only a few years before.

The second advance is a leap in theoretical knowledge. It wasn't until recent advances by Geoffrey Hinton and collaborators that the community understood that deep networks could be trained effectively by treating each layer as a Restricted Boltzmann Machine (RBM).[21, 22] Indeed, many deep learning networks are now constructed by stacking RBMs—more on these in a moment. Yann Le Cun, Yoshua Bengio, and others have made many further theoretical advances in this field, and I refer you to a review of their work to gain better insight.[23]

6.5.1 *Restricted Boltzmann Machines*

In this section, we're going to look at Restricted Boltzmann Machines (RBM). More specifically, we'll look at a specific flavor of RBM called Bernoulli RBM (BRBM). We'll get to why these are a special case of the RBM in a moment. In general, RBMs are mentioned in the context of deep learning because they're good feature learners. Because of this, they can be used in a deeper network to learn feature representations, with their output used as input to the other RBMs or a multilayer perceptron (MLP). Think back to section 6.1 and our example of car recommendation. So far, we've spent quite some time covering MLPs in general; we must now uncover the automatic feature-extraction aspect of deep learning!

---

[19] Quoc V. Le, et al., "Building High-Level Features Using Large Scale Unsupervised Learning," ICML 2012: 29th International Conference on Machine Learning (ICML, 2012): 1.

[20] Pedro Domingos, "A Few Useful Things to Know about Machine Learning," *Communications of the ACM* (October 1, 2012): 78–87.

[21] Miguel A. Carreira-Perpiñán and Geoffrey Hinton, "On Contrastive Divergence Learning," Society for Artificial Intelligence and Statistics (2005): 33–40.

[22] G. E. Hinton and R. R. Salakhutdinov, "Reducing the Dimensionality of Data with Neural Networks," *Science* (July 28, 2006): 504–507.

[23] Yann LeCun, Yoshua Bengio, and Geoffrey Hinton, "Deep Learning," *Nature* 521 (May 2015): 436–44.

To do this, we're also going to use an example from the scikit-learn documentation.[24] This example uses a BRBM to extract features from the scikit-learn digits dataset and then uses logistic regression to classify the data items with the learned features. After working through this example, we'll touch on how you might go about making deeper networks and delving further into the burgeoning area of deep learning. Before we get started, let's make sure you understand the basics—what is a BRBM?

6.5.2 *The Bernoulli Restricted Boltzmann Machine*

In general, a RBM is a bipartite graph where nodes within each partition are fully connected to nodes within the other partition. The restricted aspect comes from the fact that the visible nodes may only be connected to hidden nodes and vice versa. The Bernoulli RBM restricts each node further to be binary. Figure 6.13 shows a graphical overview of a RBM.

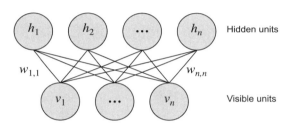

Figure 6.13 Graphical overview of a Restricted Boltzmann Machine. A RBM is a bipartite graph between hidden and visible units, with each element of each partition fully connected to other units in the opposing partition. We'll use h to refer to the vector composed of the hidden units and v to refer to the vector composed of the visible units. Note that each node may have an associated bias weight; these aren't represented here for simplicity.

That's all very well, but what is it useful for? The clue is in the naming convention. Visible nodes are something that can be observed, perhaps something you train on. Hidden nodes are something latent, with unknown or obscured meaning. Cast your mind back to the use of latent variables in chapter 3, when we performed recommendations—this is similar in many ways.

Later you'll see a concrete example of RBMs for image recognition, but as we go through the theory, it may help to have a target application in mind. For this purpose, you can think (as in chapter 3) of hidden nodes as genres and visible ones as films a person likes. Or, if you prefer, visible nodes can be songs, or painters, or whatever you want. The essence is that the hidden node captures some implicit grouping of the data—in this case, we've used user preference or affinity to movies to illustrate the point. In general, the number of visible units is defined by the problem; for a binary classification problem, you may have two. For movie recommendations, it may be the number of movies in your dataset. By increasing the number of hidden values, you increase the ability of the RBM to model complex relationships, but this comes at the price of overfitting. Hinton[25] provides a recipe for choosing the number of hidden

[24] scikit-learn, "Restricted Boltzmann Machine Features for Digit Classification," http://mng.bz/3N42.

[25] Geoffrey Hinton, "A Practical Guide to Training Restricted Boltzmann Machines" in *Neural Networks: Tricks of the Trade*, ed. Grégoire Montavon, G. B. Orr, and K. R. Muller (University of Toronto, 2012): 599–619.

units dependent on the complexity of your data and the number of training samples. Similar to MLPs with a logistic activation function, the probability of a particular visible unit firing given the value of the hidden variables is

$$P(v_i = 1 \,|\, \mathbf{h}, \mathbf{W}) = \sigma\!\left(\sum_j w_{j,i}\, h_j + b_i \right)$$

where σ is the logistic function

$$\sigma(x) = \frac{1}{1 + e^{-x}}$$

and b_i is the bias associated with that visible node. In plain terms, the likelihood of the node firing is equal to the sum of the product of the weights and values of the hidden nodes (plus a bias) passed through the logistic function. The probabilities of the hidden values are given similarly,

$$P(h_j = 1 \,|\, \mathbf{v}, \mathbf{W}) = \sigma\!\left(\sum_i w_{j,i}\, v_i + c_j \right)$$

where c_j is the bias associated with the hidden node h_j. Consider this bias carefully. This contributes to the likelihood of the hidden or visible node firing before information from its connections is considered. In many ways, it can be considered a prior. In the case of a movie/genre recommendation RBM, a hidden-node bias would associate to the prior probability that any video belonged to a particular genre. A visible-node bias would associate to the prior probability that a given movie would be liked by any given person, regardless of their genre preferences.

For practical use, RBMs must be trained—that is, the weight matrix $\mathbf{W}$ must be learned from a number of training instances. These training instances take the form of vectors of visible-node state.

Let's perform a little thought experiment to try to understand how learning will proceed. If we stick with the mental model that hidden nodes represent genres and visible nodes represent movies, then we require the weight connecting a hidden node with a visible one to be larger when the two nodes agree. Conversely, when the hidden node and the visible node disagree, we wish for the weight to be smaller (possibly negative). To understand why this works, consider a RBM with a single hidden node. Let's say that the hidden node represents an "action" genre, and the movie is *Top Gun*. If we activate the hidden node, then the only way to improve the likelihood that the visible node will fire is to have a large weight joining the two nodes. Conversely, if we activate the *Top Gun* visible node, the only way to increase the likelihood that the relevant genre will fire is to also have a large weight between the two.

RBMs can be trained using energy-based learning.[26] Training proceeds by maximizing the agreeance between connected hidden and visible nodes. We use a metric

---

[26]   Yann LeCun et al., "Energy-Based Models in Document Recognition and Computer Vision," International Conference on Document Analysis and Recognition (2007).

known as *energy*. This value decreases where there is more agreement between the hidden nodes and the visible ones; thus, decreasing the energy, *E*, results in more acceptable configurations given the training data:

$$E(\mathbf{v}, \mathbf{h}, \mathbf{W}) = -\left(\sum_i \sum_j w_{i,j} v_i h_j + \sum_i b_i v_i + \sum_j c_j h_j \right)$$

Given this, the aim of training is to minimize the $E(\mathbf{v}; \mathbf{h}, \mathbf{W})$ for a number of training examples. Once trained, we can search the latent space for the most likely vector when a given visible vector is set or, conversely, the most likely visible vector for a particular latent space configuration. Returning to our movie/genre application, this would be equivalent to inferring genre interest given a list of movies, or recommending movies given a genre space, respectively.

This is performed by converting the resulting energy into a probability and searching the probability space for an answer. LeCun shows us that obtaining a probability can be performed using the Gibbs measure.[27] For example, the likelihood of a visible vector given learned weights and hidden vector is

$$P(\mathbf{v}|\mathbf{h}, \mathbf{W}) = \frac{e^{-E(\mathbf{v}, \mathbf{h}, \mathbf{W})}}{\sum_{v \in V} e^{-E(v, \mathbf{h}, \mathbf{W})}}$$

Conversely, the likelihood of a hidden vector given learned weights and a visible vector is

$$P(\mathbf{v}|\mathbf{h}, \mathbf{W}) = \frac{e^{-E(\mathbf{v}, \mathbf{h}, \mathbf{W})}}{\sum_{h \in H} e^{-E(\mathbf{v}, h, \mathbf{W})}}$$

Consider both of these carefully. The numerator provides a number that's larger for visible and hidden configurations that are in agreeance. The denominator normalizes this over all possible states to provide a number that's between 0 and 1: that is, a probability.

So far, so good, but we've yet to understand how we go about learning our weight matrix. Also, it looks like we've got a difficult job on our hands, because we don't know anything about the hidden nodes, only the visible nodes. Remember that our training set is only a list of the visible nodes. In many cases, RBMs are trained through a method called *contrastive divergence*, attributed to Hinton.[28] We won't cover the full algorithm here, because you can find it the aforementioned reference, but we'll provide you with a sketch.

[27] Yann LeCun et al., "A Tutorial on Energy-Based Learning," in *Predicting Structured Data*, ed. G. Bakir et al. (MIT Press, 2006).

[28] Geoffrey Hinton, "A Practical Guide to Training Restricted Boltzmann Machines," version 1, internal report, UTML TR 2010-003 (August 2, 2010).

Contrastive divergence is an approximate maximum-likelihood method that proceeds through a series of phases of sampling. This iterates through the training examples and performs backward (hidden state from visible states) and forward (visible states from hidden ones) sampling. Weights are initialized to a random state; and for each training vector (visible nodes), hidden nodes are activated with the probability specified previously and a degree of agreeance measured. Hidden nodes are then used to activate the visible nodes, and a further measure of agreeance is measured. These metrics of agreeance are combined, and the weights are moved in a direction such that the network, overall, has a lower energy. More details can be found in Hinton.

6.5.3   *RBMs in action*

In this section, we'll use a modified version of the logistic classification problem presented in the scikit-learn documentation.[29] Full credit must be given to Dauphin, Niculae, and Synnaeve for this illustrative example, and we won't stray far from their material here. As in previous examples, we'll omit the import block and concentrate on the code. The full listing can be found in the supporting content.

Listing 6.11   Creating your dataset

```
digits = datasets.load_digits()
X = np.asarray(digits.data, 'float32')
X, Y = nudge_dataset(X, digits.target)
X = (X - np.min(X, 0)) / (np.max(X, 0) + 0.0001)  # 0-1 scaling
X_train, X_test, Y_train, Y_test = train_test_split(X,
    Y,test_size=0.2,random_state=0)
```

The first thing we do is to load in the dataset, but we actually do more than this. From the original dataset, we generate further artificial samples by nudging the dataset with linear shifts of one pixel, normalizing each so that each pixel value is between 0 and 1. So, for every labeled image, a further four images are generated—shifted up, down, right, and left, respectively—each with the same label: that is, which number the image represents. This allows training to learn better representations of the data using such a small dataset, specifically representations that are less dependent on the character being centralized within the image. This is achieved using the nudge_dataset function, defined in the following listing.

Listing 6.12   Generating artificial data

```
def nudge_dataset(X, Y):
    """
    This produces a dataset 5 times bigger than the original one,
    by moving the 8x8 images in X around by 1px to left, right, down, up
    """
```

---

[29] scikit-learn, "Restricted Boltzmann Machine Features for Digit Classification," http://mng.bz/3N42.

```
direction_vectors = [[[0, 1, 0],[0, 0, 0],[0, 0, 0]],
                      [[0, 0, 0],[1, 0, 0],[0, 0, 0]],
                      [[0, 0, 0],[0, 0, 1],[0, 0, 0]],
                      [[0, 0, 0],[0, 0, 0],[0, 1, 0]]]
shift = \
    lambda x, w: convolve(x.reshape((8, 8)), mode='constant',\
    weights=w).ravel()
X = np.concatenate([X] + \
    [np.apply_along_axis(shift, 1, X, vector) for vector in \
    direction_vectors])
Y = np.concatenate([Y for _ in range(5)], axis=0)
return X, Y
```

Given this data, it's now simple to create a decision pipeline consisting of a RBM followed by logistic regression. The next listing presents the code to both set up this pipeline and train the model.

Listing 6.13 Setting up and training a RBM/LR pipeline

```
# Models we will use
logistic = linear_model.LogisticRegression()
rbm = BernoulliRBM(random_state=0, verbose=True)

classifier = Pipeline(steps=[('rbm', rbm), ('logistic', logistic)])

######################################################################
# Training

# Hyper-parameters. These were set by cross-validation,
# using a GridSearchCV. Here we are not performing cross-validation to
# save time.
rbm.learning_rate = 0.06
rbm.n_iter = 20
# More components tend to give better prediction performance, but larger
# fitting time
rbm.n_components = 100
logistic.C = 6000.0

# Training RBM-Logistic Pipeline
classifier.fit(X_train, Y_train)

# Training Logistic regression
logistic_classifier = linear_model.LogisticRegression(C=100.0)
logistic_classifier.fit(X_train, Y_train)
```

This code is taken directly from scikit-learn,[30] and there are some important things to note. The hyper-parameters—that is, the parameters of the RBM—have been selected specially for the dataset in order to provide an illustrative example that we can discuss. More details can be found in the original documentation.

You'll see that beyond this, the code does very little. A classifier pipeline is set up consisting of a RBM followed by a logistic regression classifier, as well as a standalone

---

[30] scikit-learn, "Restricted Boltzmann Machine Features for Digit Classification," http://mng.bz/3N42.

logistic regression classifier for comparison. In a minute, you'll see how these two approaches perform. The following listing provides the code to do this.

Listing 6.14 Evaluating the RBM/LR pipeline

```
print("Logistic regression using RBM features:\n%s\n" % (
    metrics.classification_report(
        Y_test,
        classifier.predict(X_test))))

print("Logistic regression using raw pixel features:\n%s\n" % (
    metrics.classification_report(
        Y_test,
        logistic_classifier.predict(X_test))))
```

The output of this provides a detailed summary of the two approaches, and you should see that the RBM/LR pipeline far outstrips the basic LR approach in precision, recall, and f1 score. But why is this? If we plot the hidden components of the RBM, we should start to understand why. The next listing provides the code to do this, and figure 6.14 provides a graphical overview of the hidden components of our RBM.

Listing 6.15 Representing the hidden units graphically

```
plt.figure(figsize=(4.2, 4))
for i, comp in enumerate(rbm.components_):
    #print(i)
    #print(comp)
    plt.subplot(10, 10, i + 1)
    plt.imshow(comp.reshape((8, 8)),
      cmap=plt.cm.gray_r,interpolation='nearest')
    plt.xticks(())
    plt.yticks(())

plt.suptitle('100 components extracted by RBM', fontsize=16)
plt.subplots_adjust(0.08, 0.02, 0.92, 0.85, 0.08, 0.23)
plt.show()
```

100 components extracted by RBM

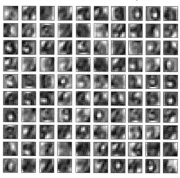

Figure 6.14 A graphical representation of the weights between the hidden and visible units in our RBM. Each square represents a single hidden unit, and the 64 grayscale values within represent the weights from that hidden value to all the visible units. In a sense, this dictates how well that hidden variable is able to recognize images like the one presented.

In our RBM, we have 100 hidden nodes and 64 visible units, because this is the size of the images being used. Each square in figure 6.14 is a grayscale interpretation of the weights between that hidden component and each visible unit. In a sense, each hidden component can be thought of as recognizing the image as given previously. In the pipeline, the logistic regression model then uses the 100 activation probabilities ($P(h_j=1|\mathbf{v}=image)$ for each j) as its input; thus, instead of doing logistic regression over 64 raw pixels, it's performed over 100 inputs, each having a high value when the input looks close to the ones provided in figure 6.14. Going back to the first section in this chapter, you should now be able to see that we've created a network that has automatically learned some intermediate representation of the numbers, using a RBM. In essence, we've created a single layer of a deep network! Imagine what could be achieved with deeper networks and multiple layers of RBMs to create more intermediate representations!

6.6   *Summary*

- We provided you a whistle-stop tour of neural networks and their relationship to deep learning. Starting with the simplest neural network model, the MCP model, we moved on to the perceptron and discussed its relationship with logistic regression.

- We found that it's not possible to represent nonlinear functions using a single perceptron, but that it's possible if we create multilayer perceptrons (MLP).

- We discussed how MLPs are trained through backpropagation—and the adoption of differentiable activation functions—and provided you with an example whereby a non-linear function is learned using backpropagation in PyBrain.

- We discussed the recent advances in deep learning: specifically, building multiple layers of networks that can learn intermediate representations of the data.

- We concentrated on one such network known as a Restricted Boltzmann Machine, and we showed how you can construct the simplest deep network over the digits dataset, using a single RBM and a logistic regression classifier.

Making the right choice 7

Given a number of options, how do we choose the one that maximizes our reward (or, equivalently, minimizes the cost)? For example, if we have two possible routes to work, how might we choose the one that minimizes the time spent traveling? In this example, our reward is based on the time it takes to get to work but could equally be the cost of fuel or the time spent in traffic.

Any problem whereby an option is tested multiple times, and where each time an option is chosen a reward is returned, can be optimized using the techniques in this chapter. In this example, the route to work is decided every day, and we can record the length of the commute in a ledger. Over time, our commuter may discover patterns in the data (route A takes less time than route B) and choose this one consistently. What then is a good strategy for the commuter to take? To consistently take route A or route B? When might they have enough data to decide which route is best? What is the optimal strategy for testing these routes? These questions are the focus of this chapter. Figure 7.1 provides a graphical overview of the problem definition

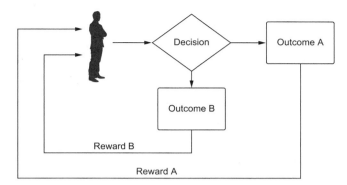

Figure 7.1 Formalizing the problem definition. In this situation, our actor is faced with a decision, and, depending on their choice, they reach an outcome. This outcome has an associated reward that is returned to the actor. Given that the user is exposed to this decision continually, how do they formulate a strategy to obtain the maximum reward (or, equivalently, the minimum cost)?

In this figure, we assume that the actor is exposed many times to a situation that requires a decision to be made. Each time a decision is made, an outcome is reached, and this outcome has an associated reward associated with it. In the case of our commuter, assuming they go to work every day, they have to choose their route every time they go to work. The outcome is the combination of all the factors on that commute, and the reward is formulated from this.

Although our toy example fits the problem perfectly, the intelligent web offers many other problems with the same format. It offers many applications where we're presented with several choices and making the correct one is crucial:

- *Landing-page optimization*—With the advent of the intelligent web, there are many more digital-only retailers. For such retailers, ensuring maximum conversion rate (the rate at which people who visit the website go on to buy products or interact with pages deeper in the site) is of key concern. The decision to be made regards the format and content of the landing page (we may have a selection of three or four to choose from). We'd like to choose the best landing page from our set that grabs the incoming users and maximizes their likelihood to interact or to buy.

- *Ad creative optimization*—As you've learned from previous chapters, online advertising provides a host of challenges that are appropriate for the application of machine-learning techniques. One of the more interesting challenges focuses on the selection of the format of the ad or aspects of the ad. Once we've decided that we want to show an ad and what price we wish to pay for it, what do we place within that space? We could test for a host of decisions. Choosing the right combination of aspects could result in an ad that performs better than those with other combinations.

7.1 A/B testing

So how do we evaluate decisions, and what strategy should we employ to test our outcomes? One example involves A/B testing. Within industry, A/B testing has gained popularity in recent years, but those with a background in statistics will recognize it simply as a two-group experiment. Let's delve a little deeper to understand the specifics.

When performing A/B testing, we do so with two groups: group A and group B. The first is a control group, and the second has some factor changed. For example, in the case of landing-page optimization, group A may be shown the existing landing page and group B a new landing page whose content or layout has changed in some way. The purpose of our A/B test is to understand whether the new layout changes the conversion rate in a statistically significant way.

It's worth noting that the assignment of users to their respective groups requires some consideration. For A/B testing, we effectively randomize assignment, so for a large number of users the cross section of the population should be the same (that is, no biases within the groups). Take care, though; for small groups of users, this won't be the case, and so other experimental designs should be considered.[1]

7.1.1   *The theory*

Given that we've constructed two large groups of users who differ only by the landing page they've arrived at, we now wish to test whether there is a statistically significant difference between the conversion rates of the two groups. Due to the large sample size, we can do this using a two-sample, one-tailed z-test, but for smaller sets we may rely on the t-test.[2]

The z-test operates under the assumption that the data is normally distributed and randomly sampled. Our aim is to test whether our test set (group B) is significantly different than that of this control set (group A). But how is this test performed?

Let's assume that we have 5,000 samples from each of group A and group B. We need a mathematical formulation to state our null hypothesis—that there is no significant positive difference in the population conversion rates of the two groups—and an alternative hypothesis that there is indeed a significant positive difference between the population conversion rates.

We can think of the sampled conversion rate as a normally distributed random variable. That is, the sampled conversion rate is an observation from a normal distribution over conversion rates. To understand this, consider that multiple experiments drawn from the same group will result in slightly different conversion rates. Each time we sample the group, we obtain an estimate of the population conversion rate. This is true of both groups A/B. We can therefor come up with a new, also normal, random variable that's the combination of random variables from groups A and B. This is the distribution of differences. Let us write X to refer to this new random variable, defined as

$$X = X_e - X_n$$

[1] Stuart Wilson and Rory MacLean, *Research Methods and Data Analysis for Psychology* (McGraw-Hill Education— Europe, 2011).

[2] Student, "The Probable Error of a Mean," *Biometrika* 6, no. 1, ed. E. S. Pearson and John Wishart (March 1908): 1–25.

where X_e is the random variable of conversion rates of our experimental group, and X_n is the random variable of conversion rates of our control group. Given this new random variable, we can now write the null and alternative hypothesis. Our null hypothesis can be stated as follows:

H_0: $X = 0$

That is, the experimental group is no different than the control group. Both random variables X_e and X_n are distributed around the same population mean, so our new random variable X should be distributed around 0. Our alternative hypothesis can be stated as follows:

H_a: $X > 0$

That is, the expectation of the random variable of the experimental group is larger than that of the control group; the population mean of this group is higher.

We can perform a one-tailed z-test on the distribution of X, under the assumption of the null hypothesis, to determine whether there is evidence to support the alternative hypothesis. To perform this, we sample X, calculate the standard score, and test against known significance levels.

Sampling of X is equivalent to running the two experiments, determining their respective conversion rates, and subtracting the control conversion rate from the experimental one. From the definition of the standard score, we may now write

$$z = (p_{experiment} - p_{control}) / SE$$

where $p_{experiment}$ is the conversion rate of the experiment, $p_{control}$ is the conversion rate of the control, and SE is the standard error for the difference in conversion rates.

To determine the standard error, we note that conversions are binomially distributed, so visits to the site can be seen as a single Bernoulli trial with an unknown chance of a positive outcome (a conversion). Provided the number of samples is large enough, we can, however, approximate this distribution as a normal using the widely adopted Wald method.[3, 4] To capture the uncertainty of the particular conversion rate, we can write the standard error (SE) for both the experimental and control groups as follows, where p is the likelihood of a conversion and n is the number of samples:

$$SE^2 - \frac{p(1-p)}{n}$$

The numerator derives from the the variance of the binomial distribution ($np(1-p)$), and the denominator captures the fact that the error in conversion rate will drop the more samples that are taken. Noting that the probability of a positive outcome is

---

[3] Lawrence D. Brown, T. Tony Cai, and Anirban DasGupta, "Confidence Intervals for a Binomial Proportion and Asymptotic Expansions," *The Annals of Statistics* 30, no. 1 (2002): 160–201.

[4] Sean Wallis, "Binomial Confidence Intervals and Contingency Tests: Mathematical Fundamentals and the Evaluation of Alternative Methods," *Journal of Quantitative Linguistics* 20, no. 3 (2013): 178–208.

equivalent to the conversion rate, and because the standard error of two variables can be combined by addition, we note the following:

$$SE^2 = SE^2_{exp} + SE^2_{control}$$

$$SE^2_{exp} = \frac{p_{experiment}(1 - p_{experiment})}{n_{experiment}}$$

$$SE^2_{control} = \frac{p_{control}(1 - p_{control})}{n_{control}}$$

By substitution, we can now write our z-test as follows. This is a formulation of the Wald (or normal) interval for the binomial distribution:

$$z = (p_{experiment} - p_{control}) / \sqrt{SE^2_{exp} + SE^2_{control}}$$

The greater the value of z, the more evidence against the null hypothesis. To obtain a 90% confidence interval for a one-tail test, our value of z would need to be greater than 1.28. What this actually says is that, under the assumption of the null hypothesis (the population mean for groups A and B is the same), the probability of this difference in conversion rates, or one larger than this, occurring by chance is less than 10%. Put another way, assuming the control and experiment conversion rates are drawn from a distribution with the same mean, if we run this same experiment 100 times, only 10 of these would have at least such an extreme value. We can provide even tighter bounds and more evidence against the null hypothesis by using a 95% confidence interval. This increases the z value required to 1.65.

It might be useful for you to think about the factors that will impact the size of z. Obviously, if we draw two conversion rates at a given point in time from an experimental set and a control set, a larger difference in these will lead to a larger z score, and therefore more evidence that they're drawn from different populations with different means. But the number of samples is also important. As you've seen, a larger number of samples will lead to an overall smaller standard error. This captures the fact that our estimate of conversion rate is more accurate the longer we run the experiment. In the following section, we'll provide an illustration of this and a worked example of A/B testing in Python using this methodology.

7.1.2   *The code*

Imagine that you're in charge of a large retail site and that your design team has just changed the landing page. You receive approximately 20,000 users per week and can quantify the conversion rate of your users: that is, what percentage goes on to buy a product. The design team assures you that the new site will drive more customers, but you aren't so sure and want to run an A/B test to see if performance will increase.

Entering users are randomly assigned to group A or group B the first time they're seen and remain in this group for the duration of the experiment. The average conversion rate of the users is assessed within the two groups at the end of the experiment and found to be 0.002 for the new landing page and 0.001 for the original landing page. You need to know whether this increase is significant enough to warrant the landing page being permanently changed to the new design. Let's look at the code that will help you answer this question.

```
import math
import random
import numpy as np
import matplotlib.pyplot as plt

n_experiment = 10000
n_control = 10000

p_experiment= 0.002
p_control = 0.001

se_experiment_sq = p_experiment*(1-p_experiment) / n_experiment
se_control_sq = p_control*(1-p_control) / n_control

Z = (p_experiment-p_control)/math.sqrt(se_experiment_sq+se_control_sq)

print Z
```

This code obtains the z value for the experiment. Given these values, we obtain a z value of 1.827. This exceeds the 92% confidence interval but not the 95% interval. We can say that there is a probability less than 0.08 that the data was drawn from the control distribution. Consequently, at this interval the data is significant. We should reject the null hypothesis that there is no difference at all between the groups and accept the alternative hypothesis, that the second group has a higher conversion rate. If we've controlled all other aspects of the user groups, this should imply that the website redesign has had a positive effect.

You should be able to see from this code that the standard error of the distributions from which the conversion rate is drawn has a direct effect on the z values returned. The higher the *SE* of the two groups, the smaller the value of z and therefore the less significant the result, given constant values of $p_{experiment}$ and $p_{control}$. We also note that, because of the definition of *SE*, z has a direct relationship with the number of samples, again for a given probability of conversion. Figure 7.2 shows this graphically.

What you see is that for a given conversion rate of the two groups, the more users in the test groups, the more confident we become of the alternative hypothesis. Intuitively, this makes sense: we should expect to become more confident the more data we collect! Note that we can also draw a similar diagram holding the number of users constant and varying the difference between the groups. We must note, however, that for the type of applications we're looking at, we shouldn't expect large magnitude changes in performance. This may indicate that we must collect a lot of data to be sure a change does lead to a significant improvement in performance. The code available for this chapter will generate the graph in figure 7.2; try generating a similar one with the difference in conversion rates across the x-axis instead!

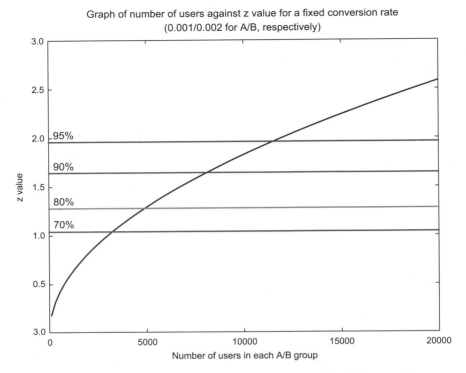

Figure 7.2 **We're given a fixed value for the conversion rates of the A/B group, the relationship between the number of users in the A/B groups, and the z value. Assuming the conversion rate wouldn't change as we collected more data, we'd need around 3,000 users in each group to hit a confidence interval of 70%. This rises to around 5,000 per group for 80%, 7,500 for 90%, and 12,000 for 95%.**

7.1.3 *Suitability of A/B*

In this section, we've given a basic introduction to a statistical method for testing called the z-test. We discussed it in the context of an A/B test, where we want to test the impact of a change in operations so as to decide whether to adopt this change permanently. What we discovered is that for very small changes in performance, similar to those that may be typical of intelligent web applications, we need to create quite large control and test groups. In the case of our imaginary retailer, depending on the number of users seen daily, it may take considerable time to reach a significant conclusion. The problem with this in a business setting is that while you're running the test, you're potentially running suboptimally because either half of your users are in an underperforming test set or half of your users are in an under-performing control set, and you have to wait for the test to finish!

This is a classic problem known as the *explore-exploit conundrum*. We need to run suboptimally to explore the space and find solutions that perform better, but once we find these solutions, we also need to exploit them as soon as possible in order to gain an advantage. What if we could exploit new solutions in a quicker fashion, without waiting for the test to finish completely? Well, we can. Enter the multi-armed bandit (MAB).

7.2 Multi-armed bandits

The name *multi-armed bandit (MAB)* comes from the popular casino game, the one-armed bandit. For those of you who have never been to a casino, this is a machine whereby you pull on a lever (the arm); depending on the values displayed by the machine, you're either paid out or (more likely) not. As you'd expect, the odds of these machines are in favor of the house, so the likelihood of being paid out is typically very small!

The (theoretical) MAB extends this formalism by imagining that you're faced with a bank of one-armed bandits, each of which is assigned to pay out with an independent probability. As a player, you're unaware of the probabilities of payout behind these machines, and the only way you can find out is by playing them. You're tasked with playing these machines and maximizing your reward. So what strategy should you use? Figure 7.3 illustrates the MAB formalism.

Figure 7.3 The multi-armed bandit problem. A user is faced with a number of one-armed bandits, each of which has a different probability of paying out. The user doesn't know what these probabilities are and may only uncover them through playing the machines. What strategy should the user employ in order to maximize their return? The user must explore the space in order to determine the probabilities of paying out, but they must also exploit machines with high probabilities of paying out in order to maximize their return.

7.2.1 Multi-armed bandit strategies

Let's define the problem more rigorously before we dive into some code! Formally, we have k bandits, with the observable probabilities of paying out equal to p_k. We assume that only one arm can be pulled at a time and that the machine either pays out or doesn't, with a value based on its associated probability. This is a finite game, with a set number of plays allowed. At any particular point in the game, the horizon H is defined as the number of remaining plays that are permissible.

The user attempts to maximize the payout over all the machines. At any given point in the game, we can assess how well the user is doing through the use of a metric known as the *regret*. This is the difference between the payout that would be received if the user had an oracle and chose the optimal bandit at every step and the actual payout so far. Formally, the regret is defined as

$$\sigma = T\mu_{opt} - \sum_{t=1}^{T} r_t$$

where T is the number of steps we've carried out so far, r_t is the reward that was received at step t, and μ_{opt} is the mean payout returned per play from the optimal bandit. The lower the value of the regret, the more optimal the strategy is. But because this metric is susceptible to chance (payouts may be greater than the expected payout playing the best bandit alone), we may choose to use the expected regret instead. Formally, the expected regret is defined as

$$T\mu_{opt} - \sum_{t=1}^{T} \mu_t$$

where μ_t is the (unobservable) mean payout from the arm chosen at time t. Because the second term is the expected payout from the selected strategy, it will be less than or equal to the expected payout from the optimal strategy, choosing the arm with μ_{opt} all the time.

In the following sections, we'll introduce a new variable to our formalism: epsilon. *Epsilon* controls the trade-off between exploring the space and exploiting the best-known solution, as you'll see in the following strategies. It's expressed as a probability.

EPSILON FIRST

Epsilon first is the simplest of the MAB strategies that can be employed and can be considered equivalent to the A/B approach outlined earlier. Given ε, we perform exploration $(1 - \varepsilon) \times N$ times, where N is the total number of trials available in the game. The remaining trials are purely exploitative.

The `update_best_bandit` method keeps a running total of the payouts for each bandit and the number of times that bandit was played. The `best_bandit` variable is updated after every play to contain the index of the bandit that so far has the best payout rate. The following pseudo-code outlines the solution.

Listing 7.2   Pseudo-code for the epsilon-first strategy

```
epsilon=0.1
best_bandit #index of the best bandit in the array
bandit_array #array containing bandit objects
total_reward=0
number_trials
current_trial=0

number_explore_trials = (1-epsilon)*number_trials

while((number_trials-current_trial)>0):
    if(current_trial<number_explore_trials):    ◁——— Explores the solution space
        random_bandit = rand(0,len(bandit_array))
        total_reward += play(bandit_array[random_bandit])
        update_best_bandit()#update the best bandit
    else:                                        ◁——— Exploits your knowledge
        total_reward +=play(bandit_array[best_bandit])

    current_trial+=1
```

EPSILON GREEDY

With the *epsilon-greedy* approach, ε acts as a probability that we'll explore the space, as opposed to exploiting the best-known arm. More formally, the following pseudo-code outlines the approach.

Listing 7.3 Pseudocode for the epsilon-greedy strategy

```
epsilon=0.1
best_bandit                    ◁─────── Index of the best bandit in the array
bandit_array                   ◁─────── Array containing bandit objects
total_reward=0
number_trials
current_trial=0

while((number_trials-current_trial)>0):
    random_float = rand(0,1)
    if(random_float<epsilon):              ◁─────── Explores the solution space
        random_bandit = rand(0,len(bandit_array))
        total_reward += play(bandit_array[random_bandit])
        update_best_bandit()
    else:                                  ◁─────── Exploits your knowledge
        total_reward +=play(bandit_array[best_bandit])

    current_trial+=1
```

Updates the best bandit

The advantage of this approach is that we don't need to wait for the explore phase to complete before we can start exploiting our knowledge of the bandit's performance—but be careful! This algorithm doesn't take into account the statistical significance of our performance data. It's possible that a peak in positive payouts for a particular bandit will result in all plays being shifted to this bandit erroneously. More on this shortly.

You can see that ε controls the probability that we explore rather than exploit. Low values of array make it less likely that we'll explore the space, whereas higher values make it more likely. There's a clear trade-off here, and the selection of our value of ε depends on many factors. Both the number of bandits and the probabilities of payouts will affect the regret, as introduced previously. One clear issue is that of bootstrapping. At the start of the experiment, we know nothing about the performance of any of the bandits (unlike in the epsilon-first strategy). Might there be a better way to do this, exploring the space more where the horizon is far away, decreasing as the horizon gets closer?

EPSILON DECREASING

The *epsilon-decreasing* strategy does just this. At the start of the experiment, we have a high value of ε, so the likelihood of exploration is high. This value is gradually decreased as the horizon goes on, making the likelihood of exploitation higher, as shown in the following listing.

Listing 7.4   Pseudo-code for the epsilon-decreasing strategy

```
epsilon=1                                    ⟵———  Starts by exploring all the time
best_bandit
bandit_array
total_reward=0
number_trials
current_trial=0

while((number_trials-current_trial)>0):
    random_float = rand(0,1)
    if(random_float<epsilon):                ⟵———  Explores the solution space
        random_bandit = rand(0,len(bandit_array))
        total_reward += play(bandit_array[random_bandit])
        update_best_bandit()
    else:                                    ⟵———  Exploits the solution space
        total_reward +=play(bandit_array[best_bandit])

    current_trial+=1
    epsilon = update_epsilon(epsilon)
```

(left margin annotation: Updates the best bandit — pointing to update_best_bandit())

Note that there are several methods to choose an optimal rate to update ε. This depends on the number of bandits, *N*, and the respective weights at which they pay out.

BAYESIAN BANDITS

As mentioned, one of the limitations of this algorithm is that we don't take into account the significance of the performance data as we explore the space. Although you might be able to exploit your knowledge sooner, you may be making erroneous decisions. That's not to say that these techniques aren't useful! But they require a careful eye for the parameters, to ensure that they don't exploit too early or explore for too long.

Enter *Bayesian bandits*. Similarly to A/B testing, we assume that the payout rate for each bandit is modeled as a distribution over payout rates. When we start out, each bandit has a very general prior (because any payout rate is equally likely for that bandit). The more we play a bandit, the more information we have about its performance, so we update its payout distribution over likely payout rates. When it comes to choosing which bandit to play, we sample from each distribution over the payout rates and choose the bandit that corresponds to the sample with the highest rate. Figure 7.4 provides a graphical overview of the knowledge held about three illustrative bandits at a given time.

Here you can see that the knowledge about the distributions of our bandits is encoded as three distributions. Each distribution has an increasing mean, with decreasing variance. Thus, we're less certain about the true rate of payout of the bandit with mean 0.1 and most certain about the bandit with an average payout of 0.4. Because the bandit to play is achieved by sampling each distribution, it's possible that the arm corresponding to the distribution around 0.1 is pulled. This will occur when the samples from bandit 2 and bandit 3 are unusually low and the sample from bandit 1 is unusually large. The following listing provides the pseudo-code for this algorithm.

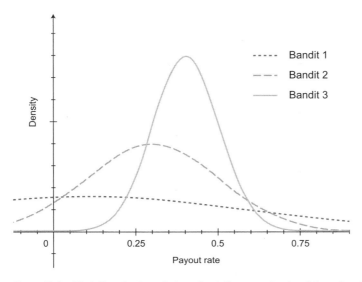

Figure 7.4 Modeling the knowledge about the payout rate of three bandits using the Bayesian bandit method. The mean payout rates for arms 1, 2, and 3 are 0.1, 0.3, and 0.4, respectively. Bandit 1 has a lower mean but a much wider variance. Bandit 2 has a higher mean and smaller variance. Bandit 3 has an even higher mean and a smaller variance. In order to choose the bandit to play, each distribution is sampled, and the bandit corresponding to the distribution from which the highest sample was drawn will be picked. After selection, the bandit is played and the respective distribution is updated. This has the effect that even bandits with a low payout rate have a chance to redeem themselves if their mean rate is uncertain (high variance).

Listing 7.5 Pseudo-code for the Bayesian bandit strategy

```
bandit_distribution_array              ◁──────  Initializes with
total_reward=0                                   suitable priors
number_trials
current_trial=0

while((number_trials-current_trial)>0):
    sample_array = sample(bandit_distribution_array)
    best_bandit = index_of(max(sample_array))
    reward =play(bandit_array[best_bandit])
    total_reward+=reward
    current_trial+=1
    update_distribution_array(best_bandit,reward)
```

You can see the elegance of this solution. Although it's simple to implement, this approach both models the uncertainly of our estimates and provides an excellent regret when compared to our previous approaches, as you'll see in the following sections.

7.3   *Bayesian bandits in the wild*

In this section, we'll set up an experiment with three arms and provide results showing that the rate of regret does indeed slow down the more the bandits are played. We'll also talk a little about the appropriateness of such an approach and the factors impacting how long the Bayesian bandit should be run for.

If you recall from the previous section, we're going to require a probability distribution to encode our belief regarding the payout rate of each arm in our experiment. Because we're dealing with a model with two possible outcomes, this can be viewed as a Bernoulli trial. The conjugate prior for the Bernoulli distribution is the beta distribution.[5] This is a distribution over distributions parameterized by two values: the number of successes and the number of failures. These parameters are given by α and β, and for $\alpha = \beta = 1$ the beta distribution is equivalent to the uniform distribution. For large values of α and β this becomes equivalent to the binomial distribution. Consequently, we'll use the beta distribution as a uniform prior over our initial belief of the payout probability for all arms ($\alpha = \beta = 1$) and update these as we play the arms and observe the outputs. First, let's consider a class that we'll create in order to encapsulate a one-armed bandit. See the next listing.

> **Listing 7.6   A class encoding a one-armed bandit**

```
class Bandit:
    def __init__(self,probability):
        self.probability=probability

    def pull_handle(self):
        if random.random()<self.probability:
            return 1
        else:
            return 0

    def get_prob(self):
        return self.probability
```

In this basic class, we have a constructor that takes the probability of payout as a parameter. The method `pull_handle` uses this probability to determine whether to pay out when the handle is pulled. Finally, a helper method allows us to access the probability of payout of an instantiated object using the `get_prob` method. This class is the basis of the example, and we'll use it extensively in the following code listings.

In listing 7.7, we'll also define the helper method that's used to sample from each distribution representing our one-armed bandits. This code will also be used extensively in order to determine which handle should be pulled next given the current status of the model.

---

[5] Eric W. Weisstein, "Beta Distribution," http://mathworld.wolfram.com/BetaDistribution.html.

Listing 7.7   Sampling the beta distributions in a Bayesian bandit strategy

```
def sample_distributions_and_choose(bandit_params):
    sample_array = \
        [beta.rvs(param[0], param[1], size=1)[0] for param in bandit_params]
    return np.argmax(sample_array)
```

This method relies on the `beta.rvs` method to sample a single random variable from each beta distribution, the parameters of which are passed in as a list. It will then return the index of the list that resulted in the highest sampled value. This is the arm pulled next in the MAB experiment.

With these two methods in place, we can run our first Bayesian bandit experiment! The following listing provides the majority of the code, and listing 7.9 illustrates the initial distribution of the priors over our belief on the payout rate.

Listing 7.8   Running the Bayes bandit

```
def run_single_regret(bandit_list,bandit_params,plays):
    sum_probs_chosen=0
    opt=np.zeros(plays)
    chosen=np.zeros(plays)
    bandit_probs = [x.get_prob() for x in bandit_list]
    opt_solution = max(bandit_probs)
    for i in range(0,plays):
        index = sample_distributions_and_choose(bandit_params)
        sum_probs_chosen+=bandit_probs[index]
        if(bandit_list[index].pull_handle()):
          bandit_params[index]=\
                    (bandit_params[index][0]+1,bandit_params[index][1])
        else:
            bandit_params[index]=\
                    (bandit_params[index][0],bandit_params[index][1]+1)
        opt[i] = (i+1)*opt_solution
        chosen[i] = sum_probs_chosen
    regret_total = map(sub,opt,chosen)
    return regret_total
```

The method `run_single_regret` takes as parameters a list of bandits, along with a list of parameters that hold the starting belief distribution of the bandits' payout rate. Also passed is the number of plays we're going to attempt. The method returns the expected regret of the executed strategy. The method starts by setting the initial values of `sum_probs_chosen` and initializing two NumPy arrays that will hold the state of the experiment at each play. For each play, the distributions are sampled, and the bandit associated with the highest sampled value is chosen. The parameters are updated in light of the outcome. Before we run this, let's take a look at the initial (prior) distributions we'll be sampling from, as shown in the next listing.

Listing 7.9   Plotting the initial priors for the Bayes bandit

```
bandit_list = [Bandit(0.1),Bandit(0.3),Bandit(0.8)]
bandit_params = [(1,1),(1,1),(1,1)]

x = np.linspace(0,1, 100)
plt.plot(x,
        beta.pdf(x, bandit_params[0][0], bandit_params[0][1]),
        '-r*',
        alpha=0.6,
        label='Bandit 1')

plt.plot(x,
        beta.pdf(x, bandit_params[1][0], bandit_params[1][1]),
        '-b+',
        alpha=0.6,
        label='Bandit 2')

plt.plot(x,
        beta.pdf(x, bandit_params[2][0], bandit_params[2][1]),
        '-go',
        alpha=0.6,
        label='Bandit 3')
plt.legend()
plt.xlabel("payout probability")
plt.ylabel("probability density of belief")
plt.show()
```

This code plots the initial distribution of our belief as to the payout rate of each arm of the bandit, using an α value and a β value equal to 1; the output can be seen in figure 7.5. We also initialize a list of Bandit objects, each instantiated to pay out different probabilities. The first pays out at a rate of 1 in 10 plays, the second a rate of 3 in 10 plays, and the final bandit pays 8 times out of 10! These are clearly very fair bandits—we personally have never played in a casino this generous.

Note that the probability density functions are equivalent: that's because we know exactly the same amount of information about each bandit (nothing at all!). You'll later see how these distributions change as we play out our strategy. Let's play a single strategy now and plot the expected regret after each play. The next listing provides the code to do this.

Listing 7.10   Plotting a single execution of a Bayes bandit strategy

```
plays=1000
bandit_list = [Bandit(0.1),Bandit(0.3),Bandit(0.8)]
bandit_params = [(1,1),(1,1),(1,1)]

regret_total = run_single_regret(bandit_list,bandit_params,plays)
plt.plot(regret_total)
plt.title("expected regret against steps in experiment")
plt.xlabel("Step in experiment")
plt.ylabel("Cumulative expected regret in experiment at this step")
plt.show()
```

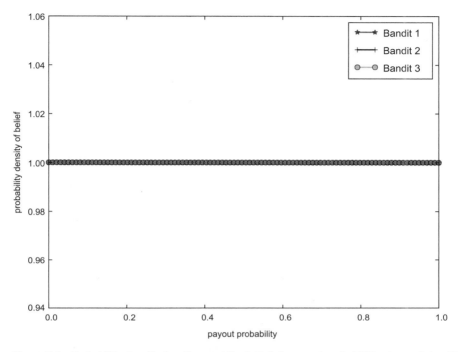

Figure 7.5 **Probability density function over the beliefs in payout probabilities for each bandit. Note that the three plots are identical and that the area under the curve is equal to 1. This illustrates our belief that all payout probabilities are equally likely for each bandit. This will change as we observe the bandits in action.**

Here we use the `run_single_regret` method, passing the same initial β values as illustrated previously as well as the same bandit payout probabilities. The output for listing 7.10 is shown in figure 7.6.

In figure 7.6, you see the cumulative expected regret for a single run of 1,000 plays. The expected regret for a step is the expected difference between the optimal and chosen payout when a decision is made, and the cumulative expected regret is the sum of this number for all prior steps. For a good solution, we would expect the rate to slow and approach a horizontal line. This would indicate that no further suboptimal decisions are being made and that the knowledge is being fully exploited. Let's now take another look at our underlying beliefs through the parameters of the beta distribution. Here's the code to generate the posterior (that is, after all the information has been used to learn) probability density functions graphically, as shown in figure 7.7.

Listing 7.11 Plotting the posterior probability density functions

```
x = np.linspace(0,1, 100)
plt.plot(x,
         beta.pdf(x, bandit_params[0][0], bandit_params[0][1]),
         '-r*',
```

```
            alpha=0.6,
            label='Bandit 1')
plt.plot(x,
         beta.pdf(x, bandit_params[1][0], bandit_params[1][1]),
         '-b+',
         alpha=0.6,
         label='Bandit 2')
plt.plot(x,
         beta.pdf(x, bandit_params[2][0], bandit_params[2][1]),
         '-go',
         alpha=0.6,
         label='Bandit 3')
plt.legend()
plt.xlabel("payout probability")
plt.ylabel("probability density of belief")
plt.show()
```

What you now see is a completely different set of distributions than those given in figure 7.5. The first (bandit 1) appears to have a maximum at a payout probability of 0, the second (bandit 2) around 0.4, and the third (bandit 3) around 0.8. Note also the width of the distributions. The beliefs for both bandit 1 and bandit 2 are much wider than the belief for bandit 3, which has a tight distribution around 0.8.

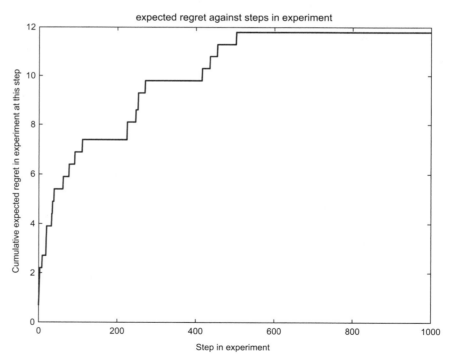

Figure 7.6   Total expected regret in a single execution of 1,000 plays. Knowledge is acquired only through play (exploration). Consequently, it's likely that suboptimal decisions will be made on the path to learning the true payout probabilities.

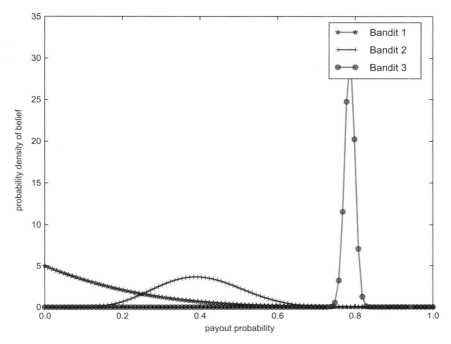

Figure 7.7 Posterior probability distributions after a single run of 1,000 plays. This represents our belief over the possible true distributions of the bandits, which have an unobservable true probability of payout equal to 0.1, 0.3, and 0.8, respectively.

If you consider figure 7.6 and figure 7.7, you may be able to understand a little better what's happening. During the very early plays, because the distributions of beliefs are almost identical, the algorithm is equally likely to choose any of the bandits to play. This leads to a cumulative regret that increases quickly to begin with. As the game goes on and the results of each play are fed back to our model, our belief in the third bandit and its payout probability being highest begins to dominate. The more we play this bandit, the more it wins, and the better our belief becomes that the true probability of payout is around 0.8. At the 1,000th play, sampling these probability density functions (PDFs) will almost always lead to a maximum value being generated from our belief in bandit 3. Thus, bandit 3 (the best bandit) will always be chosen and no further regret will be accumulated (no more wrong decisions!).

Interestingly, although the mean belief of payout for bandit 3 is almost exactly the same as the true probability, the mean beliefs for bandits 1 and 2 are some way off. This is because these bandits have been played less. In fact, we're not interested in the true value—just the likelihood that the chosen bandit performs the best overall.

What we've provided here is a snapshot of the performance of a single strategy, and because of the probabilistic nature of bandit selection, we'd expect the graph provided in figure 7.6 to be different (but similar) for each fresh execution of the same strategy. Let's plot 100 such executions to convince ourselves that independent runs are indeed similar, as shown in the next listing.

Listing 7.12   Regret for multiple executions of the Bayes bandit strategy

```
plays=1000
runs=100

for i in range(0,runs):
    bandit_list = [Bandit(0.1),Bandit(0.3),Bandit(0.8)]
    bandit_params = [(1,1),(1,1),(1,1)]
    regret_total = run_single_regret(bandit_list,bandit_params,plays)
    plt.plot(regret_total,label='%s'%i)

plt.title("expected regret against steps in experiment")
plt.xlabel("Step in experiment")
plt.ylabel("Cumulative expected regret in experiment at this step")
plt.show()
```

During each of the 100 runs, we are careful to reset the learned parameters. Figure 7.8 shows the graphical output from this code.

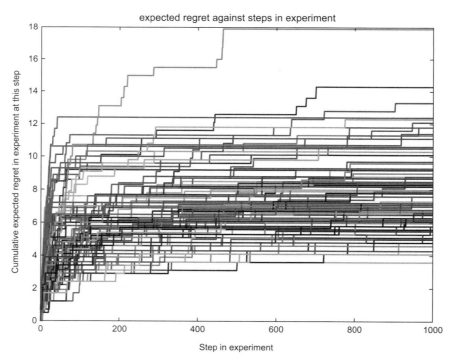

Figure 7.8   Plotting the regret for 100 runs of a 1,000-play experiment. Due to the probabilistic nature of Bayesian bandits, the outcome isn't guaranteed to be the same each time the experiment is run.

Here you can see that the outcome from an identically initialized Bayesian bandit can be dramatically different for independent executions. The cumulative regret ranges from about 4 (the expected difference between the outcome and the optimal outcome is five payouts) to 18. In most cases, the cumulative expected regret has plateaued by the end of the experiment, indicating that the optimal decision is now always being made, but this is difficult to say with certainty just by looking at the graph.

It would be better if we could provide a single, overall graph that summarizes this information over all runs of the experiment. This is exactly what we do in listing 7.13. By providing the average expected regret, we can illustrate, on average, how long it might take a Bayesian bandit to learn the best solution to a problem with this specific number of bandits and with their associated parameters.

Listing 7.13 Calculating the average cumulative expected regret

```
regret_sum=np.zeros(plays)

plays=1000
runs=100

for i in range(0,runs):
    bandit_list = [Bandit(0.1),Bandit(0.3),Bandit(0.8)]
    bandit_params = [(1,1),(1,1),(1,1)]
    regret_total = run_single_regret(bandit_list,bandit_params,plays)
    regret_sum=map(add,regret_sum, np.asarray(regret_total))

plt.plot(regret_sum/(runs*np.ones(plays)))
plt.title("average expected regret at each step over %s iterations"%runs )
plt.xlabel("Step in experiment")
plt.ylabel("Average total expected regret in experiment at this step")
plt.show()
```

As before, we create multiple runs through the experiment, each time reinitializing the learned parameters. The total cumulative expected regret is calculated at each step, and the average is calculated by dividing this array by an array containing the number of runs. This yields the output given in figure 7.9.

You can see that as the number of steps in the experiment increases, the rate at which regret is accumulated decreases. This is because the Bayesian bandit is, more often, making better decisions on average, at later stages in an individual run. Although the curve in figure 7.9 hasn't converged within 1,000 steps (that is, the gradient hasn't dropped to zero), it does look like the Bayesian bandit expects to lose somewhere in the order of 10 payouts when compared to a totally optimal strategy. If we consider that the optimal strategy pays out around $1,000 \times 0.8 = 800$ times, this isn't bad at all.

FACTORS IMPACTING THE BAYESIAN BANDIT

In the previous section, we introduced the Bayesian bandit and showed how it performs in a three-bandit problem with probabilities equal to 0.1, 0.3, and 0.8. On average and over 1,000 plays, we'd expect to lose only about 10/800 ~1.25% of payouts in

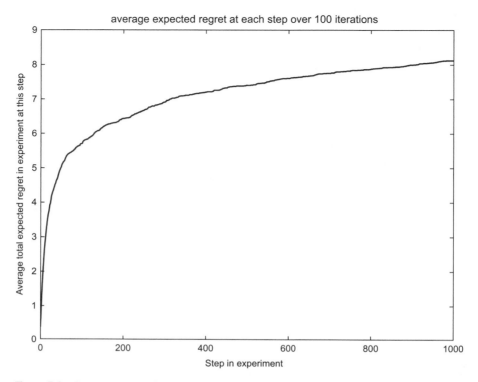

average expected regret at each step over 100 iterations

Figure 7.9   Average cumulative expected regret at each step, over 100 iterations. Note that the gradient decreases as the number of steps increases. This is because the Bayesian bandit makes comparative better choices as the experiment continues. Consequently, it's less likely to incur additional regret.

this scenario. But this is an especially good case, so let's look at some of the other factors that can impact the Bayesian bandit:

- *Similarity of probability*—As the probabilities of the bandits tend toward each other, the learned distributions tend to overlap by a large amount. This means the Bayesian bandit is more likely to "accidentally" explore; in other words, a distribution without the highest mean will generate the largest sample value. This can lead to cumulative expected regrets that are larger and take longer to reach a plateau. See figure 7.10.

- *Scale of probability*—If we repeat this experiment, replacing the probabilities with those divided by 10 (probabilities of 1 become 0.1, 0.9 becomes 0.09, and so on), then we see an interesting trend. The ordering of the cumulative expected regret inverts (see figure 7.11)! But why is this? By reducing the magnitude of the probabilities, positive events are much less likely to occur. This means several things. First, the number of steps required for our beliefs to converge is larger, because we must pull the arms more often to obtain any information

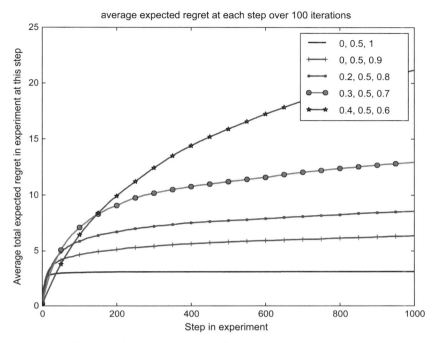

average expected regret at each step over 100 iterations

Figure 7.10 Cumulative expected regret for five experiments, each using three bandits. The overall probabilities of payouts are given in the legend. You can see that there is a tendency toward higher and longer exploration periods where the true probabilities of the bandits are closer together.

about the bandit. Second, this has the knock-on effect that the overall regret will be higher than when working with bandits with higher probabilities. The reason for the inversion of the ordering is that this is such an early stage of the regret curve. Consider figure 7.11 against the first 30 iterations of figure 7.10. Put another way, it takes 1,000 iterations in our second experiment to learn the equivalent of the first 30 iterations of our first!

- *Number of bandits*—Let's repeat our experiment by increasing the number of bandits from 1 to 10. Each will be evenly balanced in the probability space. So, for example, 1 bandit always pays out, 2 bandits pay out at rates of 1 and 0.5, 3 bandits at rates of [1,0.66,0.33], and so on. Figure 7.12 shows the equivalent output. What you see here is a tendency for an increased regret and a slower convergence, but this difference in speed isn't as marked as with the first two experiments. The speed of convergence seems to be dominated by the overall probabilities of payout and the proximity of the probability distributions to each other, not as much by the number of other bandits within the experiment.

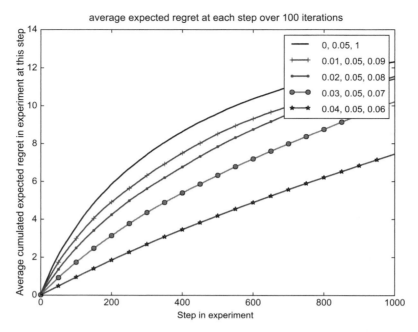

Figure 7.11 Cumulative expected regret for five experiments using scaled-down probabilities. Consider this graph in relation to figure 7.10. Note the inverse relationship and slower growth due to the reduced probabilities.

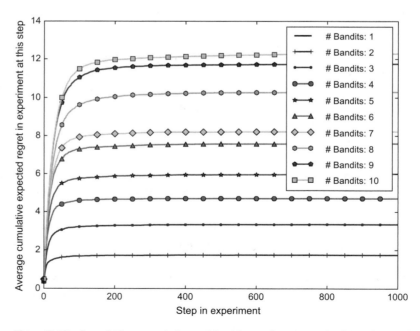

Figure 7.12 Cumulative expected regret for 10 experiments, each with an increasing number of bandits. As we increase the number of bandits, their probabilities of payout are spread equally through the space, excluding the zero-probability bandit.

7.4 A/B vs. the Bayesian bandit

So far in this chapter we've discussed several approaches to making the right choice. Much has been said in the community about MABs, and there has been a lot of hype about them—with many seeing them as a no-brainer alternative to A/B testing. After all, if you can test your choices while performing optimization, doesn't that make more sense than waiting for statistical significance with an A/B test?

Well, yes and no. As with all machine-learning techniques, there is a set of trade-offs to understand, and you should be careful to apply the right approach in the right situation. Table 7.1 provides some of the considerations you should be aware of when making the choice between a Bayesian bandit and an A/B test.

Table 7.1 Considerations of a Bayesian bandit vs. an A/B test. Remember, you should consider your application area and choose the most appropriate solution.

Bayesian bandit	A/B test
Continuous online optimization	Single-shot optimization after run
Multiple variables	Single test variable
Confidence not explicitly measured	Statistically significant result
Convergence related to the number of options, payout rates, and difference	Convergence related to the payout rate and difference between control/test sets
Accumulated regret until convergence (typically < max regret)	Max regret until answer, then zero regret
Typically slower to reach an answer	Typically quicker to reach an answer

What you should take away from table 7.1 is that A/B testing and Bayesian bandits have very different strengths, and indeed there are certain circumstances in which either one may be totally inappropriate. If nothing else, we want to draw your attention to the speed of convergence (either when we have reached statistical significance in an A/B test or where we don't incur any further cumulative regret in the Bayesian bandit case).

Let's take our initial motivational case of website optimization and discuss the appropriateness of each solution with respect to convergence speed. First, note that any change in behavior is likely to be small (<0.01), and thus we already know the Bayesian bandit will take longer to converge than with larger impact improvements. If we now add multiple choices, so that we're testing many landing pages in the same experiment, we'll further impact the convergence speed. Now, what if the underlying distribution of user conversion is changing more quickly than this model can converge? For example, seasonal trends, sales, or other external factors may affect the underlying distribution that we're assuming to be static. In such cases, it may pay dividends to think carefully and devise a statistically significant A/B test. This is not to say that Bayesian bandits aren't useful in such cases (and indeed we know otherwise), but it's imperative that you understand the characteristics of their execution. They're not a silver bullet, and you can't simply throw in as many tests as you can think of and expect the technique to perform as well as an oracle. Be careful!

7.5   *Extensions to multi-armed bandits*

As with our previous section on deep learning, what's so exciting about this area is that it's teeming with up-to-date research. At the time of writing, this is a very active area of research, and we recommend that you familiarize yourself with the literature.[6, 7, 8] In this section, we'd like to cover a few interesting developments in the MAB space. Further information and references to research can be found in each section.

7.5.1   *Contextual bandits*

Contextual bandits[9] are an important extension to the typical approach, because they allow you to encode additional information as an input that influences the strategy of the player. This lends itself to approaches whereby the bandits don't pay out based on a fixed probability but also depend on the context or situation. Figure 7.13 provides a graphical illustration of this paradigm.

Solutions to such a problem have immediate application in the advertising world. Earlier in this chapter, we discussed the use of bandits to choose the most suitable ad property, such as color or shape. Solutions to this problem will allow for the optimization of global ad properties but can't take into account specifics of the user to whom we're showing the ad. Progress in the field of contextual bandits may help us change this.

Vector of attributes assigned to a particular user and situation changes payout probabilities.

Figure 7.13   A contextual bandit. The payout probability isn't fixed and is dependent on the context or situation. One way to think about this is that the player has assigned to them a vector of attributes at a given time, and, depending on those attributes, the payout probabilities of the machine will change. The best strategy must minimize the cumulative regret with this in mind.

---

[6]   John Myles White, *Bandit Algorithms for Website Optimization* (O'Reilly, 2012).

[7]   Richard Weber, "On the Gittins Index for Multiarmed Bandits," *Annals of Applied Probability* (1992): 1024–1033.

[8]   J. C. Gittins, *Multi-armed Bandit Allocation Indices* (John Wiley and Sons, 1989).

[9]   John Langford, "Contextual Bandits," *Machine Learning (Theory)*, October 24, 2007, http://hunch.net/?p=298.

7.5.2 *Adversarial bandits*

If you recall from previous sections, up until now we've made the implicit assumption that the payout distribution is always static. That is, these distributions don't change as we play the bandits. Solutions to the *adversarial bandits* problem[10] don't make this assumption. In this formalism, the play proceeds as follows:

1 The adversary selects a vector: the size of the number of bandits. This contains the rewards for each bandit at that step.
2 The player, without knowledge of the adversary's selection, chooses a bandit to play based on their strategy.
3 In the full-information game, the player then may see the entire reward vector. In the partial-information game, the player sees only the reward associated with their chosen bandit.

Play continues in this way over a fixed number of steps, and the player must maximize their reward and minimize their regret. Figure 7.14 provides a graphical overview of the problem.

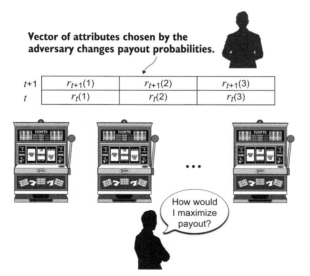

Figure 7.14 The adversarial bandit problem. In this variant of the MAB problem, solutions make no assumptions about the underlying distributions of the rewards. Instead, the problem is modeled as a game between a player and an adversary. At each time step, the adversary selects a reward vector before the player chooses an arm. In one variant of the game (full information), the player gets to see the full reward vector, and in another (partial information) the player sees the reward of their chosen bandit.

---

[10] P. Auer, N. Cesa-Bianchi, Y. Freund, and Robert E. Shapire, "Gambling in a Rigged Casino: The Adversarial Multi-armed Bandit Problem," *Foundations of Computer Science* (1995), Proceedings of the 36th Annual Symposium on Foundations of Computer Science (IEEE, 1995): 322–31.

7.6   *Summary*

- We covered several methods for making the right choice. Put simply, we looked at strategies for making a choice when faced with a multitude of options.
- We also covered the use of the z-score in an A/B test and discussed the implications of statistical significance.
- You've seen that the more data you collect, the more certain you can be about a potential change in performance.
- We demonstrated the other factors that impact significance: the variance of the two groups and the absolute differences in their rates.
- You were introduced to the concept of the multi-armed bandit. MABs allow us to use early information (before statistical significance is reached) to probabilistically modify the distribution of our choices.
- You saw how MABs can lead to an overall lower regret.
- We noted that MABs aren't a panacea and that many factors can affect their convergence rate. We explored some of these factors and highlighted some common pitfalls to watch out for.

The future of
the intelligent web

> **This chapter covers**
> - Summary and review
> - Future applications of the intelligent web
> - Social implications of the intelligent web

In this book, we've presented to you the current state of the intelligent web and walked you through the basics, teaching you what an intelligent algorithm is and how to evaluate one. Your eyes should now be open to the plethora of intelligent algorithms you're interacting with on a daily basis! You've learned about design considerations and the key pitfalls you should try to avoid in your work.

The current philosophy of machine learning is that "more data beats a cleverer algorithm."[1] As you've seen in the case of deep learning, it's been possible to make great advances due to the changing nature of computing and the internet. So much information is available on the web that channeling and accessing it appropriately becomes of utmost importance. This is the focus of the appendix. Although it may

---

[1] Pedro Domingos, "A Few Useful Things to Know about Machine Learning," *Communications of the ACM 55*, no. 10 (October 2012): 78–87.

seem removed from what many consider an intelligent algorithm, we can't stress enough the importance to the enthusiast of having at least a passing interest in this area. Future practitioners in this space will absolutely need to know the magnitude, velocity, and availability of their real-time data.

We've covered what we consider some of the most pervasive topics in intelligent algorithms: extracting structure; providing recommendations; classification, click prediction, and deep learning; as well as selection and testing. These topics aren't completely unrelated, and we've drawn parallels between concepts wherever possible. Think of these as design patterns—or blueprints for a particular solution. If in the future you're faced with something that feels like a recommendation problem, refer to chapter 3. Or if you need to write a system to choose among several options, refresh your memory with chapter 7.

Remember, though, that this book is by no means comprehensive. Intelligent algorithms are a huge topic covering several related fields, and it would be foolish of us to attempt to cram all of this knowledge into these pages! Instead, we hope you put down this book with a flavor of how you might approach problems with an intelligent algorithm in mind and with a feel for what has been done before. The good news is that that this really is still a fledgling area. There are many application-specific problems to be solved and lots of well-researched techniques to do so. As a practitioner in the area, you'll have a responsibility to connect the dots, be aware of the limitations, and find a path forward. Good luck!

8.1   *Future applications of the intelligent web*

We started this book with a an outline of how a real intelligent web application might work—the Google Now product—so it seems fitting that we draw a line from here into the future and highlight some of the application areas we feel will provide fertile ground for the creation of new algorithms. Some of the applications are on the cusp of mainstream, but others are some way off. We'll leave it to you to decide what is science fact and what is science fiction.

8.1.1   *The internet of things*

The internet of things is an umbrella term for a new wave of computing whereby all devices are online and attached to the internet. It's a realization of Marc Weiser's vision of ubiquitous computing,[2] whereby computing power has shrunk to the level that it has disappeared into the background of our daily lives. The internet of things has largely remained conceptual to date because the path forward is strewn with issues around standardization of communication and security. Ultimately, you might argue that we have seen some progress in this area through consumer products in home automation,[3] but what about a fully connected house that does the shopping for you,

---

[2] Marc Weiser, "The Computer for the 21st Century," *Scientific American*, September 1, 1991: 66–75.
[3] Nest Thermostat, 01/01/2015, https://nest.com/thermostat/meet-nest-thermostat/.

makes appointments, interacts with your smartphone, starts dinner, and activates the washing machine? This appears to be some way off yet. Many intelligent algorithms would need to be designed to realize this vision, and thus there are many likely avenues of work to pursue.

8.1.2 Home healthcare

Extending the idea of the self-aware home, what if we went a step further and built a home that was interested in the health of its occupants? This might be especially useful for the elderly, the infirm, or people on home release from the hospital. Such a house could monitor general behavior and activity trends[4, 5] or provide periodic monitoring of vital signs of occupants. This would move us from a world in which medical practitioners see only a snapshot of your health to providing a more holistic view of your health status (perhaps available only on a private network). Ultimately, it could give many increased security and independence away from the hospital environment. In such a world, algorithms would need to be developed to understand and detect acute incidents or abnormal vital signs. Such algorithms would need to have a low false-negative rate and be aware of the privacy concerns of the monitored individuals.

8.1.3 The self-driving vehicle

As most readers will know, Google's self-driving car has been in development for some time now.[6] In the future, you might imagine a totally distributed taxi network that seeks to algorithmically maximize the throughput of customers and minimize their journey times. What if we went a step further and imagined that all road vehicles were autonomously controlled and connected to the same network? Provided the right security measures were met, this would help maximize the flow of traffic, reduce traffic incidents, and increase safety—all through the use of intelligent algorithms. You might argue that we're already moving toward such a world, because several insurers are providing reduced (or more appropriate) insurance premiums through the use of data-monitoring boxes in the insured cars.[7, 8]

8.1.4 Personalized physical advertising

Several times in this book we've talked about the personalization of online advertising. What if this personalization were to jump off the screen and into real life? You

---

[4] Douglas McIlwraith, "Wearable and Ambient Sensor Fusion for the Characterisation of Human Motion," International Conference on Intelligent Robots and Systems (IROS) (IEEE, 2010): 505–510.

[5] Julien Pansiot, Danail Stoyanov, Douglas McIlwraith, Benny Lo, and Guang-Zhong Yang, "Ambient and Wearable Sensor Fusion for Activity Recognition in Healthcare Monitoring Systems," IFMBE proc. of the 4th International Workshop on Wearable and Implantable Body Sensor Networks (IFMBE, 2007): 208–212.

[6] Google Self Driving Car Project, https://www.google.com/selfdrivingcar/.

[7] Adam Tanner, "Data Monitoring Saves Some People Money on Car Insurance, But Some Will Pay More," *Forbes*, August 14, 2013, http://mng.bz/PWgf.

[8] Leo Mirani, "Car Insurance Companies Want to Track Your Every Move—And You're Going to Let Them," *Quartz*, July 9, 2014, http://mng.bz/1elQ.

may have already seen an illustration of this in the film *Minority Report*,[9] where personalized ads are presented physically as people interact with their environment. Farfetched, you think? Well, in 2013, in the city of London, smart refuse bins fitted with advertising screens were found to be using an open Wi-Fi network to count footfall—by counting the number of unique MAC addresses that had connected to its network. In this way, the advertiser could determine whether the same person had walked past multiple times and potentially tailor ads to them.[10] The practice was stopped almost immediately,[11] but it does provide an interesting proof of concept and food for (ethical) thought.

Solutions in this application space might migrate away from localized pods and onto the web, bridging the gap between the digital and the physical. Click prediction might then be based on other factors, such as your movement in the physical world or whether you had seen an ad on your morning stroll to work.

8.1.5 *The semantic web*

The World Wide Web contains a vast amount of information, but the way in which we interact with it is, for the most part, still rather primitive. We rely heavily on one of several search engines to make sense of our requests (keywords) and find us pages or documents that are relevant to the search. This model works but is far removed from the natural sorts of interactions that we enjoy with our family, friends, and colleagues.[12] Even simple relationships between objects (for example, a cat is a type of animal) may not be encoded, so keyword searches can't use this implicit information that we as humans have available at the time of the search.

It would be a much richer experience if we could ask questions of the web, and, through a series of relationships, an answer could be derived by deduction or a table of information returned or an action performed. This is the vision of the *semantic web*, a term coined by Tim Berners-Lee et al. in 2001.[13] Their vision of the semantic web relies on knowledge being *encoded* into web resources through a markup language and the existence of a set of *ontologies* to bind facts together and make them more easily manipulated by logic. *Agents* operate over the semantic web, extracting information and performing actions based on a set of deductions or proofs. One of the key benefits of such an approach is that the deductions reached are explainable by the agent in a language that is close to our own. Should a user disagree with the information returned by an agent, the deductive rules and ontologies used can be returned so the user can inspect the logical steps in deduction.

---

[9] Andrew Orlowski, "Facebook Brings Creepy 'Minority Report'-Style Ads One Step Closer," *The Register*, November 09, 2015, http://mng.bz/ML01.

[10] Siraj Datoo, "This Recycling Bin Is Following You," *Quartz*, August 08, 2013, http://mng.bz/UUbt.

[11] Joe Miller, "City of London Calls Halt to Smartphone Tracking Bins," *BBC News*, August 12, 2013, http://mng.bz/k56c.

[12] Although as we have seen, this is changing rapidly—consider Google Now and Apple's Siri. www.apple.com/uk/ios/siri/.

[13] Tim Berners-Lee, James Hendler, and Ora Lassila, "The Semantic Web," *Scientific American*, May 1, 2001: 34–43.

We might be some way from the fluid and natural user experience with the web as described in the opening example of the aforementioned paper, but much research toward this is finding application in industry. What we can be sure of is that any attempt to provide richer semantics to the vast amount of information available on the web can only be a good thing for designers of intelligent algorithms, allowing us access to knowledge as opposed to just data.

8.2   *Social implications of the intelligent web*

In the previous sections, we've provided several potential areas for the development of intelligent applications. Whether our visions will come to pass is up for debate, but one thing is for sure: the technology exists or is being created to make these visions a reality. The major question is one of adoption and legislation. Just because something can be done, that doesn't mean it should be. There are many social implications to consider before leaping headfirst into such a future.

 The underlying concerns regarding most intelligent algorithms seem to be focused on privacy and security. Users have the right to expect a degree of privacy with respect to their actions both online and offline. Similarly, users have a reasonable expectation that data held about them is secure and safe from malicious intent. Thus, designers of intelligent applications should respect these requirements and neglect them at their peril! Ultimately, we believe the question boils down to utility. Users are willing to give away some of their rights to control their data if they're provided with some measurable benefit that outweighs the risk and are reasonably assured that it's in safe hands.

Consider the adoption of mobile phones as a case in point. These devices allow your movements to be tracked precisely and in real time across the globe, with this data held by a company that, on paper, has no interest in the specifics of your movements. In return, you're provided with the ability to communicate with similarly connected users at the touch of a button. Here we see a trade-off in the extreme: detailed movement information for access to a killer application. We believe the adoption was so swift because of the rewards associated with instant real-time communication. We predict that we'll witness even more extreme examples of detailed and personal information being given freely, provided the intelligent application that it powers helps in the lives of the users it serves.

We believe that we are now at a crossroad for the intelligent web. Users are more informed than ever before and demand to know how their data is being used. It's our job to provide meaningful advances to their experience in line with their privacy and security expectations. Thus, developers of intelligent algorithms hold much power and are obliged to wield it responsibly.

appendix
Capturing data on the web

As you've learned in this book, *intelligent applications* are those that can change their behavior based on information. It follows, then, that we must have a mechanism for the capture and access of data. Because we're talking about web-scale processing, it stands to reason that we may need a system designed with the following in mind:

- *Volume*—Our system should be capable of dealing with web-scale data.
- *Scalability*—Our system should be configurable with changing load.
- *Durability*—Outages or network blips shouldn't affect the eventual consistent state of data.
- *Latency*—We shouldn't expect to wait long periods of time between data being generated and data being processed.
- *Flexibility*—Access to the data should be flexible, allowing multiple services to read and write from the data platform, each at different states of progress.

Typically, in the internet industry, these are issues relating to *logging* in the sense that when an event occurs, it has traditionally been written down in a log, or log file. In the coming sections, we'll discuss in detail the implications of the log file before providing an alternative, which we can assess against the previous points. To set the scene, and to provide an illustrative example to refer to throughout the remainder of this appendix, we introduce a use case from the world of online advertising.

A motivating example: showing ads online

Although many may despair at the prevalence of ads when browsing the web, nobody can deny that ads are here to stay! With revenues in the billions,[1] these numbers look set to increase steadily as the number of people using electronic devices to consume media continues to grow.

At its core, the concept of online advertising is simple, but behind this simplicity hides significant complexity. In its simplest form, advertisers either pay a publisher to show an ad or pay to have an ad shown if it's interacted with. There are more complicated models, but we don't want to confuse matters here. The first case is

---

[1] *Internet Advertising Bureau*, "Digital Ad Revenues Surge 19%, Climbing to $27.5 Billion in First Half of 2015," October 21, 2015, http://mng.bz/Ud70.

paid for on a cost per mille (CPM) basis; that is, for every thousand ads shown, an amount is paid from the advertiser to the publisher. The latter is charged on a cost per click (CPC) basis, where payment is exchanged every time a consumer sees and subsequently clicks an ad.

The complexity arises in the process by which this all occurs. Rather than advertisers working with publishers directly, these interactions can occur on an open market, or exchange. In these cases, the ad opportunity is commoditized, encouraging competition. This in turn drives more relevant ads and an arguably better experience for the web user.

You may have noticed that in the CPC case, there exists an opportunity for arbitrage. Operating on the demand (advertiser's) side, you could operate a service that uses the data collected from users and their interaction habits to target ad opportunities in order to improve the interaction or click-through rate (CTR). Such parties can buy ad opportunities cheaply on a CPM basis and use their data about web and ad interaction to provide an above-average performance. These ad placements can then be sold on a CPC basis at a profit. Figure A.1 illustrates this process. What we've just described is a simplified version of a demand-side platform (DSP) operating an intelligent algorithm, discussed in chapter 5. This example will also serve us well to demonstrate the world of data collection.

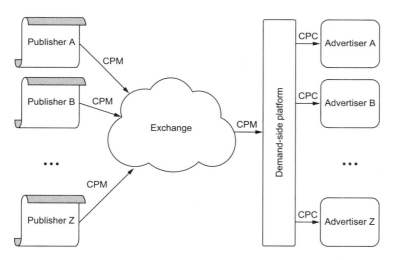

Figure A.1 Overview of a demand-side platform. DSPs use their knowledge of the user to provide better interactions. Consequently, they can arbitrage content bought on a CPM basis, selling this on a CPC basis.

Data available for online advertising

As you know, intelligent algorithms run on data, so let's delve a little deeper into the data that can be collected for ad targeting. Every time our fictional DSP interacts with an exchange, it performs cookie synchronization. That is, either the exchange will pass the DSP a user ID known to the DSP, or the exchange will pass its own ID and the DSP will have to look up its own ID accordingly. The reasons for this have to do with the security of the page and the scope of the identifiers; an exact explanation lies outside the scope of this example. Suffice to say that the DSP can obtain an ID in the DSP's format to look up information regarding user behavior.

What information does the DSP store? Essentially, any interaction with associated users, sites, and ads. To illustrate, let's work through an example. Say you visit Adidas online, while Adidas is working with our imaginary DSP. You become associated with the DSP in rather a complicated way. All interactions with that site and any partner sites become accessible to the DSP. So if you look at the running-shoe collection, a message is sent back to the DSP informing it so. If you also look at the casual footwear selection, similar information is transmitted. If you're shown an ad by the DSP, or if you click one of its ads, the DSP is similarly notified. Where it gets interesting is that these messages aren't limited in scope to Adidas alone. If you visit another of the DSP's partners—say, Walmart—this information is also sent back to the DSP and stored against your identifier. We talk more about how this information is used to perform segmentation in chapter 5; for now, all you need to know is that for every interaction on the web, a lot of information is being stored about you. For a DSP, this presents a significant challenge in collection and storage.

Data collection: a naïve approach

As always, there's a really simple approach we could use to collect and process data, but as you may expect, it's suboptimal. To understand what's happening under the hood, let's look at the hypothetical naïve data-processing architecture of a simple DSP. Figure A.2 shows a visual overview.

Interactions are recorded by the browser and sent back to the DSP's servers for processing. As shown, the receiving server will have many concurrent connections and

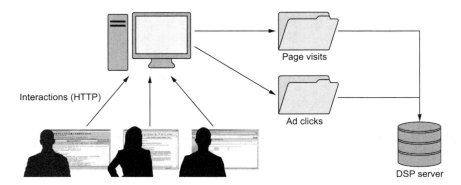

Figure A.2 Overview of the log-processing architecture of a typical DSP. Web page interactions are recorded by the browser and sent back to the DSP's server(s) via HTTP. Depending on the interaction type, these will be written to different files and stored in different locations. Over time, these files are collated and imported to a database for downstream processing.

will have to be configured to deal with a high connection load. Once interactions are received, a number of things need to happen. First, as you can see, depending on the interaction type, the event is logged into different folders. The reason has to do with priority. Click logs equate to money, so minimizing the latency of this data makes good business sense.

For the purposes of *log shipping*, where log files are sent on to the database, it makes sense to periodically finalize files and start new ones so that we can send the data as soon as possible. Consequently, files need to be continually created, finalized, and recycled while data is entering and flowing through the system.

At this stage, finalized data is shipped to the database for import. Here we must deal gracefully with the several possible failure cases. First, corrupt files must be ring-fenced for manual intervention. Processed files must be separated for archival, and transmission failures must be retried. It's imperative that data be received by the database in a consistent state, because without this, billing and reporting can't happen effectively.

Managing data collection at scale

What we've just described is an extremely simple and hypothetical example of a DSP log-processing pipeline. In reality, significant complexity is added in several areas. Let's return to our required properties as stated at the start of this appendix and investigate the suitability of this solution.

To achieve high volume in such a system, the connection thresholds of the receiving machine need to be maximized; but going beyond this, we must find a way to parallelize log processing at the receiver. There are many patterns by which this can be achieved. Processing can be performed by machines with local affinity (to the site or to the user) or that are randomly balanced. Although this allows for horizontal scaling, files must be recombined at some point. This can happen either during an intermediate stage or at the database after shipping. The problem with such an approach is it introduces several points of failure. It also introduces a layer of coordination between the nodes and the database. For example, the database may need to wait for a failed node to come up before files can be combined and imported.

Although such a system is scalable, how this is achieved is closely tied to the chosen architecture. For example, it's much easier to add a processing node to a system that's randomly balanced, rather than one that has been carefully built to manage a particular load profile (for example, where site locality is considered). Scalability certainly isn't guaranteed or automatic.

Durability has to be designed into the system. We've already mentioned transmission failure and corruption, and as you can see, this requires a high degree of logic and coordination between different stages of the processing pipeline. Although not impossible to get correct, the problem is complex enough that it requires some care in implementation.

Latency in this system is closely related to several aspects of its design. In order for an event to be shipped to the database, it must first have reached the file writer and been written to a file, and that file must be closed. When this happens will depend on the load and queuing capability of the receiving server as well as the maximum file size for a log file. After shipping, the file must again wait, to be imported by the database application.

In terms of flexibility, there's only a single consumer of the data: the database. Multiple consumers would result in an increase in transmission bandwidth, because log files would have to be sent to all consumers. This would have an associated impact on the logic required to keep the data consistent. If consumers were allowed to be at different states of progress, enabling logic would have to be borne by the log-shipping code.

Hopefully, this simple example is illustrative enough to convince you that data capture at web scale isn't easy! This, of course, all depends on your application and its requirements, but striving to achieve the properties at the start of this appendix will lay the groundwork for the rest of your application. Each property has an associated knock-on effect to your intelligent algorithm and its deployment lifecycle. For example, if your training data reaches your algorithm with low latency, you can train and deploy more-relevant models more quickly. If access is flexible, multiple algorithms can consume the data in different ways in parallel. Wouldn't it be nice if there were a system that was designed and built for this purpose?

Introducing Kafka

As it happens, there is a system built for this purpose! Apache Kafka is a distributed log-processing platform for dealing with high volumes at low latency. At its core, Kafka is a distributed cluster of brokers. Producers of data can publish messages to a topic (a stream of messages of a given type) that are stored at a set of brokers. Consumers can then subscribe to one or more topics and consume data directly from the brokers. Before delving further into the details of this powerful framework, let's get our hands dirty—it's time for some code!

First, you'll need to get the latest version of Apache Kafka up and running on your system. At the time of writing, version 0.10.0.0 is the current stable release and can be downloaded directly from the Kafka project home page (http://kafka.apache.org/). Be sure you download the binary version built for the version of Scala you have installed. For this appendix, we've tested against Scala 2.10.4. Once you've downloaded the file, unzip it to a convenient location and navigate to the root of the archive. You can then start Kafka using the default configuration with the following two commands:

```
./bin/zookeeper-server-start.sh ./config/zookeeper.properties &
./bin/kafka-server-start.sh ./config/server.properties
```

This will start up Kafka and will by default bind to port 9092, as specified in the server.properties file. You'll also notice that something called Zookeeper is started and bound to port 2181. This is a centralized service that's used to share Kafka configuration—more on this later. To communicate with Kafka, you'll need bindings in your particular language of choice. Because we're using Python throughout this book, we'll use David Arthur's kafka-python[2] to connect to our Kafka instance (v0.9.5). In order to run the examples in this appendix, we're going to assume that you've made this available to your favorite Python environment already. More details on installation can be found in the book's associated requirements document, included with the code available at the book's website (www.manning.com/books/algorithms-of-the-intelligent-web-second-edition). The following listing provides the Python code to send your first set of messages to your Kafka instance.

Listing A.1   Kafka simple publish

Imports the relevant definitions from the kafka-python module

Creates a KafkaClient object that points to your local Kafka instance

```
from kafka import KafkaClient, SimpleProducer
kafka = KafkaClient("localhost:9092")
producer = SimpleProducer(kafka)

producer.send_messages("test", "Hello World! ")
producer.send_messages("test", "This is my second message")
producer.send_messages("test", "And this is my third!")
```

Creates a SimpleProducer instance that will be used to publish messages

Sends messages to kafka under the "test" topic

Run each line of listing A.1 in a Python prompt. All being well, you should see output that resembles the following:

```
[ProduceResponse(topic='test', partition=0, error=0, offset=1)]
[ProduceResponse(topic='test', partition=0, error=0, offset=2)]
[ProduceResponse(topic='test', partition=0, error=0, offset=3)]
```

So, what just happened? Let's go through this line by line. After initial imports from the kafka-python module, a KafkaClient object is created. We then instantiate a SimpleProducer using this and send three messages to the "test" topic before exiting.

Let's investigate this a little further. The send_messages method returns a list of ProduceResponse objects, one for each message submitted by the method. Each object has topic, partition, error, and offset attributes. We've already mentioned topic, but what about the other attributes? Figure A.3 shows the relationship among topics, partitions, and offsets.

---

[2]   David Arthur, kafka-python, https://github.com/dpkp/kafka-python.git.

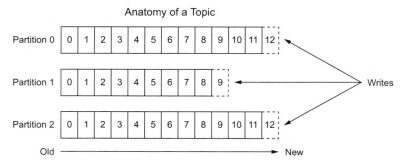

Figure A.3 Anatomy of a topic, taken from the Kafka documentation.[3] Topics consist of a partitioned log, which can only be appended to. The partitions are immutable: they can't be changed once committed.

Topics comprise multiple partitions. Each partition must be held on the same broker, but the partitions for a single topic can be spread over multiple brokers. This serves several purposes. First, it allows topics to scale beyond the size of a single server. Although each partition must physically fit on the machine that hosts it, the logical unit—the topic—can grow to be much larger than a single machine. It also provides a level of redundancy and parallelism. Duplicate partitions can be held, and multiple partitions can be read from and serviced by different machines. The number contained in the partition illustrates the offset in figure A.3. This uniquely identifies an element in the partition; hence the immutability constraint.

The cluster keeps all messages published for a length of time that is configurable by topic, after which logs are deleted to free up space. This means any consumer can go back in time to data that has already been processed. This is achievable because state regarding log processing can be held by the consumer itself; it equates to the offset in each partition.

Returning to our response from the send_messages method, we can now make sense of these attributes. The topic and partition attributes are the topics and partitions written to. The offset provides the datum's place in the partition. Any errors occurring while writing will be captured in the error attribute. Now that you understand the internals of Kafka a little more, let's revisit our example and see if you can find those messages. The following listing provides the code to achieve this.

Listing A.2 Kafka simple subscribe

```
from kafka import KafkaClient, SimpleConsumer          Creates a KafkaClient object

kafka = KafkaClient("localhost:9092")
consumer = SimpleConsumer(kafka,"mygroup","test")      Instantiates a SimpleConsumer
for message in consumer                                 with the KafkaClient object
        print(message)
                                                        Prints each message
```

---

[3] Apache Kafka Documentation, *Apache Projects*, http://kafka.apache.org/documentation.html.

Here we create a `SimpleConsumer`, which takes as arguments a `KafkaClient` as well as two string arguments. The first is known as a *consumer group*, and the second relates to the topic the consumer is to consume from. The concept of a consumer group allows multiple consumers to coordinate, such that a single message published to a topic is only ever delivered to a single member of a consumer group. In this example, there's only a single consumer in our group, titled `mygroup`, and it will receive all messages destined for this group.

There's something else you should know about the `SimpleConsumer` that may not seem obvious at first. Notice that we haven't specified any partitions or offsets from which to start reading. This is because `SimpleConsumer` takes care of this for us. For each partition in the topic, and for each consumer and consumer group, the offset to which that consumer reached is recorded. This is stored in Zookeeper, which if you recall was started at the same time as Kafka. Thus, multiple executions of the previous code won't start from offset zero but instead will pick up at the position after the last successful read. Try it and see!

Replication in Kafka

One of Kafka's features is its ability to hold replica partitions, for the purposes of both parallelism and durability. Let's now store our log data with a replication level of 3. That is, for each partition, the data is stored on three separate brokers.

This requires a bit of setup when starting Kafka. In order to achieve a replication level of 3, we need to have at least three brokers running. In our initial example, we used the stock server.properties file. Now we need to modify this and create two additional configuration files. See the next listing for the sections in server.properties that need to be changed.

> **Listing A.3   Configuration changes in server.properties for broker 2**

```
broker.id=1                              ◁─────┐   Must be set to a unique
port=9093                                       │   integer for each broker
log.dirs=/tmp/kafka-logs-1
```

We need to change three separate parameters in order to use the properties file to create multiple Kafka instances. First, we need to change `broker.id`. This is the unique identifier of the broker in the Kafka cluster. Second, because each of the three brokers will run on the same host, we must change the port. Finally, each instance needs an exclusive location in which to store its data. The location of this data is specified by the `log.dirs` parameter. The example in listing A.3 provides the changes for the relevant sections in the case of the second broker. We'll leave it as an exercise for you to create the third server.properties file. Once it's created, you can add two more brokers to your cluster using the following commands, assuming you've matched the naming convention and location of our new configuration files:

```
./bin/kafka-server-start.sh ./config/server-1.properties
./bin/kafka-server-start.sh ./config/server-2.properties
```

Note that because we haven't modified Zookeeper details in server.properties, they will all communicate with the same Zookeeper instance. No further configuration is required to ensure that they work as part of the same cluster. You'll require some configuration to create a topic with a new replication level, however. Navigate to your Kafka folder, and input the following:

```
bin/kafka-topics.sh --create --zookeeper localhost 2181 \
    --replication-factor 3 --partitions 1 --topic test-replicated-topic
```

This will create a new topic called `test-replicated-topic`. This topic has one partition and a replication level of 3. To confirm this, issue the following command:

```
./bin/kafka-topics.sh --describe --zookeeper localhost:2181
```

All being well, you should see some output that looks remarkably like the following listing.

Listing A.4 Kafka topic summary

```
Topic:test
PartitionCount:1
ReplicationFactor:1
Configs:
        Topic: test
        Partition: 0    Leader: 0    Replicas: 0    Isr: 0

Topic:test-replicated-topic
PartitionCount:1
ReplicationFactor:3
Configs:
        Topic: test-replicated-topic
        Partition: 0    Leader: 0    Replicas: 0,1,2    Isr: 0,1,2
```

Let's take a minute to step through this, because it will help further on in this appendix. The output of this command summarizes what we've done to date. In listing A.1, we automatically created the test topic, with the default parameters as specified in the server.properties file. At the time of writing, this is a default of one partition per topic and a replication factor of 1: no replication. The final column heading, `Isr`, stands for In-Sync-Replicas, and we'll discuss this, along with leaders, in the next section. You also see the recently added `test-replicated-topic` topic. As expected, this has only a single partition but with a replication level of 3. In order to publish to our new topic, let's modify the existing code from listing A.1.

Listing A.5 Kafka publish to cluster

```
from kafka import KafkaClient, SimpleProducer

kafka = KafkaClient("localhost:9092")
producer = SimpleProducer(kafka,
        async=False,
        req_acks=SimpleProducer.ACK_AFTER_CLUSTER_COMMIT,
        ack_timeout=2000)
```

SimpleProducer with optional parameters. Here we use synchronous calls and wait for the entire cluster to acknowledge a sent message, subject to a 2-second timeout.

```
producer.send_messages("test-replicated-topic","Hello Kafka Cluster!")
producer.send_messages("test-replicated-topic","Message to be replicated.")
producer.send_messages("test-replicated-topic","As is this!")
```

We provide an alternative construction of `SimpleProducer`. Here we specify synchronous communication, blocking until the entire cluster has acknowledged a new message before `SimpleProducer` returns a success. Note that it's also possible to set `async=True`, in which case `SimpleProducer` won't wait for a response.

After running listing A.5, kill the broker that's using the server-1.properties file, and rerun listing A.2, replacing `"test"` with `"test-replicated-topic"`. What do you notice? In this scenario, you'll still receive the three new messages, starting with "Hello Kafka Cluster!" But why? Let's delve a little deeper. By querying the topics (via the `./bin/kafka-topics.sh` command issued previously), you should now see an updated summary as given in the next listing.

Listing A.6   Kafka topic summary (dead replica)

```
Topic:test
PartitionCount:1
ReplicationFactor:1
Configs:
     Topic: test   Partition: 0   Leader: 0   Replicas: 0   Isr: 0

Topic:test-replicated-topic
PartitionCount:1
ReplicationFactor:3
Configs:
     Topic: test-replicated-topic   Partition: 0   Leader: 0   Replicas:
0,1,2   Isr: 0,2
```

You can see that `Isr` has gone from `0,1,2` to `0,2`. You might also notice (although it isn't shown here) that the leader has changed. Both of these are a direct consequence of the unavailability of broker 1, which was just killed. We'll discuss this in more detail in the following sections.

MESSAGE ACKNOWLEDGEMENT

Before we continue to discuss the low-level details of replication, let's take a little time to understand message transmission and the different levels of acknowledgments available as we produce our cluster. To start with, we have two types of communication: asynchronous and synchronous. The implication of operating synchronously is that messages are dispatched on the same thread that's calling the producer. The producer has the opportunity to block, waiting for a response before sending the next message. Conversely, with asynchronous communication, new threads are fired up to dispatch messages in parallel without the overhead of blocking. Although this is the least-safe way to produce messages, it allows for extremely high throughput (messages are batched to amortize communication overhead); thus, where some failure can be tolerated, asynchronous communication may be the most appropriate configuration.

For this example, let's assume we're going to operate synchronously. We then have three options available when instantiating `SimpleProducer`:[4]

- `ACK_NOT_REQUIRED`—`SimpleProducer` isn't dispatching multiple threads for delivery; neither is it waiting for acknowledgement from the leader of the topic being written to. This almost offers the worst of all worlds, because the lack of acknowledgment means no delivery guarantees can be made, whereas the lack of asynchronous delivery provides the majority of load on a single thread.

- `ACK_AFTER_LOCAL_WRITE`—Guarantees that the leader has written the data to its local log (although not committed it) before sending a response to the producer. Note that this doesn't guarantee consistency across the replicas, because should this leader immediately fail after the record has been acknowledged, replicas will never receive the new data. This is an intermediate guarantee that provides some trade-off between write speed and durability.

- `ACK_AFTER_CLUSTER_COMMIT`—Using this ensures that the leader will return an acknowledgment only when its local message has been committed: that is, the full set of in-sync replicas (note that this differs from the full set of replicas) has responded to acknowledge their committed data, and the data has been committed locally. This offers the strongest guarantee of availability, but, predictably, the latency between producer message submit and acknowledgement is higher. Provided at least one of the in-sync replicas remains available, this guarantees data availability.

Figure A.4 provides a graphical overview of these acknowledgement modes.

UNDER THE HOOD: REPLICATION, LEADERS, AND IN-SYNC REPLICAS

We've already touched on Kafka's replication model, but now it's time to delve further into the details. So far, we know that topics are made up of partitions, and each of these must reside on a single broker. We also know that topics can be created with a replication factor, which controls the level of data redundancy.

Although replication may be specified at the topic level, it's controlled at the partition level. If you refer back to listing A.6, you'll see an entry per partition. It just so happens that our replicated topic has only a single partition for demonstration purposes. Here, partition 0 has three replicas, but only two are in sync. The leader is replica 0. Let's look at this state from the broker's perspective.

For each partition, a leader is assigned. This is, in some sense, the owner of that partition. All read/write operations for this partition are mediated by the leader. Thus, when a producer publishes a message to a partition, it's sent first to the leader, which may or may not wait for commits to its own log and other replicas' logs before issuing a response. We described the protocol and options for this earlier.

Note that the concept of message acknowledgment and the internal mechanisms of synchronization are different but related concepts. These two principles are decoupled in the sense that any level of message acknowledgement can be requested, but this will

---

[4] http://kafka-python.readthedocs.org/en/latest/usage.html.

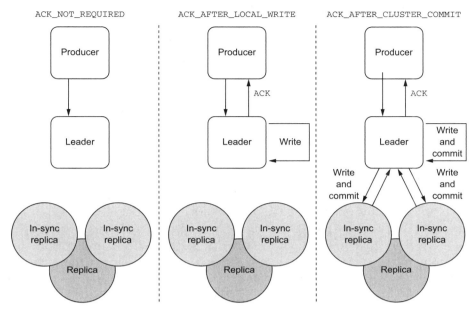

Figure A.4   The different levels of acknowledgments in Kafka. From left to right, they offer increasing degrees of availability at the cost of acknowledgement latency.

have no effect on the attempts made by the cluster to achieve consistency. They do, however, allow the producer to block on different events within the replication protocol and modify downstream behavior dependent on certain outcomes. How replica synchronization is achieved, even in the case of temporary or permanent network failure, is best demonstrated with an example of in-sync replicas (ISRs) that we reproduce from a paper by Jun Rao[5] and show in figure A.5.

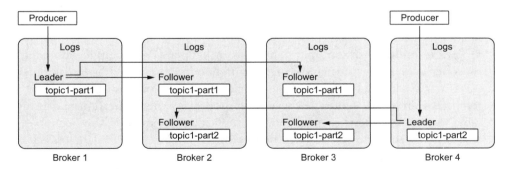

Figure A.5   Kafka replication, reproduced from Rao. In this example, we have four brokers and one topic with two partitions. Broker 1 leads partition 1, and broker 4 leads partition 2.

---

[5]   Jun Rao, "Intra-cluster Replication in Apache Kafka," February 2, 2013, http://mng.bz/9Z99.

In figure A.5, we present a Kafka cluster of four brokers. This cluster manages a single topic with two partitions. The replication factor of this topic is set to 3. Imagine that we're going to write some data to partition 1. Data is forwarded on to broker 1, and the three brokers, 1, 2, and 3, achieve consistency through the use of in-sync replica sets.

In-sync replicas are those whose commit log is up to date with respect to the leader. Consequently, the leader always has to be in the ISR. When a message is published to the leader, it sends the message to the followers and waits until all replicas in the ISR have committed the message. If any of the replicas fail to commit, those replicas will be dropped from the ISR, and the commit will complete with under-replication.

To take a concrete example from figure A.5, if our producer is to write to `topic1-part1`, it will first communicate with broker 1. The type of acknowledgement the producer will block for will depend on the acknowledgement level; but regardless of this, the replica set will now proceed to obtain synchronization. Under normal operation, the ISR will be equal to the replica set for that partition. Thus, broker 2 and broker 3 will communicate with broker 1 to transfer, write, and commit the entering data. Once this is done, broker 1 will commit this message locally, and the operation will conclude. If, however, broker 3 can't be reached (say, some timeout is hit), then broker 1 will remove broker 3 from the ISR, commit the message locally and at broker 2, and terminate. In this scenario, brokers 1 and 2 have commit logs that are in sync, but broker 3 is out of sync.

Should broker 3 reemerge, it will need to catch up with the rest of the replica set. It does this by communicating with the leader, broker 1, to see what it missed. For this purpose, the leader maintains a high watermark (HW), which is a pointer to the last committed message in the ISR. Broker 3 will truncate its commit log at this point, catch up with the leader, and be added back to the ISR. There's another possibility here: that the leader fails. Because Zookeeper is used to detect failures and manage the configuration of the cluster, it's relied on to reelect new leaders in the event that the original leader failed. If this occurs, Zookeeper must inform all replicas of the new leader so they know which broker to follow.

It's interesting to note that data loss can happen. For example, should a leader become unavailable, any data written but not committed would be lost upon election of a new leader. Kafka was designed for high throughput and primarily for redundancy within a data center, because its approach to synchronization makes it unsuitable where high latencies exist between replicas. Consequently, the likelihood of ISR set change and/or leader reassignment is low. A small amount of data loss is therefore acceptable for most logging applications given the throughput that can be achieved. The article from which this example is taken provides a much more comprehensive treatment of replication, so we refer you to Rao for more information.

Consumer groups, balancing, and ordering

In listing A.2, we introduced the concept of Kafka consumer groups. This abstraction allows Kafka to be used either as a queue, whereby multiple consumers process items from the head, with each message going to a single consumer, or as a publish-subscribe system, in which each message is broadcast to all consumers.

Recall that a single message published to a topic is guaranteed to be delivered only to a single consumer of a consumer group. So where we have one topic and one group, this emulates the behavior of a queue. Where each consumer is a member of its own group, this provides the same behavior as a publish-subscribe system—each group receives the same set of messages.

Each partition is assigned to a single consumer in a group, such that this is the only consumer in the group to receive messages from it. As you'll see, provided the partitions are well balanced, this also balances the load on consumption, although it does mean the maximum number of consumers that can consume data from a topic is limited to the number of partitions.

It's worth noting that Kafka provides ordering guarantees only over a partition, the intuition being that if a was written before b within a partition, it will also be consumed in this order. It provides no guarantee on ordering between partitions: when reading from multiple partitions, it may be possible to read a message that was written before another, but this would have to come from a different partition. In this sense, Kafka relaxes some of the guarantees made by a queue in order to achieve high throughput via parallelism. In practice, and for most logging applications, provided you can specify how data is partitioned, this should be sufficient. For example, you may choose to partition incoming web-click logs by some modulo of cookie/user ID. This ensures that partitions will be balanced and that all logs from a given user will be guaranteed to be in the same partition. You can then use ordering on this partition when trying to understand how users interacted with your ads. We'll look at this in more detail in the next section.

Putting it all together

In this section, we're going to bring everything together to provide an example that illustrates all the concepts introduced so far. We'll again use a single topic, which we'll call `click-streams`. This topic will be split into three partitions with level 3 replication. We'll operate with two consumers groups: one containing a single consumer and the other containing three consumers. These will be named `group-1` and `group-2`, respectively. Finally, we'll ensure that all clicks from the same user end up in the same partition. Figure A.6 provides an overview of our final Kafka setup.

We previously presented the code required to bring up a new cluster consisting of any number of brokers and to create a new topic and specify the number of partitions and replication level. We also specified in listing A.2 how to bring up a consumer within a consumer group. What we don't specify, however, is how to perform custom partitioning, because previously this was taken care of by `SimpleProducer`. To demonstrate this

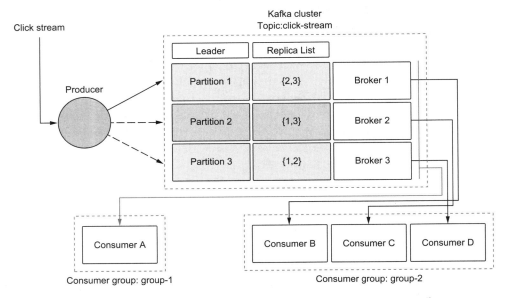

Figure A.6   Our final Kafka cluster. In this example, we use a low-level producer to perform our own partitioning of the stream of data. This cluster is operating with three brokers, three partitions, and level-3 replication. Two consumer groups exist, one with a single consumer called group-1 and the other with three consumers, known as group-2.

concept, we'll introduce a schema of data as illustrated in the following listing. This can also be found in the additional resources available at this book's website (as file A1.data), should you wish to follow the example programmatically.

Listing A.7   Click user data

> Adview, clicks, and convert, all from the same user and within a short period of time

```
381094c0-9e45-424f-90b6-ad64b06cc184    2014-01-02 17:33:07    click
6615087e-ea19-492c-869c-28fc1fa77588    2014-01-02 17:33:20    view
d4889090-942b-4790-9831-362051b0847b    2014-01-02 17:34:01    adview
e6688db5-d31f-4ede-985a-115fb51836fb    2014-01-02 17:35:06    adview
e6688db5-d31f-4ede-985a-115fb51836fb    2014-01-02 17:35:30    click
e6688db5-d31f-4ede-985a-115fb51836fb    2014-01-02 17:37:01    click
e6688db5-d31f-4ede-985a-115fb51836fb    2014-01-02 17:39:00    convert
ae6ae5c9-acb2-479b-adcb-0c29623d921b    2014-01-02 17:40:00    adview
1ac384c1-1b2d-4ed0-b467-7c90b7ac42d8    2014-01-02 17:40:01    adview
280bfa16-07ac-49ed-a1a5-9ab50a754027    2014-01-02 17:40:03    click
dda0e95d-9c30-4f60-bb6a-febf05526b83    2014-01-02 17:40:05    adview
8a1204f1-5076-4d4c-8b23-84c77ad541d8    2014-01-02 17:40:10    adview
3bdb8f17-11cc-49cb-94cf-75676be909b7    2014-01-02 17:40:11    adview
69b61156-6c31-4317-aec5-bd48908b4973    2014-01-02 17:40:13    adview
69722471-0532-4f29-b2b4-2f9007604e4f    2014-01-02 17:40:14    adview
00e5edf6-a483-48fa-82ed-fbfac8a6b1e6    2014-01-02 17:40:15    adview
```

```
9398d369-6382-4be0-97bc-182b3713745f    2014-01-02 17:40:17    convert
f40c1588-e4e1-4f7d-8ef5-5f76046886fb    2014-01-02 17:40:18    adview
54823527-fe62-4a81-8551-6282309b0a3f    2014-01-02 17:40:20    click
46d6f178-7c11-48c1-a1d7-f7152e7b2f1c    2014-01-02 17:40:26    adview
4c4e545b-d194-4531-962f-66e9d3b6116d    2014-01-02 17:41:00    convert
42b311f5-ba84-4666-a901-03063f7504a9    2014-01-02 17:41:01    adview
bfa28923-c358-4741-bcbf-ff99b640ee14    2014-01-02 17:42:06    adview
54c29b39-5640-49b8-b610-6f2e6dc6bd1b    2014-01-02 17:42:10    convert
edf6c5d2-1373-4dbb-8528-925d525b4a42    2014-01-02 17:43:03    click
f7f6752f-03bf-43f1-927c-8acdafd235e2    2014-01-02 17:43:11    adview
f4b7c0a6-b209-4cc4-b4e7-395489e0e724    2014-01-02 17:43:19    click
```

This is a fictitious and simplified dataset based on page interaction. Note that the schema has three distinct columns. The first is a uniquely identifying code, or globally unique identifier (GUID); the second is the time of the interaction; and the third is the interaction type. There are only three possible types of interaction: adview, which corresponds to the action that an ad has been seen by a user; click, which denotes a click by a given user; and convert, which is set if the user buys a product.

We might imagine a payment method whereby our DSP gets paid a certain amount for every click, with the caveat that any clicks from the same user that happen within a set period of time (say, five minutes) should be counted only once. A quick glance at listing A.7 shows that the annotated user viewed an ad and was recorded as clicking twice before converting (perhaps buying the product in the ad they saw!). It also shows that the clicks happened within a few minutes of each other. Consequently, some downstream processing would need to occur if we were to discount the second click, leaving only a single click in our interaction stream.

If we revisit the example from the start of this appendix, listing A.1, we published to a single partition topic called test. What we'd like to do, though, is to have multiple partitions and somehow ensure that all information regarding a single user ends up at a single partition. As a secondary requirement, it would be ideal if the data were balanced across the available partitions. The next listing provides the code to do this.

Listing A.8 Custom partitioning with a producer

```
from kafka import KafkaClient
from kafka.common import ProduceRequest
from kafka.protocol import KafkaProtocol,create_message

kafka = KafkaClient("localhost:9092")
f = open('A1.data','r')

for line in f:
    s = line.split("\t")[0]
    part = abs(hash(s)) % 3
    req = ProduceRequest(topic="click-streams",
        partition=part,messages=[create_message(s)])
    resps = kafka.send_produce_request(payloads=[req],
        fail_on_error=True)
```

Opens the data file that contains the example click-stream data

Iterates through the data

Splits the file by tab, and pulls out the first column, which contains the GUID of the user

Hashes the GUID and modulo 3 to obtain a number between 0 and 2, inclusive

Creates a ProduceRequest object that specifies the click-streams topic and partition

Sends this data, with responses stored in the resps object

This toy producer partitions by user GUID. In a production implementation of such a system, the click stream would come directly from a web browser or associated code, but for the purposes of illustration this data comes directly from a file.

If your broker from listing A.6 is still dead, restart it now. If you wish to run this example, you'll need to create the click-streams topic with replication level 3. Make sure you do this before you run the code in listing A.8; otherwise, you'll end up automatically creating a topic with too few partitions:

```
bin/kafka-topics.sh --create \
                    --zookeeper localhost 2181 \
                    --replication-factor 3 \
                    --partitions 3 \
                    --topic click-streams
```

Recall that we wish to ensure that all click streams from the same user end up at the same partition. Working through listing A.8, you can see that each GUID has the modulo operator applied to it (modulo 3), and the resulting number is used to determine the partition to publish to. Thus, all entries for the same user result in the same output (modulo 3) and will end up at the same partition! This partition isn't exclusive for that user—other users' data will also end up there—but this isn't a requirement for the system, because the number of partitions is much less than the number of users. This method of custom partitioning has another useful property. Assuming the GUIDs are randomly distributed, then so will the result, modulo 3. This means users will be, in the limit, evenly balanced across the partitions. This is important in order to distribute both the publish and subscribe loads among the available resources.

From the perspective of consumer groups in figure A.6, let's work through the partition assignment to ensure that a single consumer really does obtain all the data for a given user. In group-1, consumer A is the only member and thus will receive all the data for the topic click-streams. It does this by periodic communication with the leaders of all partitions of the topic. Because this consumer acquires data from all partitions, for any given user, all data will end up with a single consumer.

Perhaps more interesting is group-2, containing consumers B, C, and D. Recall that the consumer group guarantee is such that a given message is to be received by only a single consumer within a consumer group and that this is achieved through the assignment of a partition to a consumer. In this case, the leader of each partition communicates with a single consumer. Broker 1 (leading partition 1) is assigned to consumer B, broker 2 to consumer C, and broker 3 to consumer D. Note that this is the maximum number of consumers possible in this example because the number of consumers in a group can't exceed the number of partitions in the topic it's consuming from.

Because of our custom partitioning strategy, it's now guaranteed that a single consumer consumes the messages from a given user. It would be possible to do things like click de-duplication (to remove erroneous clicks and work out how much the DSP should bill its client) at the consumer, because all relevant data is processed by that consumer and also because the ordering guarantees provided by Kafka ensure that events that are published in order at a partition will be retrieved in that same order.

There's also an intermediate example, which we haven't illustrated here. In the case where we have two consumers and three partitions, one of the consumers will be responsible for two of the partitions. This assignment will be random, and it does impact the load-balance on the consumers; but it again ensures that a single consumer obtains all the data for a given user.

Evaluating Kafka: data collection at scale

Thus far, we've presented Kafka along with the kafka-python client, which can be used to communicate with your cluster via Python. We present this as an alternative to a bespoke log-shipping service, which, although simple to understand, has been demonstrated to be non-optimal for our purposes. For completeness, and to illustrate the design of Kafka, we'll compare a solution based on Kafka against our naïve yardstick—illustrating how it has the potential to perform better with respect to each of the metrics introduced at the start of this appendix.

One of the most important features for a web application is the ability to deal with large volumes of data. When assessing our naïve solution, we noted that in order to parallelize, we'd need to add a degree of coordination into the system that might be difficult to get correct. We also noted that data processed in parallel would need to be recombined at some point. Kafka takes care of this for us. By partitioning the data, we immediately add a level of parallelism in the order of the number of partitions. Zookeeper takes care of discovery and management, and combination can occur at the consumer. In order to get the highest level of parallelism, Kafka should be configured with distinct and unrelated topics, whose consumption patterns are independent from each other. This allows consumer groups to operate in parallel, potentially transforming that data as it's consumed.

Scalability was considered a major sticking point in our naïve solution, because it was tied quite tightly to the chosen architecture. More clicks in a region might mean regional server processing power might need to be increased, but this might have a downstream effect when aggregating logs. Kafka can help in this situation, because it's possible to add additional brokers to a cluster and rebalance partitions. It's also possible to increase the number of partitions to make the best use of the broker pool. This centralizes scaling to the cluster, rather than distributing throughout the log-shipping pathway. As an aside, Kafka can also be configured for multicluster operation through mirroring. This provides a higher-latency link between clusters, suitable for cross–data center synchronization.

Durability is a strong point of Kafka. We've already discussed how Kafka replicates data, which provides fault tolerance where replica factors greater than 1 are used. In these cases, brokers can fail completely without affecting data flow within the system. To compare this to our naïve solution, we'd need to manually create and manage copies. Again, although not impossible, this adds a significant amount of complexity to a file-management service.

In our naïve approach, latency isn't a tunable parameter. When an event occurs, we must wait until it has been logged, that file has been closed, and the data eventually reaches its destination before we can consider that event to be processed. In contrast, if we look at Kafka, both read and write latency can be parameterized individually. In the write case, we can choose the level of acknowledgement that we require before continuing to write (see the earlier section "Replication in Kafka"), and we can even choose to write asynchronously, not waiting for acknowledgements at all. Here we're trading write latency for consistency. We can get low-latency writes, but we must deal with the possibility that a leader failure may cause a small amount of data loss as the new leader is elected. In terms of read latency, because reads start from the last recorded offset, leaders can wait as short or long a period as they wish (up to the data storage window of the cluster) before running again and reading from the offset where they left off.

The naïve solution presented assumed by design that there was a single consumer. It was a pipeline in the sense that generated data would eventually emerge in a database at some point in the future. It was also very much a push-based system. No provision was made to store data in any location other than its final resting place, so replaying data—or having multiple processes consume data—is a departure from the norm. In comparison, Kafka has been designed with these properties in mind. It's easy for multiple processes to consume data; we simply fire up an additional consumer group. It's also easy to replay data, provided it's within the window of storage offered by the cluster. These properties are excellent for prototyping and deploying intelligent algorithms, because relevant data is always available on tap. This means we can train, deploy, and test algorithms quickly, tightening the loop between data generation and decisions made from that data.

Kafka design patterns

To consolidate some of the content covered here, we'll finish by taking a look at some standard design patterns for the use of Kafka. So far, we've determined that Kafka is great as a data-brokerage platform; but to develop useful applications, this alone isn't enough. Now that we've tamed the act of moving data from A to B, it's imperative that we be able to do something useful with that data. Toward this end, we'll present two potential use cases that may be of interest to you as you think about how to implement the algorithms introduced in the later chapters of this book.

In the first use case, we'll deal with how to perform data transformations in flight. In the second, we'll look at how we might extract data ready for querying in some batch data platform. Note, however, that these aren't necessarily mutually exclusive! Stream processing could occur before data is transferred to a batch-processing engine, or these steps could occur in parallel.

Kafka plus Storm

Kafka alone can't perform any transformations to the data it ingests. If we wish to perform in-stream transformations, we must couple Kafka with an additional technology, such as Storm.[6] Storm is a distributed, real-time system for processing stream data. This allows us to process data in arbitrary and complex ways through the use of several simple literals, two of which are the *spout* and the *bolt*. The spout acts as a source of data, whereas the bolt is a processor of data that can consume a number of streams and do some processing, possibly emitting a new stream. These literals, when combined with several ways to group and relay data between stages (shuffle randomly to the next stage, partition by a particular field, send to all, and so on), provide a powerful way to process data in flight. Such combinations are known as *topologies.*

For example, using the combination of Kafka and Storm, it would be possible to remove duplicate clicks from our `click-streams` topic, as mentioned earlier. This would be achieved using a Kafka spout, such as `storm-kafka`, which extracts data from Kafka and acts as a data source for a topology. Figure A.7 shows an example.

In this configuration, we're using the power of Kafka plus Storm to deduplicate clicks in our click stream that occur within a short time of each other. The consumer

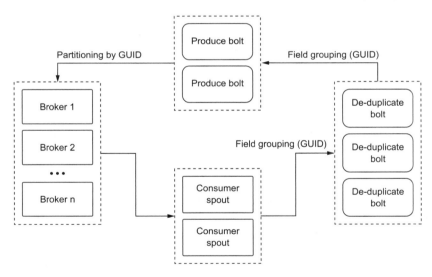

Figure A.7   In this example, a consumer group of spouts is consuming from the Kafka cluster that has been partitioned by GUID. This ensures that each consumer spout receives all the data for a given user. Through Storm's field grouping, we can also partition data on GUID as we send this data to one of several deduplication bolts that operate on the incoming clicks. Field grouping again on GUID, we can send these to one of several producers that will write these back into a new, deduplicated topic, again partitioned by GUID.

---

[6]   Sean T. Allen, Matthew Jankowski, and Peter Pathirana, *Storm Applied: Strategies for Real-Time Event Processing* (Manning, 2015).

group illustrated consists of Storm consumer spouts, which pull data from Kafka in the same way as any other consumer but forward information in a way that's configurable to Storm. In this case, we use the Storm *field grouping* on GUID, sending the data on to three bolts that will perform the deduplication. Much in the same way that Kafka works, this grouping ensures that all user data for a given user will end up at a single bolt. This is necessary to enable us to perform the deduplication. The output from each of the bolts is a stream minus the duplicate data, and in this case we choose to use the field grouping again to send the data to the producers. This keeps per-user event ordering within a given producer. The producers then send messages back into the cluster, partitioning by GUID into a new topic, which will contain the deduplicated data. Because the data is processed in the order in which it arrives, per-user deduplicated data should arrive at its particular partition in more or less the same order as the duplicate data.

You'll notice that we say "more or less." This doesn't sound very strict! Storm allows for several levels of guarantees with respect to ordering. In its simplest mode, messages may be dropped—or even replayed if the message times out—creating multiple entries in the output. For *exactly-once semantics*, Storm Trident must be used, which is an abstraction to provide enhanced guarantees on topology execution. Using this abstraction, we could guarantee that our new deduplicate topic would be in exactly the same order as the original, minus the duplicate clicks.

Note the scalability here. Each of the four steps can theoretically be scaled in parallel without breaking the semantics of the system. Using Kafka plus Storm with field groupings ensures parallel processing pipelines for subsets of the GUID space, which facilitates efficient scaling as the number of users in the system increases.

Just a quick note on the deduplicate bolt. Removing duplicate clicks is a fairly simple process if we can use the ordering of arriving data. For each click that occurs for a given user, we can store this in local memory, listening for any further clicks for that user within a given timestamp offset, dropping these messages if they occur, and throwing away that item from memory after an item greater than that window has been seen for that user. This works only if the per-user ordering is guaranteed throughout the system (consider what would happen if a message was replayed into one of the deduplicate bolts out of order, especially if that were outside the deduplicate window). If we were to choose this pattern, we'd need to give careful consideration to the number of bolts required and the memory required by each bolt.

Kafka plus Hadoop

Working with data in flight is a powerful mechanism. This allows data to be transformed as it flows into our system. The downsides to such an approach, however, are that we need to know the type of transformations up front! In our previous example, we knew all about deduplication and so could deploy this within a stream-processing architecture quite easily.

There are many cases where we don't know in advance what we'd like to calculate, and this forms much of the workload of a traditional analyst. In order to facilitate this, we need to present the data to Kafka in a queryable manner, and to illustrate this we've chosen Hadoop (with some other enabling technologies).

Apache Hadoop (https://hadoop.apache.org) is a software framework that allows large datasets to be processed in parallel across many machines. It uses a simple processing paradigm known as MapReduce to perform computation in a distributed fashion much more quickly than could be achieved on a single machine. Hadoop is an extremely powerful framework, and we urge you to refer to the associated literature to get a better feel for its use.

Integral to Hadoop is the Hadoop Distributed File System (HDFS), which creates a file-system abstraction on top of a distributed cluster of machines. Data residing here can be operated on using MapReduce to generate results from extremely large datasets in reduced time frames. Consequently, getting data from Kafka and into HDFS for processing might be something you want to do!

Figure A.8 shows a simple architecture that makes this a possibility using the Camus project (https://github.com/linkedin/camus). Camus has been built as a MapReduce job to read data from topics in Kafka and write into HDFS in a distributed fashion.[7] In short, this allows for parallel loading of data from one system to the other. This is an extremely powerful feature when you're working with very large datasets. From the point of view of Kafka, Camus is just another consumer. Upon execution, Camus performs topic discovery, loads in its own partition offsets from HDFS, and allocates the partitions to a fixed number of tasks (MapReduce executions)—these consume the data and write to HDFS. As with other consumers you've encountered so far, Camus is based on pull semantics, and thus a scheduler must trigger execution.

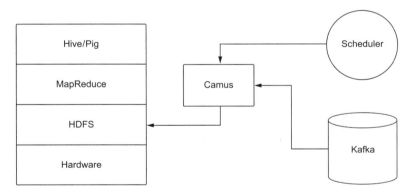

Figure A.8 Overview of Kafka plus Hadoop integration. Camus is used to generate MapReduce jobs, which extract data from Kafka in parallel, placing the data in HDFS. Camus jobs must be executed periodically; hence the scheduler. High-level languages such as Hive and Pig can then be used to query the imported data.

---

[7] At the time of writing, Camus is being phased out and replaced by a next-generation project called Gobblin (https://github.com/linkedin/gobblin). This extends Camus and unifies it with several other LinkedIn data-ingestion projects.

With data residing in HDFS, it will now be possible to run MapReduce jobs or register the data with a higher-level query language, such as Apache Hive (https://hive.apache.org) or Pig (https://pig.apache.org). Such languages provide a familiar programming paradigm for analysts running ad hoc queries over the imported data.

index